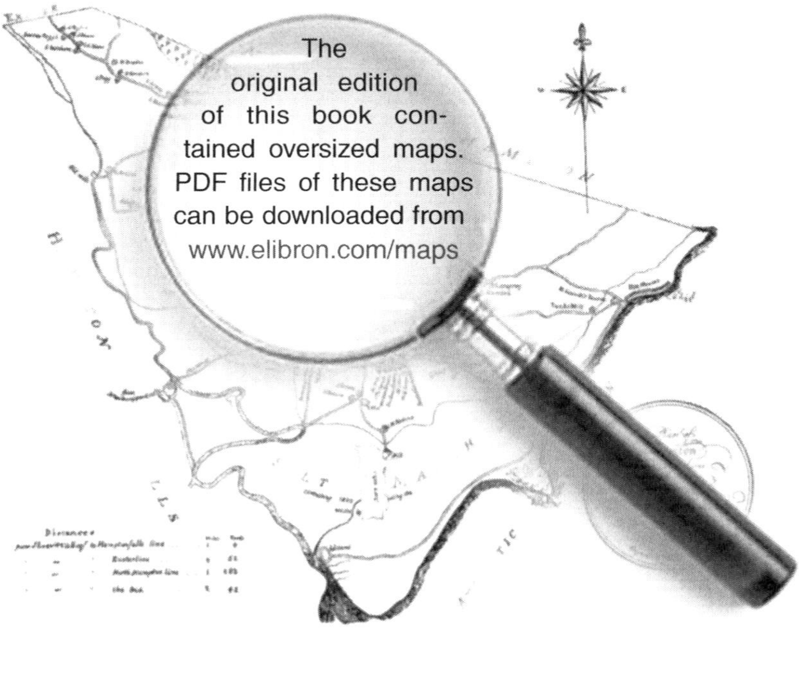

The original edition of this book contained oversized maps. PDF files of these maps can be downloaded from www.elibron.com/maps

M. HENRY MOUHOT

TRAVELS

IN THE

CENTRAL PARTS OF INDO-CHINA (SIAM), CAMBODIA, AND LAOS,

DURING THE YEARS 1858, 1859, AND 1860

VOLUME II

Elibron Classics
www.elibron.com

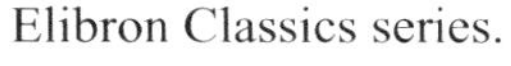
Elibron Classics series.

ISBN 1-4021-8172-8 (paperback)
ISBN 1-4021-2909-2 (hardcover)

This Elibron Classics Replica Edition is an unabridged facsimile of the edition published in 1864 by John Murray, London.

TRAVELS

IN THE

CENTRAL PARTS OF INDO-CHINA

(SIAM),

CAMBODIA, AND LAOS.

Vol. II. p. 112.

BIVOUAC OF M. MOUHOT IN THE FORESTS OF LAOS.

Drawn by M. Bocourt, from a Sketch by M. Mouhot.

TRAVELS

IN THE

CENTRAL PARTS OF INDO-CHINA

(SIAM),

CAMBODIA, AND LAOS,

DURING THE YEARS 1858, 1859, AND 1860.

BY THE LATE

M. HENRI MOUHOT,

FRENCH NATURALIST.

IN TWO VOLUMES.—VOL. II.

WITH ILLUSTRATIONS.

LONDON:

JOHN MURRAY, ALBEMARLE STREET.

1864.

LONDON: PRINTED BY WILLIAM CLOWES AND SONS, STAMFORD STREET,
AND CHARING CROSS.

CONTENTS OF VOL. II.

CHAPTER XIII.

CHAPTER XIV.

CHAPTER XV.

CHAPTER XVI.

CHAPTER XVII.

CHAPTER XVIII.

APPENDIX.

ILLUSTRATIONS TO VOL. II.

TRAVELS IN INDO-CHINA,

ETC.

CHAPTER XIII.

ONGCOR THÔM (ONGCOR THE GREAT)—SURROUNDING WALL—TRIUMPHAL ARCH.

HALF-A-MILE beyond Bakhêng are the ruins of Ongcor-Thôm. A partly-destroyed road, hidden by thick layers of sand and dust, and crossing a large ditch, half filled with blocks of stone, portions of columns, and fragments of sculptured lions and elephants, leads to the gateway of the town, which is built in the style of a triumphal arch.

These remains are in a tolerable state of preservation, and are composed of a central tower, 18 metres high, surrounded by four turrets, and flanked by two other towers connected together by galleries. At the top are four immense heads in the Egyptian style; and every available space is filled with sculpture. At the foot of the great tower is a passage for carriages; and on each side of it are doors and staircases communicating with the walls, the whole building being constructed of sandstone.

The outer wall is composed of blocks of ferruginous stone, and extends right and left from the entrance. It is about 24 miles square, 3 met. 80 centimet. thick, and 7 met. high, and serves as a support to a glacis which rises almost from the top. At the four cardinal points are doors, there being two on the east side. Within this vast enclosure, now covered with an almost impenetrable forest, are a vast number of buildings, more or less in ruin, which testify to the ancient splendour of the town. In some places, where the heavy rains have washed away the soil, or where the natives have dug in search for treasure, may be seen immense quantities of porcelain and pottery.

PREA SAT LING POUN.

Within the enclosure of Ongcor Thôm, and two miles from the west gate, are to be seen through the trees the tops of the high towers of a building called by the Cambodians "Prea sat Ling poun," that is to say, "The Pagoda where they play hide and seek." It is a collection of 37 towers of unequal size, connected by galleries which cross each other perpetually, and form a labyrinth through which it is not easy to find one's way. A long shallow ditch, crossed by four roads leading to the principal entrances, surrounds it on all sides. Beyond the ditch rises the wall of a gallery, of which the exterior colonnades and the roof are only a mass of ruins, over which you must climb to reach the interior. This wall is still intact: it is about 120 metres long, and forms a square round the pagoda. About 1 metre from the ground are visible, in places where the blocks fallen from the roof have not hidden everything, various bas-reliefs carved in the thickness of the wall: they are not surmounted by cornices as at Ongcor-Wat, by which it would seem as if they had never been finished.

Besides the four principal entrances there were other doors at unequal distances in this gallery, but singularly enough many of them have been walled up. The gallery was connected with the main body of the building by four smaller ones opposite each of the great doors, and forming a covered way to the interior; but all these galleries are destroyed.

The second enclosure is 65 metres square, and each front is composed of five towers, connected by galleries. The central and corner towers are the largest: they are about 13 metres high. High galleries connect the centre tower with the intermediate ones, which again are connected with those at the corners by galleries of a less elevation.

On each side are seven staircases, of six steps each, and leading either to towers or galleries: these galleries are covered by a triple roof: a central one 7 metres high, resting on an outer wall, and on columns 2 metres in height; an exterior roof on a double row of columns; and a third resting on a very low wall, pierced with numerous large windows looking on to a narrow interior court.

On the exterior of the wall, which on one side sustains

the high roof, are a series of bas-reliefs, surrounding the whole gallery. They are sculptured in the thickness of the wall, and are curious from the scenes and costumes they represent. These scenes are drawn more from the sacred books of the people than from their history; for men with ten heads and twenty arms, fantastic animals, griffins and dragons, are favourite subjects. The men all wear the langouti, and often nothing beside, and have the ears pierced and hanging on their shoulders: many have long beards.

In the vestibules of the towers, and in the high galleries near them, are kings and queens seated on a rich dais, with a numerous court, and surrounded by persons carrying parasols, fans, standards, and caskets: there are likewise many musicians with drums, flutes, and harps.

In the galleries are represented several boats' crews fighting; while underneath are fishes disputing for the bodies of the slain. There are also in the same galleries persons in attitudes of adoration, with clasped hands, before a figure of Samonakodom.

In another part is a long procession: the king is in a large open carriage, divided into three compartments, he being in the centre one, and his wives in the two others. This carriage has six wheels and two shafts, which rest on the shoulders of eight men. The chiefs are mounted on elephants or horses, or seated in carriages drawn by four led horses, and by their side march a numerous company bearing standards, parasols, and caskets.

The bas-reliefs at the east and north sides represent

similar scenes, as well as many of the fabulous men and animals which are to be seen in those at Ongcor-Wat. In numerous places the water, trickling through holes in the roof, has so obliterated the carving that the subjects can no longer be recognised. This gallery, with its sixteen towers, is connected with another only 3 metres distant; and this last has five towers on each side, of which the three in the middle face the exterior towers. The interior of the gallery with its three roofs receives no light but by the doors, and is so dark that torches are necessary when it is visited. The gallery, sustained by two rows of columns and by an exterior wall, has no bas-reliefs. The towers, which are built at equal distances, are thus disposed: the largest at the angles, two smaller ones next to them, and one of medium size in the centre.

The middle of the terrace is occupied by a large tower connected with the gallery by two others, only about a metre distant. The central tower is circular at the base, is 20 metres in diameter, and nearly 40 metres high, and has on each side a turret. A colonnade supporting a roof, now in ruins, surrounds it: the columns, each of which is hewn out of a single block of stone more than 40 metres high, are still standing. Four doors lead to the interior. Outside this tower, between each two doors, are three chapels, constructed out of the thickness of the wall, and having no communication with each other, nor with the exterior. In nearly every one of them is a full-length statue of Samanokodom seated on a pedestal.

On visiting this place you behold on every side the tops

of these numerous towers, and the roofs of the galleries, intermingled with large trees, creepers, and thistles, which invade the courts, the terraces, and other parts; and you have at first some difficulty in comprehending the arrangements of the different buildings. It is only after a long examination that you perceive the symmetry of them as a whole, and that these thirty-seven towers and numerous galleries are all in regular order. Some parts are in good preservation; others have been dealt hardly with by time, in spite of the immense size of the blocks of stone, and the skill with which they are united; and the condition of this stone, ready to crumble to powder, seems to prove that this structure was anterior to Ongcor-Wat.

Like it, it is built of sandstone, and the roofs are very similar, only that, in place of the pointed stones ranged in courses at Ongcor, these are embellished, at about two-thirds of their height, with four gigantic sculptured heads.

The roof is terminated by a very elegant embrasure, a feature not belonging to the other temple. Every door in the building is sunk, and many of them are admirably carved, displaying scenes full of expression, skilfully arranged, and exquisitely delicate in detail. They represent various subjects: worshippers prostrated before their idols, musicians and comedians performing pantomimes, chariots filled with warriors standing up, and drawn by horses galloping: in some instances they appear to be running races.

Not far from this labyrinth are three platforms close

together, each occupied by a colossal idol of stone, and gilt. These idols appear to be of modern date; but at their feet are assembled a number of others, some uninjured, some broken, collected from among the ruins. On one of the platforms are several stones fixed in the ground; on one of which is a long undecipherable inscription.

PHIMÉNAN ACA. THE PALACE OF THE ANCIENT KINGS.

Three walls at some distance from each other, and each bounded by a moat, surround what remains of the palace of the ancient kings. Within the first enclosure are two towers connected by galleries, which form four sides, like a triumphal arch. The walls are of ferruginous stone, and the length of each block forms the thickness of the wall. The towers and galleries are of sandstone.

A hundred metres from the angle of the square formed on the north side by the wall, is a singular building, consisting of two high terraces, and communicating with the outer wall by another terrace half in ruins.

In a cavity recently made by excavations, are visible large sculptured blocks, which seem to have fallen from the top. The walls, still intact, are covered with bas-reliefs, disposed in four rows, one above another, each representing a king seated in the Oriental fashion, with his hands resting on a broken poignard, and by his side a number of women. All these figures are covered with ornaments, such as very long earrings, necklaces, and bracelets. Their costume is the langouti, and all wear high head-dresses terminating in a point, and apparently composed of precious stones, pearls, and gold and silver ornaments.

On another side the bas-reliefs represent combats; and here are children with long hair tied up like the savages of the East. Everything here, however, yields in beauty to the statue of the leprous king, which is at the end of the terrace. The head, admirable in its nobility, regularity of feature, and gentle yet proud expression, must have been the work of the most skilful sculptor of the country, in an age when many, doubtless, evinced great talent. A small moustache covers his upper lip, and his hair falls in long curls over his shoulders; but the whole body is naked, and without ornament. One foot and one hand are broken.

PREA SAT SOUR PRÔT.

About 1200 metres in front of the building just described is one called "Prea sat sour prôt," and said to have been the royal treasury. It is square, and consists of sixteen towers connected by galleries, but nearly all in ruins: the doorways and walls are ornamented with sculpture, as in the other remains. It served, they say, as a depository for the crown jewels. The Cambodians also believe that ropes were stretched from one tower to another, on which dancers exercised their skill in the presence of the king, who, seated on one of the neighbouring terraces, enjoyed their performances. All traditions being lost, the natives invent new ones, according to the measure of their capacity.

The centre of the interior of the third enclosure is occupied by an immense esplanade, supported by walls formed of magnificent blocks of stone, sculptured and surrounded by staircases. The ground is level; but in the excavations that had been made I remarked large masses of carved stone.

Not far from this esplanade is a square building in tolerable preservation, the basement composed of great blocks of ferruginous stone, as are the staircases, of which there are four, one on each side; but they are so steep, narrow, and worn away that it is difficult to climb them. The base supports small galleries, very narrow, and having windows with carved bars. The stones and every doorway are covered with inscriptions.

In the centre of the gallery rises a ruined tower, approached by four staircases, as awkward to ascend as the others just mentioned. Near the doors are some figures of women, standing with flowers in their hands. This building appears very old: the stone is crumbling away like rotten wood.

PREA SAT FIAO SAÏE.

On the banks of the river which skirts the eastern side of Ongcor Thôm are several remains. The first you come to is Fiao Saïe, two or three hundred metres from the water's edge. Large and deep ditches surround it on all sides; and when these have been crossed you arrive in front of a terrace 45 metres long, and 2 metres 50 centimetres in width. Four rows of columns 1 metre high are all that is left standing. Those in the middle rows are square, the others are fluted, with capitals. This terrace leads to a square formed by four galleries, each 20 metres long: the one facing the terrace has three porticoes with doors and staircases, while in the centre, and at each corner of the gallery, are towers.

Another gallery, 40 metres long, leads from the central tower to another larger one, where, on a high pedestal, is placed the principal idol. On each side of this tower are three staircases, with porticoes projecting four or five metres, and supported by six high columns. All the windows have been ornamented with twisted bars, many of which still remain. By the side of each door are carved columns, every block being cut and polished with infinite patience and art. There are some bas-reliefs portraying a lion devouring a stag, dances, pantomimes, worshippers before idols, &c. As at Ongcor-Wat, the building is entirely composed of great blocks of sandstone.

PREA SAT IHEUR MANONE TIREADA, OR THE TEMPLE OF THE ANGELS.

This little pagoda is only about 150 metres from the preceding, and, according to tradition, was formerly a celebrated school for Buddhist theology. At the east is the principal entrance, which consists of a gallery 18 metres long, with a portico in the centre, and staircases. A second gallery, 30 metres long, terminated by a tower, extends from the centre of the other, and at about two-thirds of its length open out on either side porticoes and staircases. There are two other small buildings north and south, and a third behind the tower. That on the south is in good preservation, but receives no light except through a single door. This pagoda has been built with smaller stones than the other temples: in its architecture and details it much resembles Fiao Saïe.

THE BRIDGE.

Near Iheur Manone Tireada is a bridge of very ancient date, in a fair state of preservation, excepting the parapet and a portion of the roadway, which are a mass of ruins; but the piers and arches still remain. The piers are formed of sandstone, some of the blocks being long, others square, and placed irregularly; a few only are carved.

This bridge, with its fourteen narrow arches, may be about 42 or 43 metres in length, and 45 metres wide.

The river, instead of flowing under its arches, runs now along the side, its bed having been altered by the shifting of the sand, which has so accumulated around the piers and fallen stones, that a great portion of the former is concealed.

This bridge must have served as a communication between Ongcor the Great and the high road, which, traversing the province from east to west, took afterwards a southerly direction.

Prea sat Kéo.

Two hundred metres from the bridge rise, amidst the forest, the imposing ruins of Prea sat Kéo, to reach which you have to cross a deep moat. This done, you arrive at the exterior wall, which has four entrances formed by elegant pavilions, with staircases of eight steps leading to a terrace raised nearly 2 metres from the ground; from this you pass into a low narrow gallery with numerous interior windows ornamented with twisted bars. This gallery surrounds the building, and you ascend to it by a staircase leading to a second terrace. Three other terraces, each more than 3 metres 50 centimetres wide, rise one above another, supported on blocks of well-cut sandstone.

Each terrace forms a perfect square, the sides of the first measuring each 30 metres in length. A staircase, 15 metres high and 3½ metres wide, leads to the top; and a wide parapet to the staircase serves as a pedestal for four statues of lions, more or less injured. In the centre of the upper terrace is a lofty tower, and there are four smaller ones at the corners. Each tower has four porticoes with staircases, which rest on a base 7 metres high, and these towers are reached by staircases of twenty-two steps. From them a magnificent view is obtained over the surrounding forest. They, as well as their bases and staircases, are built of great blocks of granite arranged in regular tiers, and joined together in the most perfect manner. There is little sculpture, and the doorways have been left unfinished. The towers are without roofs, and perhaps never had any. The whole building appears very ancient, judging by the condition of the stone, which in many places is falling to pieces.

PONTÉEY TA PROUM.—TOWN OF TA PROUM.

On the road before mentioned are two towns containing some remarkable buildings. These towns, each of which is enclosed by walls forming a square, almost touch each other, being only about 20 metres apart. The walls are of ferruginous stone, surmounted by a coping of carved sandstone resembling a cornice, above which are serrated stones, giving a very finished appearance to the wall.

The smallest of these towns is called Pontéey Kedey (Town of Kedey); the other, Pontéey ta Proum.

The town of Ta Proum has seven gateways in the style of triumphal arches, formed by a central tower at the entrance and by lateral galleries. As at Ongcor the Great, a deep track is worn in the roadway beneath by the passage of vehicles. The interior of the town is completely deserted; no one enters it except the Cambodians from a hamlet outside the enclosure, who cultivate a few rice-plantations. In the centre are the ruins of a large and splendid monument, which has suffered greatly by the hand of time, and perhaps also from barbarous invasions. The ruins are surrounded by a double wall of ferruginous stone and by deep moats; and at every entrance are galleries with porticoes. A long gallery, 120 metres on each side, and with porticoes at the middle and at each end, goes quite round the building. Exteriorly, on each side, are two detached towers about 10 or 15 metres from the ruins. This gallery is formed by an interior wall and colonnades supporting a vaulted roof, which in many places has fallen in, and most of the columns are overthrown.

On the opposite wall are large bas-reliefs, forming series of subjects, set in a magnificent framework, which is in so good a state of preservation that the delicacy of the execution can be appreciated. As for the bas-reliefs themselves, they are much injured, not so much by time as by some barbarous hand, for everywhere are marks of the hammer or pickaxe. Leaving this gallery on the western side, you enter a long court, in which are three detached towers, and on the opposite side are similar towers.

Several of these, which are from 8 to 10 metres high, and well preserved, are real works of art. The mandarins of the provinces of Ongcor and Battambong are at present occupied in taking two of them to pieces, in order to transport them to Bangkok, the king having issued orders to that effect, and appointed one of the mandarins to carry them out.*

---

* In a letter from M. Silvestre, missionary at Battambong, to M. Mouhot, but which he never received, the murder of this mandarin is mentioned.

Beyond, extends a second rectangular gallery, connected with the first by three parallel galleries and two transverse ones. At the points where they intersect are ten towers, placed, like the galleries, in an odd and unsymmetrical fashion. The perfect preservation of several parts of these last, and the ruinous state of others, seem to mark different ages.

One of the towers and several of the galleries are constructed of ferruginous stone, the others of sandstone. The architecture of the galleries is the same as that of Ongcor-Wat, a double roof with colonnades. All the building is on one floor. This temple, which, after Ongcor-Wat, is the largest of all, is situated in a desert place, and lost amidst a forest; an exuberant vegetation has overgrown everything, galleries and towers, so that it is difficult to force a passage.

RUINS IN THE PROVINCE OF BATTAMBONG.

The principal ruins of this province are those of Bassette, Banone, and Watêk. I visited Bassette twice, before going to Ongcor and after; but all I could bring away was the design of a bas-relief in perfect preservation, carved on a block of sandstone 1 metre 50 centimetres long, forming the top of a doorway in a brick tower. The whole place is so ruinous, that one might suppose some enemy had done his utmost to demolish it, or that one gazed at the results of an earthquake. A thick vegetation, the haunt of fierce animals, has sprung up, and we found it quite impossible to discover the plan of the buildings. Galleries have disappeared under the ground, and the bases of doorways are to be seen 2 metres above.

The only portion which remains at all perfect is an erection 25 metres long and 6 metres wide, divided in two parts by an interior wall, the ends of which are in the form of a tower. It is built entirely of stone, and the exterior bears traces of fine carving on the tops of the doors and on the cornices; inside, the walls are bare, and almost all the stones chipped and injured. The windows have been ornamented with twisted bars, of which only a few traces remain.

On the ground inside lies a large broken stone, 5 decimetres wide and 2 thick, having on each side inscriptions apparently similar; this, and two small fractured idols are the sole remains of Buddhism at Bassette. The subjects, most frequently occurring over the doors, represent men with long beards, seated, and wearing high conical head-dresses, the hands either resting on the hilt of a poignard or crossed one over another, elephants with four heads, and other fanciful creatures.

A little beyond this enclosure is another, bounded by a wall of sandstone, a single block forming the thickness; it appears to have been only 75 centimetres high, and to have served as a kind of terrace. Within this enclosure are some magnificent columns, some still standing, others overthrown; doorways, the upper portions of which alone are visible above the ground; here and there fragments of sculptured stone, towers and walls nearly destroyed, and a beautiful dry basin, 18 metres square and above 2 metres deep, to which you descend by flights of steps extending the entire length of each side.

Bassette is believed to have been the occasional residence of the ancient sovereigns. Battambong is comparatively modern. It is scarcely a century since Bassette was the centre of a numerous Cambodian population, which has entirely disappeared in consequence of the frequent hostilities between Cambodia and Siam, the inhabitants being led away captive by the conquerors, who often employed this method of peopling the desert parts of their country. It is thus that, in Siam and Laos, entire provinces are to be found, of which the great mass of the population are of Cambodian origin.

The river which formerly flowed near Bassette has been banked up, and a new settlement, peopled from Penom-Peuh, Udong, and other places, formed in the place now called Battambong. Bassette is nine miles from this place, and about as far from the mountains.

Banone.—Ascending the river again for about forty miles from Battambong in a southerly direction, you arrive at a mountain standing somewhat isolated, but forming part of the ramifications of the great chain of Pursat. At the foot is a miserable pagoda of recent origin, and in the environs a few hamlets, while on the summit are the ruins of Banone.

Eight towers are connected with galleries, and communicate on two sides by a wall with a central tower nearly 8 metres in diameter. The buildings are all on one floor, and built of sandstone, and appear of the same date as Bassette. Although there is nothing about them especially remarkable, what remains of the galleries displays fine workmanship, and great taste and skill in construction.

Banone must have been a temple, for there are still in the central tower, and in two smaller ones connected by a gallery, a great number of enormous Buddhist idols, probably as ancient as the building itself, and surrounded by many divinities of less size. At the foot of the neighbouring mountains is a deep cavern in the limestone rock, from the roof of which hang some beautiful stalactites. The water dropping from these is considered sacred by the Cambodians, who attribute to it, amongst other virtues, that of imparting a knowledge of the past, present, and future. Devotees consequently resort hither in pilgrimage, from time to time, to gain information as to their own fate or that of their country, and address their prayers to the numerous idols scattered about on the ground or placed in the cavities of the rocks.

Wat-Ek.—This temple is about six miles on the other side of Battambong, and is in tolerably good preservation. The architecture of the galleries is full of beauty, and that of the tower very imposing; but neither here nor at Banone are you met by the singular grandeur and magnificence which make so great an impression on you in visiting Ongcor and most of the other ruins.

Wat-Ek is situated in an immense plain, bounded north and east by the beautiful mountains of Pursat and ramifications of those of Chantaboun.

CHAPTER XIV.

Remarks on Cambodia and its Ruins.

A knowledge of Sanscrit, of "Pali," and of some modern languages of Hindostan and Indo-China, would be the only means of arriving at the origin of the ancient people of Cambodia who have left all these traces of their civilization, and that of their successors, who appear only to have known how to destroy, never to reconstruct. Until some learned archæologist shall devote himself to this subject, it is not probable that aught but contradictory speculations will be promulgated. Some day, however, the truth will surely appear and put them all to flight. I myself, having nothing but conjecture to rest upon, advance my own theory with diffidence.

Nokhor has been the centre and capital of a wealthy, powerful, and civilized state, and in this assertion I do not fear contradiction from those who have any knowledge of its gigantic ruins. Now, for a country to be rich and powerful, a produce relatively great and an extended commerce must be presumed. Doubtless, Cambodia was formerly thus favoured, and would be so at the present day under a wise government, if labour and agriculture were encouraged instead of despised, if the ruling powers exercised a less absolute despotism, and, above all, if slavery were abolished—that miserable institution which is a bar to all progress, reduces man to the level of the brute, and prevents him from cultivating more than sufficient for his own actual wants.*

The greater part of the land is surprisingly fertile, and the rice of Battambong is superior to that of Cochin China. The forests yield precious gums, gum-lac, gamboge, cardamoms, and many others, as well as some useful resins. They likewise produce most valuable timber, both for home use and for exportation, and dye-woods in great variety. The mines afford gold, iron, and copper.

Fruits and vegetables of all kinds abound, and game is in great profusion. Above all, the great lake is a source of wealth to the whole nation; the fish in it are so incredibly abundant that when the water is high they are actually crushed under the boats, and the play of the oars is frequently impeded by them. The quantities taken there every year by a number of enterprising Cochin Chinese are literally miraculous. The river of Battambong is not less plentifully stocked, and I have seen a couple of thousand taken in one net.

Neither must I omit to mention the various productions which form so important a part of the riches of a nation, and which might be here cultivated in the greatest per-

---

* This is equally true of Cambodia and of Siam, the former country being tributary to the latter.

fection. I would especially instance cotton, coffee, indigo, tobacco, and the mulberry, and such spices as nutmegs, cloves, and ginger. Even now all these are grown to a certain limited extent, and are allowed to be of superior quality. Sufficient cotton is raised to supply all Cochin China, and to allow of some being exported to China itself. From the little island of Ko-Sutin alone, leased to the planters by the King of Cambodia, the transport of the cotton produce employs a hundred vessels. What might not be accomplished if these were colonies belonging to a country such, for example, as England, and were governed as are the dependencies of that great and generous nation?

Battambong and Korat are renowned for their silken "langoutis" of brilliant and varied colours, both the material and the dyes being the produce of the country.

A glance at the map of Cambodia suffices to show that it communicates with the sea by the numerous mouths of the Mekong and the numberless canals of Lower Cochin China, which was formerly subject to it; with Laos and with China, by the great river.

These facts being established, whence came the original inhabitants of this country? Was it from India, the cradle of civilization, or was it from China? The language of the present natives is that of the old Cambodians or Khendome, as they call the people who live retired at the foot of the mountains and on the tablelands, and it is too distinct from Chinese to render the latter supposition possible. But whether this people originally came from the north or from the west, by sea, and gradually making their way up the rivers, or from the land, and descending them, it seems certain that there must have been here other ancient settlers, who introduced Buddhism and civilization. It would appear as though these had been succeeded by some barbarous race, who drove the original inhabitants far into the interior, and destroyed many of their buildings. At all events, it is my belief that, without exaggeration, the date of some of the oldest parts of Ongcor the Great may be fixed at more than 2000 years ago, and the more recent portions not much later. The state of decay of many of these structures would indicate even a greater age; but they probably date from the dispersion of the Indian Buddhists, which took place several centuries before the Christian era, and which led to the expatriation of thousands of individuals.

All that can be said respecting the present Cambodians is, that they are an agricultural people, among whom a certain taste for art still shows itself in the carved work of the boats belonging to the better classes, and their chief characteristic is unbounded conceit.

It is not so among the savages of the east, called by the Cambodians their elder brothers. I passed four months among them, and, arriving direct from Cambodia, it seemed like entering a country comparatively civilized. Great gentleness, politeness, and even sociability—which, to my fancy, bore evidence of a past refinement—struck me in these poor children of nature, buried for centuries in their deep forests, which they believe to be the largest portion of the world, and to which they are so strongly attached that no inducement would tempt them to move. At the risk, then, of this portion of my notes being passed over by many readers, I shall enlarge a little upon these people, my own observations being aided by the information afforded me by the missionaries who have for years resided among their different tribes.

When looking at the figures in the bas-reliefs at Ongcor, I could not avoid remarking the strong resemblance of the faces to those of these savages. And besides the similar regularity of feature, there are the same long beards, straight langoutis, and even the same weapons and musical instruments.

Almost all the fruit-trees of the neighbouring countries are found, though in small numbers, among them; and they have some good species of bananas, which are unknown beyond the limits of their forests.

Having a great taste for music, and being gifted with ears excessively fine, with them originated the tam-tam, so prized among the neighbouring nations; and by uniting its sounds to those of a large drum, they obtain music tolerably harmonious. The art of writing is unknown to them; and as they necessarily lead a wandering life, they seem to have lost nearly all traditions of the past. The only information I could extract from their oldest chiefs was, that far beyond the chain of mountains which crosses the country from north to south are other "people of the high country"—such is the name they give themselves; that of *savage* wounds them greatly—that they have many relations there, and they even cite names of villages or hamlets as far as the provinces occupied by the Annamite invaders. Their practice is to bury their dead.

I extract the following account of the Bannavs—which applies to most of the tribes inhabiting the mountains and table-lands between Tonquin and Laos, Cochin China and Cambodia—from a letter of M. Comte, missionary in Cochin China, who recently died amongst them after a residence of several years:—

"To what race do the Bannavs belong? That is the first question I asked myself on arriving here, and I must confess that I cannot yet answer it; all I can say is, that in all points they differ from the Annamites and Chinese; neither do they resemble the Laotians or Cambodians, but appear to have a common origin with the Cédans, Halangs, Reungao, and Giaraïe, their neighbours. Their countenances, costumes, and belief are nearly the same; and the language, although it differs in each tribe, has yet many words common to all; the construction, moreover, is perfectly identical. I have not visited the various tribes of the south, but from all I have heard I conclude that these observations apply to them also, and that all the savages inhabiting the vast country lying between Cochin China, Laos, and Cambodia belong to the same great branch of the human family.

"The language spoken by the Bannavs has nothing

in common with that of the Annamites. Very simple in its construction, it is soft, flowing, and easy.

"These people manufacture the saucepans in which they cook their rice and wild herbs, the hatchets, pick-axes, and pruning-bills, which comprise all their agricultural instruments, the sabres which serve them as weapons, and the long-handled knives used for various kinds of work in which they excel. Their clay calumets, tastefully ornamented with leaves or other devices, are the production of the most skilful among the tribe. The women weave pieces of white or black cloth, which they use for coverings, and which, coarse as they are, form the principal article of commerce between the Bannavs and the Cédans.

"The villagers who live on the banks of the river Bla make light canoes, which are both solid and graceful, out of the trunks of trees. Such are the principal articles produced by the Bannavs, who are more backward than any of the other tribes, having little inventive genius.

"The Giaraïe, their neighbours on the south, show much taste and aptness in all they do; their clothes are of a finer texture than those spun by the Bannavs, and are sometimes embellished with designs which would be admired even in Europe. The iron which they forge is also wrought into more elegant forms, and is more finely tempered; and they manufacture some articles in copper. Very superior to the Reungao, they do not perhaps surpass the Halangs.

"The Cédans are a tribe of iron-workers, their country abounding in mines of this metal. The inhabitants of more than seventy villages, when their agricultural labours are over, busy themselves in extracting and working the ore, which they afterwards dispose of in the shape of hatchets, pickaxes, lances, and sabres.

"Amongst all the dwellers in a Bannav village, even more than among the other natives, there exists a very decided spirit of community. Thus, no family will drink wine without inviting others to join them, as long as the quantity will hold out; and on killing a pig, goat, or buffalo, the possessor divides it into as many portions as there are families, reserving for himself a share very little larger than the others. No one is forgotten in this distribution, from the youngest child to the oldest man. The deer and wild boar taken in the chase are divided in the same way, the hunters retaining only a rather larger portion in consideration of their labour and fatigue. I have actually seen a fowl divided into forty or fifty parts. Even if the children catch a serpent, a lizard, or a mouse in their little expeditions, you will see the oldest of them, on returning, portion it with strict impartiality amongst the party. These customs might have been borrowed from the early Christians had these savages ever heard of them. The other tribes also observe them, but less scrupulously.

"Not only does general censure follow any criminal act, but severe penalties, such as slavery or exile, are imposed for lying. Even suicide—instances of which you occasionally find among them—has a stigma affixed to it in their penal code; any one who perishes by his own hand is buried in a corner of the forest far from the graves of his brethren, and all who have assisted in the sepulture are required afterwards to purify themselves in a special manner.

"This legislation is far from being deficient in morality and wisdom, but unfortunately on certain points it is tainted with superstition, and has opened a large door to numberless injustices, and sometimes provoked cruel strife. On the subject of witchcraft they are particularly credulous: nearly every misfortune is attributed by them to the malice of certain persons whom they believe gifted with the power of influencing their fate; superstition serves as a guide to seek out the guilty individual, and when he is supposed to be discovered, he is usually sold for a slave, or a heavy ransom is exacted.

"The Bannavs believe in the existence of a multitude of spirits, some mischievous to man, others beneficent. According to their creed, every large tree, every mountain, every river, every rock, almost everything, has its particular genius; but they seem to have no idea of a superior being, sovereign and Creator of all things.

"If you ask them respecting the origin of mankind, all they tell you is, that the father of the human race was saved from an immense inundation by means of a large chest in which he shut himself up; but of the origin or creator of this father they know nothing. Their traditions do not reach beyond the Deluge; but they will tell you that in the beginning one grain of rice sufficed to fill a saucepan and furnish a repast for a whole family. This is a souvenir of the first age of the world, that fugitive period of innocence and happiness which poets have called the golden age.

"They have no very fixed ideas on the subject of rewards and punishments in a future life. They believe in the immortality of the soul, which, after leaving the body, they imagine wanders about the tombs and adjacent mountains, often terrifying the living by nocturnal appearances, and finally loses itself for ever in the shadowy depths of the regions of the south.

"All their religion consists of sacrifices and vows, vain and endless observances performed in the hope of warding off misfortune, alleviating suffering, and retarding the hour of death; for, as with all Pagans, the foundation of their religion is terror and egotism."

On my return from my excursion amongst the Stiêns, M. Fontaine, whom I met at Pinhalú, was so kind as to present me with his journal, kept during a residence of twenty years among various savage races, and which I hope some day will see the light; and he likewise favoured me with the following remarks on the dialects of several of these tribes:—

"The language of the Giaraïe and that of the Redais bear a strong resemblance to each other: the two tribes are only separated from each other by the river Bong, which flows between them in a westerly direction, after running for some distance from south to north and watering the lands of the Candians or Bihcandians, whose language also resembles in some degree that of the tribes just mentioned. The dialect of the Bonnavs or Menons does not appear to me to have any similitude to the others, nor even to those of the tribes farther north.

"After a sojourn of several years among these tribes, I was forced, on account of my health, to go to Singapore. I was astonished, after a little study of Malayan, to find in that language a number of Giaraïe words, and many more bearing a strong resemblance to words in that dialect; and I doubt not this similarity would be found still more remarkable by any one who thoroughly studied both languages. The resemblance also of the language of the Thiâmes, the ancient inhabitants of Isiampa, now in the province of Annam, to that of these tribes, leads me to believe that they must all have sprung from the same root."

The information I obtained from the Stiêns accords perfectly with these remarks of M. Fontaine:—"The Thiâmes," they said, "understand our language very well, but the Kouïs, who live beyond the great river, speak exactly the same language as ourselves." M. Arnoux, another missionary in Cochin China, who has long resided amongst these savage tribes, speaks in the same way respecting the language. To M. Arnoux also I owe the exact latitude of many places on the map, and a great deal of topographical information about the whole country; and it affords me great pleasure here to express my gratitude and my esteem for his character.

"The languages of the Sedans," says he, "of the Reungaos, and of the Italhans are almost identical, although often varying slightly even in the same tribe: the dialect of the northern Sedans is somewhat different from that of the southerns, and the Stiengs of Brelum speak differently from those farther to the east.

"The Bannav and the Bannam are nearly the same; the Bannav and Sedan much alike; generally only the terminations differ, but there are words in each not to be found in the other. M. Fontaine found that the Ieboune and Braon strongly resemble the Bannav. I cannot speak personally about the Giaraïe, Nedais, Bonous, and Bih; but doubtless others can."

I myself remarked many Stiên words like the Cambodian, especially in the western districts, where there exists some commerce between the two countries. To all this must be added that the Siamese, Laotian,* and Cambodian seem to be sister languages: more than a fourth part of the words, especially those expressing intellectual things, are exactly the same in each.

In the course of this work I have cited several passages from the Life of the Abbé Gagelin, who died a martyr in Cochin China, and which was published by Abbé Jacquenet: in it mention is made of savage races on the coast of Siam and in the environs of Kompat (Cambodia). I have sought in vain for them, and no one has ever heard them spoken of. Probably the missionary was

---

* Lao means ancient.

deceived by his servants, who were Annamites, and they always call the Cambodians and Siamese savages (Noye Uhen, inhabitants of the woods), while they give themselves the appellation of citizens.

Notwithstanding all my efforts to discover the traces of the probable migrations of the Jewish people through Siam and Cambodia, I have met with nothing satisfactory excepting a record of the judgment of Solomon, which, as I before stated, was found by M. Miche, Bishop of Laos and Cambodia, to be preserved *verbatim* in one of the Cambodian sacred books. To all my questions on this subject I received the same answer, "There are no Jews in the country." Nevertheless, among the Stiêns, I could not but be struck by the Hebrew character of many of the faces.

In 1670 Cambodia extended as far as Isiampa; but the provinces of Lower Cochin China, as Bien-hoa, Digne-Theun, Vigue Laon, Ann Djiann, and Ita-Tienne—all at one time conquered and annexed—have, for more than a century, shaken off their dependence on Cambodia; and the language and ancient Cambodian race have entirely disappeared in those districts. The different states have now their limits and sovereigns entirely independent of each other. Cambodia is, however, to a certain extent tributary to Siam, but in no degree to Annam; and I cannot understand how, at the present day, the French newspapers, even the 'Moniteur de la Flotte,' still less how our admiral in those seas, should habitually confound these two countries.

The suppositions of the Abbé Jacquenet, which I have already quoted and to which I was disposed to give credence, seem to fall before the more accurate information which I have obtained concerning the religion of the Thiâmes or Isiampois. It must be allowed that the only vestiges of Judaism found among them are equally met with amongst Mahometans. They have priests, temples, practise circumcision, abstain from pork, and frequently pronounce, with the greatest veneration, the words Allah and Mahomet. They themselves declare that their present religion was brought to them from Malaisia—that priests still come to them from thence and visit them from time to time. I had this information from some Cambodians of Battambong, who, having been taken prisoners in the wars with the Cochin Chinese, passed eight years in Isiampa. One of them, a blind man, who appeared to me to be remarkable for good sense and judgment—an exceptional case in this country—seemed especially to merit confidence. These facts, and others which I collected regarding the religion of the Thiâmes, who until 1859, the time of their flight, inhabited Cambodia, lead me to infer that the Abbé Gagelin was in error. I was certainly told of two sects into which the tribe was divided; but the only distinguishing point between them was that one ate pork and the other did not.

The Thiâmes must formerly have occupied several important districts in Cambodia, principally on the banks of the tributary of the Me-kong. Thus, on the shores of Touli Sap, or the great lake, not far from Battambong, is a place called Campong Thiâme (shore of the Thiâmes). More to the south, near Campong Tchnam, the village where the custom-house of Cambodia is erected, is an island called Isle of Thiâmes. According to tradition, the whole banks of the river, as far as Penom-Peuh, were formerly inhabited by these people; and to this cause is to be attributed the complete absence of remains in these localities.

The mountains of Dom-rêe, situated a little way to the north of Ongcor, are inhabited by the Khmer-dôme, a gentle and inoffensive race, although looked upon as savages by their brethren of the plain. These latter are the Somrais: they speak the Cambodian language, but with a different pronunciation. Beyond are the provinces, formerly belonging to Cambodia, but now Siamese, of Souréne, Song Kac, Con Khan, Nan Kong, and Ongcor-Eith or Korat.

According to popular belief, the king, if he should cross the great lake, is sure to die in the course of the year.

Whilst the present sovereign was prince he paid a visit to Ongcor, and seeing some of the Somrais, said, "These are my true subjects, and the stock from which my family sprang." It seems that, in fact, the present dynasty did so.

The Cambodians give the following account of the introduction of Buddhism among them. Samanokodom left Ceylon and went to Thibet, where he was very well received; from thence he went among the savages, but, not meeting with encouragement from them, he took refuge in Cambodia, where he was welcomed by the people.

A circumstance worthy of remark is that the name of Rome is familiar to nearly all the Cambodians: they pronounce it Rouma, and place it at the western end of the world.

There are among the Giaraïe two great nominal chiefs, called by the Annamites Hoa-Sa and Thorei-Sa, the king of fire and the king of water. The kings of Cambodia and Cochin China send to the former chief, every four or five years, a small tribute as a token of respectful homage, in consideration of the ancient power of which their ancestors have despoiled him. The king of fire, who appears to be the more important of the two, is called Eni (grandfather) by the savages, and the village where he resides bears the same name. When this "grandfather" dies, another is chosen, sometimes one of his sons, sometimes a stranger, the dignity not being hereditary. His extraordinary power is attributed, according to M. Fontaine, to Beurdao, an old sabre wrapped in rags, and having no other sheath. This sabre, say the Giaraïe, is centuries old, and contains a famous spirit (Giang), who must certainly have a good digestion to consume all the pigs, fowls, and other offerings brought to him. It is kept in a certain house, and whoever ventures to look at it dies suddenly, the sole exception being Eni himself, who has the privilege of seeing and handling it unharmed. Every inhabitant of the village has to act as sentinel in turn at this house.

Eni wages war on no one, and is assailed by none; consequently his attendants carry no arms when they go round to collect offerings. Most of the people give something, cloth, wax, pickaxes; anything is accepted.

I have written these few notes on Cambodia, after returning from a long hunting expedition, by the light of a torch, seated on my tiger-skin. On one side of me is the skin of an ape just stripped off; on the other, a box of insects waiting to be arranged and packed; and my employment has not been rendered easier by the sanguinary attacks of mosquitoes and leeches. My desire is, not to impose my opinions on any one, especially with regard to the wonderful architectural remains which I have visited, but simply to disclose the existence of these monuments, which are certainly the most gigantic, and also to my mind display a more perfect taste than any left to us by the ancients; and, moreover, to collect all the facts and traditions possible about these countries, hoping they may be useful to explorers of greater talent and fortune. For, I doubt not, others will follow in my steps, and, aided by their own government and by that of Siam, advantages denied to myself, will gather an abundant harvest where I have but cleared the ground.

But, after all, my principal object is natural history, and with that study I chiefly occupy myself. I have written, as I said before, in leisure hours, when resting from my fatigues, with a desire to implant in the breasts of others a love for the great works of Nature, and to benefit those who, in the quiet of their homes, delight to follow the poor traveller; who, often with the sole object of being useful to his fellow-men, or of discovering some insect, plant, or unknown animal, or verifying some point of latitude, crosses the ocean, and sacrifices family, comfort, health, and, too often, life itself.

But it is pleasant to the man devoted to our good and beautiful mother, Nature, to think that his work, his fatigues, his troubles and dangers, are useful to others, if not to himself. Nature has her lovers, and those alone who have tasted them know the joys she gives. I candidly confess that I have never been more happy than when amidst this grand and beautiful tropical scenery, in the profound solitude of these dense forests, the stillness only broken by the song of birds and the cries of wild animals; and even if destined here to meet my death, I would not change my lot for all the joys and pleasures of the civilised world.

CHAPTER XV.

KHAO SAMROUM—PROVINCE OF PECHABURI OR PHETXABURI.

AFTER a sojourn of three weeks within the walls of Ong-cor-Wat in order to make drawings and plans, I returned to Battambong. There I inquired for some means of transport to Bangkok, but, on different pretexts, I was detained more than two months before I could get away, in spite of the assistance of the viceroy. At last, on the 5th March, I set off with two waggons and two pair of powerful buffaloes, which had been taken wild, and trained up to the yoke, and were strong enough to sustain the fatigues of a journey at this season.

This time I carried along with me a complete menagerie; but of all my prisoners a pretty young chimpanzee, which, after slightly wounding it, we had succeeded in taking alive, was the most amusing. As long as I kept him in my room, and he could amuse himself with the numerous children and other visitors whom curiosity brought to look at him, he was very gentle; but as I was obliged on the journey to fasten him at the back of one of the waggons, he became frightened, and used ever effort to break his chain, continually screaming, and trying to hide himself. After a time, however, he got accustomed to his position, and was quiet and docile as before.

Our guns on our shoulders, I and my young Chinese Phrai followed or walked before the waggons, occasionally finding some sport as we skirted the forest. As for my other servant, when we reached Pinhalú he begged to be allowed to return to Bangkok by our former route; so, not wishing to retain him against his will, I paid his expenses home, and wished him happiness.

Scarcely had we proceeded a mile when our drivers asked my permission to stop for supper, saying that afterwards we could set out again, and travel part of the night. I at once consented, knowing it to be a custom with the Cambodians, before departing on a long journey, to make their first halt not far from their village, that they may return home to shed a last tear, and partake of a farewell glass.

Before the oxen were even unyoked, the families of our drivers were all collected round me, the whole party talking at once, and begging me to take care of their relations, to save them from robbers, and give them medicine if they had a headache. They all then took their evening meal together, washing it down with some glasses of arrack which I gave them; after which we resumed our journey by a magnificent moonlight, but treading in a bed of dust which reached to our ankles, and raised a thick cloud round our waggons.

We encamped part of the night near a small piece of water, where some custom-house officers are stationed—

three poor wretches—whose duty it is to arrest the depredators who lie in wait for the buffaloes and elephants coming down here from the lake and neighbouring districts. Those among us who had mats, spread them on the ground, and lay down; those who had none, piled up grass and leaves for beds.

For three days we travelled northward until we reached Ongcor-Borige, chief town of a province of the same name; but, surprised by darkness and a heavy storm, we were compelled to halt at the outskirts. The next morning, as we were leaving the place, we fell in with a caravan of thirty waggons conveying rice to Muang-Kabine, whither we were ourselves going; so my Cambodians fraternised with the party, all breakfasting together, and two hours afterwards we set off again at the head of this line of waggons.

There is here an immense plain, almost a desert, which in the best season takes six days to cross with elephants, and twelve with waggons. As for us, we set out on the 5th March, and only reached Muang-Kabine on the 28th; and oh! what we suffered from ennui, from heat, from attacks of mosquitoes, and want of water. In addition to these miseries my feet became like a jelly; and, when we arrived at our destination, I could scarcely drag myself along, or keep up with the slow but regular step of the buffaloes.

Some days before reaching Muang-Kabine we had to ford a small river, the Bang-Chang, and here we obtained some good water; but all the rest of the journey we had

Drawn by M. Sabatier, from a Sketch by M. Mouhot.

VIEW IN THE GULF OF SIAM.

nothing but the water from the muddy pools, serving for baths and drinking-places to all the buffaloes of the caravan. When I drank it, or used it for cooking or tea, I purified it with a little alum, a better method than filtering. Every day some accident happened to our waggons, which was one cause of our being so long on the road.

On our arrival at Muang-Kabine we found great excitement prevailing on account of a recent discovery of gold-mines, which had attracted to the place a number of Laotians, Chinese, and Siamese. The mines of Battambong, being less rich, are not so much frequented. From Muang-Kabine I continued my route to Paknam, where I hired a boat to take me to Bangkok.

The first day's navigation was very tedious, the water being shallow, and the sand-banks in many places bare, but the day following we were able to lay aside our poles, and take to the oars. The stream takes a bend towards the south, and empties itself into the gulf a little above Petrin, a district which produces all the sugar of Siam, which is sold at Bangkok.

This canal connects the Menam and the Bang-Chang, which afterwards takes the name of Bang-Pakong; it is nearly sixty miles in length, and was the work of a clever Siamese general, the same who, twenty years ago, retook Battambong from the Cochin-Chinese. He is also noted for having constructed a fine road from Paknam to Ongcor-Borige, the place where the great inundations have their limit. This road I could not make use of, for at this season I should have found neither water nor grass for my oxen.

On the banks of the Bang-Pakong are several Cambodian villages, peopled by prisoners from Battambong; and along the canal, on either side, is a mixed, and for this country numerous population, of Malays, Laotians from the peninsula, and Laotians from Vien-Chan, a district on the banks of the Mekong, north-east of Korat, and now depopulated by frequent revolts.

Although overburdened with taxes, yet, to judge from their clean and comfortable dwellings, and a certain air of well-doing which reigns in these villages, the inhabitants must enjoy some degree of prosperity, especially since the impulse given to commerce by the Europeans settled in the capital.

The water was so thickly covered with weeds that our progress was much impeded, and we were three days in the canal; while, after May, it only takes the same time to go from Paknam to Bangkok.

On the 4th April I returned to the capital, after fifteen months' absence. During the greater part of this time I had never known the comfort of sleeping in a bed; and throughout my wanderings my only food had been rice or dried fish, and I had not once tasted good water. I was astonished at having preserved my health so well, particularly in the forests, where, often wet to the skin, and without a change of clothes, I have had to pass whole nights by a fire at the foot of a tree; yet I have not had a single

Vol. II. p. 44.

Drawn by M. Bocourt, from a Sketch taken by M. Mouhot in the residence of the Prime Minister.

CEREMONY, ON A YOUNG SIAMESE COMING OF AGE, OF THE REMOVAL OF THE TUFT.

attack of fever, and been always happy and in good spirits, especially when lucky enough to light upon some novelty. A new shell or insect filled me with a joy which ardent naturalists alone can understand; but they know well how little fatigues and privations of all kinds are cared for when set against the delight experienced in making one discovery after another, and in feeling that one is of some slight assistance to the votaries of science. It pleases me to think that my investigations into the archæology, entomology, and conchology of these lands may be of use to certain members of the great and generous English nation, who kindly encouraged the poor naturalist; whilst France, his own country, remained deaf to his voice.

It was another great pleasure to me, after these fifteen months of travelling, during which very few letters from home had reached me, to find, on arriving at Bangkok, an enormous packet, telling me all the news of my distant family and country. It is indeed happiness, after so long a period of solitude, to read the lines traced by the beloved hands of an aged father, of a wife, of a brother. These joys are to be reckoned among the sweetest and purest of life.

We stopped in the centre of the town, at the entrance of a canal, whence there is a view over the busiest part of the Menam. It was almost night, and silence reigned around us; but when at daybreak I rose and saw the ships lying at anchor in the middle of the stream, while the roofs of the palaces and pagodas reflected the first rays of the sun, I thought that Bangkok had never looked so beautiful. However, life here would never suit me, and the mode of locomotion is wearisome after an active existence among the woods and in the chase.

The river is constantly covered with thousands of boats of different sizes and forms, and the port of Bangkok is certainly one of the finest in the world, without excepting even the justly-renowned harbour of New York. Thousands of vessels can find safe anchorage here.

The town of Bangkok increases in population and extent every day, and there is no doubt but that it will become a very important capital: if France succeeds in taking possession of Annam, the commerce between the two countries will increase. It is scarcely a century old, and yet contains nearly half a million of inhabitants, amongst whom are many Christians. The flag of France floating in Cochin China would improve the position of the missions in all the surrounding countries; and I have reason to hope that Christianity will increase more rapidly than it has hitherto done.

I had intended to visit the north-east of the country of Laos, crossing Dong Phya Phai (the forest of the King of Fire), and going on to Hieng Naie, on the frontiers of Cochin China; thence to the confines of Tonquin. I had planned to return afterwards by the Nékong to Cambodia, and then to pass through Cochin China, should the arms of France have been victorious there. However, the rainy season having commenced, the whole country was inundated, and the forests impassable; so it was neces-

VIEW OF THE PORT AND DOCKS OF BANGKOK. Drawn by M. Sabatier, from a Sketch by M. Moubot.

sary to wait four months before I could put my project in execution. I therefore packed up and sent off all my collections, and after remaining a few weeks in Bangkok I departed for Pechaburi, situated about 13° north lat., and to the north of the Malayan peninsula.

On the 8th May, at five o'clock in the evening, I sailed from Bangkok in a magnificent vessel ornamented with rich gilding and carved-work, belonging to Khrom Luang,

Drawn by M. Bocourt, from a Photograph.

PORTRAIT OF KHROM LUANG, ONE OF THE BROTHERS OF THE KING OF SIAM.

one of the king's brothers, who had kindly lent it to a valued friend of mine. There is no reason for concealing the name of this gentleman, who has proved himself a real friend in the truest meaning of the word; but I rather embrace the opportunity of testifying my affection and gratitude to M. Malherbes, who is a French merchant settled at Bangkok. He insisted on accompanying me for some distance, and the few days he passed with me were most agreeable ones.

The current was favourable, and, with our fifteen rowers, we proceeded rapidly up the stream. Our boat, adorned with all sorts of flags, red streamers, and peacocks' tails, attracted the attention of all the European residents, whose houses are built along the banks of the stream, and who, from their verandahs, saluted us by cheering and waving their hands. Three days after leaving Bangkok we arrived at Pechaburi.

The king was expected there the same day, to visit a palace which he has had built on the summit of a hill near the town. Khrom Luang, Kalahom (prime minister), and a large number of mandarins had already assembled. Seeing us arrive, the prince called to us from his pretty little house; and as soon as we had put on more suitable dresses we waited on him, and he entered into conversation with us till breakfast-time. He is an excellent man, and, of all the dignitaries of the country, the one who manifests least reserve and hauteur towards Europeans. In education, both this prince and the king are much advanced, considering the state of the country; but in their manners they have little more refinement than the people generally.

Our first walk was to the hill on which the palace stands. Seen from a little distance, this building, of

HALL OF AUDIENCE, PALACE OF BANGKOK. Drawn by M. Thérond, from a Photograph

European construction, presents a very striking appearance; and the winding path which leads up to it has been admirably contrived amidst the volcanic rocks, basalt, and scoria which cover the surface of this ancient crater.

About twenty-five miles off, stretches from north to south a chain of mountains called Deng, and inhabited by the independent tribes of the primitive Kariens. Beyond these rise a number of still higher peaks. On the low ground are forests, palm-trees, and rice-fields, the whole rich and varied in colour. Lastly, to the south and east, and beyond another plain, lies the gulf, on whose waters, fading away into the horizon, a few scattered sails are just distinguishable.

It was one of those sights not to be soon forgotten, and the king has evinced his taste in the selection of such a spot for his palace. No beings can be less poetical or imaginative than the Indo-Chinese; their hearts never appear to expand to the genial rays of the sun; yet they must have some appreciation of this beautiful scenery, as they always fix upon the finest sites for their pagodas and palaces.

Quitting this hill, we proceeded to another, like it an extinct volcano or upheaved crater. Here are four or five grottoes, two of which are of surprising extent, and extremely picturesque. A painting which represented them faithfully would be supposed the offspring of a fertile imagination; no one would believe it to be natural. The rocks, long in a state of fusion, have taken, in cooling, those singular forms peculiar to scoria and basalt. Then, after the sea had retreated—for all these rocks have risen from the bottom of the water—owing to the moisture continually dripping through the damp soil, they have taken the richest and most harmonious colours. These grottoes, moreover, are adorned by such splendid stalactites, which, like columns, seem to sustain the walls and roofs, that one might fancy oneself present at one of the beautiful fairy scenes represented at Christmas in the London theatres.

If the taste of the architect of the king's palace has failed in the design of its interior, here, at least, he has made the best of all the advantages offered to him by nature. A hammer touching the walls would have disfigured them; he had only to level the ground, and to make staircases to aid the descent into the grottoes, and enable the visitor to see them in all their beauty.

The largest and most picturesque of the caverns has been made into a temple. All along the sides are rows of idols, one of superior size, representing Buddha asleep, being gilt.

We came down from the mountain just at the moment of the king's arrival. Although his stay was not intended to exceed two days, he was preceded by a hundred slaves carrying an immense number of coffers, boxes, baskets, &c. A disorderly troop of soldiers marched both in front and behind, dressed in the most singular and ridiculous costumes imaginable. The emperor Soulouque himself would have laughed, for certainly his old guard must have made a better appearance than that of his East Indian

Drawn by M. Bocourt, from a Photograph.

GROTTO AT PECHABURI.

brother. Nothing could give a better idea of this set of tatterdemalions than the dressed-up monkeys which dance upon the organs of the little Savoyards. Their apparel of coarse red cloth upper garments, which left a part of the body exposed, in every case either too large or too small, too long or too short, with white shakos, and pantaloons of various colours; as for shoes, they were a luxury enjoyed by few.

A few chiefs, whose appearance was quite in keeping with that of their men, were on horseback, leading this band of warriors, whilst the king, attended by slaves, slowly advanced in a little open carriage drawn by a pony.

I visited several hills detached from the great chain Khao Deng, which is only a few miles off. During my stay here it has rained continually, and I have had to wage war with savage foes, from whom I never before suffered so much. Nothing avails against them; they let themselves be massacred, with a courage worthy of nobler beings. I speak of mosquitoes. Thousands of these cruel insects suck our blood night and day. My body, face, and hands are covered with wounds and blisters. I would rather have to deal with the wild beasts of the forest. At times I howl with pain and exasperation. No one can imagine the frightful plague of these little demons, to whom Dante has omitted to assign a place in his infernal regions. I scarcely dare to bathe, for my body is covered before I can get into the water. The natural philosopher who held up these little animals as examples of parental love was certainly not tormented as I have been.

About ten miles from Pechaburi I found several villages inhabited by Laotians, who have been settled there for two or three generations. Their costume consists of a long shirt and black pantaloons, like those of the Cochin Chinese, and they have the Siamese tuft of hair. The women wear the same head-dress as the Cambodians. Their songs, and their way of drinking through bamboo pipes, from large jars, a fermented liquor made from rice and herbs, recalled to my mind what I had seen among the savage Stiêns. I also found among them the same baskets and instruments used by those tribes.

The young girls are fair compared with the Siamese, and their features are pretty; but they soon grow coarse, and lose all their charms. Isolated in their villages, these Laotians have preserved their language and customs, and they never mingle with the Siamese.

Drawn by M. Bocourt, from a Sketch by M. Mouhot.

VIEW OF THE MOUNTAINS OF PECHABURI.

Drawn by M. Therond, from a Sketch by M. Mouhot.

PAVILION CONTAINING THE ASHES OF THE LATE KING OF SIAM IN THE GARDENS ATTACHED TO THE PALACE AT BANGKOK.

CHAPTER XVI.

RETURN TO BANGKOK — PREPARATIONS FOR A NEW EXPEDITION TO THE NORTH-EAST OF LAOS — PHRABAT — PAKPRIAU — SAOHAÏE.

AFTER a sojourn of four months among the mountains of Pechaburi, known by the names of Makaon Khao, Panam Knot, Khao Tamoune, and Khao Samroun, the last two of which are 1700 and 1900 feet above the level of the sea, I returned to Bangkok to make the necessary preparations for my new expedition to the north-east of Laos, my intended route being to the basin of the Mekong, towards the frontier of China. I had an additional motive for coming here again, namely, to get cured of that annoying complaint the itch, which I caught at Pechaburi; how, I really cannot guess, for, in spite of the mosquitoes, I bathed regularly two or three times a day; but I hope that a short course of rubbing with sulphur ointment, and proper baths, will effect a cure. This, one of the ills of a traveller's life, is, however, trifling in comparison with the misfortune of which I have just heard. The steamer 'Sir James Brooke,' in which Messrs. Gray, Hamilton, and Co., of Singapore, had sent off all my last boxes of collections, has foundered at the entrance of that port. And so all my poor insects, which have cost me so much care and pains for many months, are lost for ever — some of them rare and valuable specimens, which, alas ! I shall probably never be able to replace.

Two years ago, about this same season, I was nearly in the same place where I now am, on the Menam, some leagues north of Bangkok. The last floating shops, with their almost exclusively Chinese population, are beginning to disappear, and the banks of the river are assuming a monotonous aspect, although from time to time, through the brushwood and foliage of the bananas, the roof of some hut is visible, or the white walls of a pagoda, prettily situated, and surrounded by the modest dwellings of the priests.

It is the season of fêtes; the stream is covered with large and handsome boats, decorated with gilding and carved work, with true oriental gorgeousness; and among them the heavy barges of the rice-merchants, or the small craft of poor women going to the market with bananas and betel-nuts. It is only on festivals, and a few other occasions, that the king, princes, and mandarins display their riches and importance. The king was on his way to a pagoda to offer presents, followed by his whole court. Each of the mandarins was in a splendid barge, the rowers being dressed in the most brilliant colours. A number of pirogues were filled with soldiers in red coats. The royal barge was easily to be distinguished from the rest, by the throne surmounted by a canopy terminating in a pinnacle, and by the immense quantity of carving and

Drawn by M. Sabatier, from a Sketch by M. Mouhot.

THE BAR OF THE RIVER MENAM.

Drawn by M. Catenacci, from a Sketch by M. Mouhot.

CLOCK TOWER AT BANGKOK.

gilding about it. At the king's feet were some of his children, and he waved his hand to every European whom he saw.

All the ships at anchor were adorned with flags, and every floating house had an altar covered with various objects, and with odoriferous woods burning on them. Amidst all these fine barges, one was remarkable for its simplicity, and the good taste with which the rowers were dressed,—a uniform of white cloth, with red cuffs and collar. It belonged to Khrom Luang, the king's brother, a good, courteous, and intelligent prince, ever ready to protect Europeans to the utmost of his power; in a word, a gentleman.

Most of the dignitaries, generally fat men, were lying lazily on triangular embroidered cushions, in their splendid boats, upon a kind of dais, surrounded by officials, women, and children, kneeling, or lying flat, in readiness to hold out the golden urns which serve them for spittoons, or their betel-boxes or teapots, all made of the same precious metals by the goldsmiths of Laos and Ligor. The boats have generally from eighty to a hundred rowers, with the head and greater part of the body bare, but wearing a large white scarf round the loins, and a brilliant red *langouti;* they all raise their paddles simultaneously, and strike the water in regular time, while at the prow and stern are stationed two other slaves, one dexterously managing a long oar which serves as a rudder, the other on the watch to prevent a collision with any other boat. The rowers continually raise a wild, exulting cry, "Ouah! ouah!" while the steersman utters a louder and more prolonged one, which rises above the voices of the rest. Many boats also are to be seen crowded with women, musicians, or parties carrying presents. The *coup d'œil* is certainly charming.

Drawn by M. Sabatier, from a Sketch by M. Mouhot.

SCENE ON THE RIVER MENAM, NEAR BANGKOK.

From time to time appears, amidst the picturesque assemblage, the boat of some European, always to be recognised by his "chimney-pot" or silk hat.

Drawn by M. Sabatier, from a Sketch by M. Mouhot.

A PRIEST IN HIS BOAT.

All these scenes passed rapidly away, and, before long, I could only hear the distant sounds of the music, and see a few scattered boats adorned with streamers, passing up or down the river, being often skilfully managed by girls and very young children, who amused themselves by racing. It is evident, from the careless gaiety of these people, that they do not suffer the frightful poverty but too often met with in our large cities. When his appetite is satisfied—and, for that, all that is necessary is a bowl of rice, and some fish seasoned with capsicum—the Siamese is lively and happy, and sleeps without care for the morrow; he is, in fact, a kind of Lazzaroni.

My friend M. Malherbes accompanied me for a few hours' sail from Bangkok, and then we parted with a warm clasp of the hand, and, I confess, not without tears in both our eyes, trusting that destiny might reunite us here or elsewhere. My friend's light boat glided rapidly down the stream; in a few minutes he was out of sight, and I was again left alone—for how long a period being quite uncertain. I rarely allow myself to dwell on the subject; but separations are painful to the traveller who has left behind him all he holds most dear in the world,—family, country, home, and friends,—to visit countries inhospitable, and in many ways dangerous, without comfort or companionship. It is equally painful to think that, during long months, his impatient family are living in anxiety, and forming a thousand conjectures as to his fate. I know what awaits me, having been warned both by the missionaries and the natives. During the last twenty-five years, only one man, as far as I know, a French priest, has penetrated to the heart of Laos, and

Drawn by M. Thérond, from a Photograph.

THE NEW PALACE OF THE KING OF SIAM, BANGKOK.

he only returned to die in the arms of the good and venerable prelate, Mgr. Pallegoix. I know the discomfort, fatigue, and tribulations of all sorts to which I am again about to expose myself; the want of roads, the difficulty of finding means of conveyance, and the risk of paying for the slightest imprudence by a dangerous or even fatal illness. And how can one be prudent when compelled to submit to the hardest life of the forest, to suffer many privations, and to brave all inclemencies of the weather? Nevertheless, my destiny urges me on, and I trust in the kind Providence which has watched over me until now.

Only a few hours before my departure from Bangkok, the mail arrived, and I received news of my dearly loved family, which consoled me for the misfortune I sustained in the loss of my collections. Thanks, thanks, my good friends, for the pleasure you gave me before starting, by the expression of your warm and constant affection; I shall not forget you in my solitude.

I shall continue during my journey to take notes of all my little adventures, very rare, alas! for I am not one of those travellers who kill a tiger and an elephant at one shot; the smallest unknown shell or insect is more interesting to me; however, on occasion, I do not object to a meeting with the terrible inhabitants of the forest, and more than one have known the range of my rifle and the calibre of my balls.

Every evening, enclosed in my mosquito curtains, either in some cabin or at the foot of a tree, in the jungle

Drawn by M. Rousseau, from a Photograph.

KUN MOTTE, A SIAMESE NOBLE AND SAVANT.

or by the river bank, I shall talk to you, my friends; you shall be the companions of my journey, and it will be my greatest pleasure to confide to you my impressions and thoughts.

Scarcely had my friend M. Malherbes left me, when I discovered, in the bottom of my boat, a box, which he had contrived to place, unknown to me, among my packages; a fresh proof of his kindness, for he had already sent me three cases when I was at Pechaburi. I found it to contain some dozens of Bordeaux, as much cognac, boxes of sardines, biscuits, and a number of other things, which would recall to me, were I ever likely to forget it,

Drawn by M. Catenacci, from a Photograph.

BUILDING FOR THE INCREMATION OF THE QUEEN OF SIAM.

the true and considerate friendship of my countrymen, so valuable to one far from home.

I also carry with me most agreeable *souvenirs* of another excellent friend, Dr. Campbell, of the Royal Navy, attached to the British Consulate; and am very grateful to Sir R. Schomberg, the English Consul, who has shown me much attention and sympathy. Here let me, likewise, express my obligations to Mgr. Pallegoix, to the American Protestant missionaries, and, indeed, to most of the Consuls and resident strangers, who have all shown me kindness; and I would particularly mention the name of M. D'Istria, the new French Consul.

Let me say, in passing, that I am cured of the itch, which I suspect my servants had caught in wandering about the villages, and had communicated to me, in spite of my scrupulous cleanliness.

The banks of the Menam are covered with splendid crops, the periodical inundations rendering them as fertile as those of the Nile. I have four Laotian rowers; one of them was in my service for a month two years ago, and he now begged to be allowed to attend me throughout my journey, telling me I should find him very useful. After a little hesitation I have engaged him, so now I shall have three servants. My good and faithful Phrai has never left me, luckily for me, for I should find it difficult to replace him; and, besides, I am attached to the lad, who is active, intelligent, industrious, and devoted to me. Deng — which means "The Red"—his companion, is another Chinese whom I brought from Pecha-

Drawn by M. Bocourt, from a Photograph.

SAYA VISAT, HEAD OF THE CHRISTIANS AT BANGKOK.

buri. He knows English pretty well; not that incomprehensible jargon of Canton, "You savee one piccey boy, lartel pigeon," &c. (You know a clever boy, &c.) He is very useful to me as interpreter, especially when I wish to comprehend persons who speak with a great piece of betel between their teeth. He is likewise my cook, and shows his skill when we want to add an additional dish to our ordinary fare, which occasionally happens when some unfortunate stag comes within range of my gun, or I bring down a pigeon, or even a monkey, a kind of game not much to my taste, though highly esteemed by my Chinese, as well as wild dog and rat. Every one to his taste.

This attendant of mine has one little defect, but who has not in this world? He now and then takes a drop too much, and I have often found him sucking, through a bamboo cane, the spirit of wine from one of the bottles in which I preserve my reptiles, or laying under contribution the cognac presented to me by my friend Malherbes. A few days ago he was seized with this devouring thirst, and, profiting by my absence for only a few minutes, he opened my chest, and hastily laid hands on the first bottle which presented itself, great part of the contents of which he swallowed at one gulp. I came back just as he was wiping his mouth with his shirt-sleeve, and it would be impossible to describe his contortions and grimaces as he screamed out that he was poisoned.

He had had the bad luck to get hold of my bottle of ink; his face was smeared with it, and his shirt pretty well sprinkled. It was a famous lesson for him, and I think it will be some time before he tries my stores again.

The wages I give at present are ten ticals each per month, which, allowing for exchange, amounts to nearly forty francs per month. This in any other country would be good pay; but here I should find great difficulty in finding any other men to accompany me, were I to offer them a tical a day.

I soon reached the mountains of Nephaburi and Phrabat, with their pure clear atmosphere, the weather being pleasant and a fresh wind blowing. All nature looks smiling, and I feel exhilarated and happy. At Bangkok I felt stifled and oppressed. That town does not awaken my sympathies. Here my heart dilates, and I could fancy I had grown ever so much taller since I arrived. Here I can breathe, I live, amid these beautiful hills and woods; in cities I seem to suffocate, and the sight of so great a number of human beings annoys me.

I stopped yesterday at Ayuthia to see Father Larmandy, and, after a night passed beneath his hospitable roof, proceeded on my way towards Pakpriau. The whole day after our departure we passed by fields and rice-plantations on both sides of the river. All the country, till within two miles of Ayuthia, is inundated; there, only, the ground begins to rise a foot above the waters. Already, in several places they are beginning to cut the rice, and in a fortnight the whole population, male and female, will be busy with the harvest.

At present most of them are availing themselves of the short time left them to enjoy the "far niente," or visit the pagodas with offerings to the priests, which consist principally of fruit and yellow cloth; the latter intended to afford a supply of raiment for them while they are travelling; as, during several months of the dry season, they are allowed to quit their monasteries and go where they like.

October 20.—Having reached Thama Triestard at night, we slept at the entrance of the village, and early this morning I stopped my boat before the house of Khun

PORTICO OF THE AUDIENCE HALL AT BANGKOK.

Drawn by M. Clerget, from a Photograph.

Pakdy, the kind chief who, two years ago, accompanied me to Phrabat. The worthy man was not a little surprised to see me, and could scarcely believe his eyes, for he had heard that I had died at Muang-Kabuic. We soon renewed our acquaintance, and I was pleased to find that his regard for me, especially when stimulated by a glass of cognac, had survived the lapse of time. Poor Khun Pakdy! if I were King of Siam—which Heaven forbid!—I would name you Prince of Phrabat, or rather resign my throne to you.

He gave immediate orders to prepare breakfast for me; then, on finding that I was going to Korat, he remembered that he had promised again to be my companion if I brought him a gun from Bangkok. "If it were only worth three ticals it would do," said he; but seeing only the same percussion guns, "You have not brought me one," he observed; "but never mind, I will go with you all the same." It was only when I told him that I should make but a very short stay at Korat, and intended to proceed farther on into places where he would doubtless have to "tighten his belt," and that I did not wish him to lose his comfortable mandarin's *embonpoint*, that I succeeded in checking his enthusiastic devotion. But when he heard that we should be obliged to sleep among the woods by the light of the stars, he turned the conversation.

As soon as we had breakfasted I returned to my boat to escape his rather too demonstrative conversation, and the noisy eulogiums he continued to pour upon me.

From hence are visible the beautiful chain of hills which extend from Nephaburi, and which, I conjecture, join those of Birmanie and the Deng mountains, which do not appear more than fifteen miles off, and awaken a host of agreeable recollections. I feel sure the fine season has arrived; the air is pure, the sky serene, and the sun shines almost constantly.

Saohaïe, October 22.—I have not yet reached Pakpriau, and already I have met with, and begun to suffer from, the annoyances inevitable in a country like this, inundated during a great part of the year, and in which the means of travelling are so difficult to obtain, particularly when one is burdened with an extra, though indispensable, quantity of luggage.

During the two days I have been here I have lodged in the boat of a Chinese who was at first afraid to receive me; and I may consider myself fortunate in meeting with any resting-place. Yesterday I paid a visit to the governor, who resides in an old hut, repulsively dirty, about two miles from the spot where I landed. Although this is the most important place in Saraburi, this wretched dwelling, and a few scattered huts belonging to agriculturists, are all the houses I have seen; there is no bazaar, and no floating shops. From time to time petty merchants come to sell or exchange salt and other articles of absolute necessity; or a few Chinese with small stocks of *langoutis*, arrack, cloth, Siamese dresses, and bowls, which they barter for skins, horns, or rice. These dealers sometimes go as far as Boatioume.

The current was so strong, that in a quarter of an hour we reached the residence of the mandarin whose acquaintance I had made on my former journey, and who, in return for a present I had given him, had promised me, in the event of my going to Korat, to furnish me with even a hundred attendants, if I needed as many. I announced to him my intention of visiting Khao-Khoc, fixed upon two years ago by the King of Siam as a desirable place for a fortress to which he might retire, in case the too active Europeans should seize upon his capital—which, let me whisper, would be very easy to do, and would only require a handful of our brave Zouaves accustomed to an African sun.

I was all the better received by the mandarin, that I asked for nothing; for I had already engaged a boat, the owner of which wished to return to Khao-Khoc in two days. I had projected a trip to Patawi, but at this season the roads are impassable, so that I was forced to abandon the idea.

A great number of the inhabitants of this province are natives of Laos, and are principally captives brought from Vien Chang after the insurrection there. The provinces of Boatioume and Petchaboune are peopled by Siamese, for Laos proper only commences at M'Lôm. Boatioume, Petchaboune, Sôm, and some other provinces in the north and east, are governed by Siamese mandarins of rank more or less elevated; that is to say, several of them have the power of life and death, and are then considered as viceroys. The most distant provinces belong to the empire of Siam, and form a part of it.

Petchaboune is particularly noted for its tobacco, which is reckoned the best in Siam; and a commerce in this article is carried on with Bangkok in spite of the extreme difficulty of communication; for in the time of the inundations, when boats of some size are able to come up here, the contending against a very strong current is the labour of a month; while in the dry season only very small boats can be used, as, frequently, they have to be dragged over the sand, or carried past the rocks, which in many places cause rapids and obstruct the navigation. This commerce is chiefly in the hands of the Siamese of Petchaboune, who arrive at Pakpriau towards the end of the rainy season, to exchange their tobacco for betel and other articles.

The province of Saraburi is very populous, and in the southern districts a great quantity of rice is produced, but the quality of it is inferior to that of Pechaburi, which is considered very good, and is regularly bought by the Siamese dealers, who afterwards carry it to Bangkok. As is the case all over the country, there is great difficulty in arriving at a correct estimate of the population, which is scattered along the banks of the stream.

Saohaïe is the starting-point for all the caravans going to Korat. Another road, from Muang-Kabuic, also leads to this ancient Cambodian town; but it is little frequented, except by the Laotians of the locality.

Whilst writing I was interrupted by the unexpected visit of the governor, who was on his way to a pagoda to make an offering of dried fruits, and passed an hour in my cabin. He was in a large and elegant pirogue more than 30 metres long, for which I would have given his house and all its appurtenances. He sent for the owner of the boat which was to take me to Khao-Khoc, and gave him some instructions for the chief of that place, adding, "I have sent no letter, because I know that M. Mouhot made himself respected when here two years ago, and will doubtless do the same there." I could not but offer him some small presents in acknowledgment of this slight service, which might or might not be of use to me. I therefore gave him a pair of spectacles mounted in tortoiseshell, a bottle of scent, and one of brandy; and I prepared for him a sedative mixture, as he begged for some medicine for his rheumatism. Happy Raspail! who, with his "system," can assuage suffering even in these distant lands.

In return, he promised to give me a pony when I wanted to go to Korat, besides other useless things; but he will probably forget these promises, for here it is the custom of the rich to accept everything even from the poorest, but very rarely to give away. However, were it not for peculation and presents, how could these mandarins live? Their salary—when they have one—would condemn them to a state of leanness which would not only drive them to despair, but cause them to be looked upon as unsuitable for their places.

VOYAGE TO KHAO-KHOC.—DONG PHYA PHAI (FOREST OF THE KING OF FIRE).

I am now en route for Khao-Khoc, in the boat of a Chinese merchant, a worthy person, who, luckily for me, does not intoxicate himself with opium or arrack. He intends going as far as Boatioume, but the current is so strong that I doubt if he will be able to proceed higher up the river than Khao-Khoc; for, in spite of his four rowers, and the aid of my two men—(I sent away my Laotian, who found it too great fatigue to row, and preferred sleeping and smoking)—we have been nearly carried away at every bend of the river and at the frequent rapids.

The weather, which I trusted was settled, has changed during the last three days, and every afternoon, about four or five o'clock, we have a violent shower. Last evening I was seized with a more severe headache than any I have had since I entered the country, and my first impression was that I had been attacked by fever, which, in the rainy season, there is so much cause to dread in the neighbourhood of Dong Phya Phai. It proceeded, however, only from the heat of the sun, to which I had been all day exposed, and was dissipated by the freshness of the night air at the prow of the boat. In the morning I felt as well as usual.

They tell me that to-morrow I shall see Khao-Khoc, and I shall not be at all sorry. The little boat is so encumbered with our united baggage, that the fraction of space left for me forces me to all sorts of constrained and uncomfortable positions; and these twelve days of tedious navigation have fatigued me much. And what a place this is! The air is damp, unwholesome, and dreadfully heavy; one's head burns, while one's body is at one time covered with perspiration, and at another a cold shivering comes on.

After four days of excessive toil we entered a gorge through which the river passes, which, even at this season, is here not more than 90 metres wide. Torrents of rain, bursting suddenly upon us, forced us to stop rowing, and take refuge under our roof of leaves. The rain lasted all night, and a wretched night it was for the poor men, who, having yielded to me the front of the boat, were all crammed together in the cabin, and, after all their fatigues under a burning sun, were unable to obtain a moment's sleep, but lay groaning under the suffocating atmosphere and the attacks of legions of mosquitoes.

At daybreak about a hundred strokes of the oar brought us past a new bend in the river, and we found ourselves before Khao-Khoc. This place has, in my humble opinion, been badly chosen by the kings of Siam for their stronghold and retreat in case of an European invasion of the south. In the event of this occurring, they would abandon Bangkok; and, certainly, as whoever possesses that town is master of the whole country, no one would be likely to come and molest the kings in their solitude.

Two or three miles below Khao-Khoc I observed a kind of landing-place, and a house of mediocre appearance, bearing the pretentious appellation of palace, although built only of leaves and bamboo. This is Rabat Moi. At Khao-Khoc, although the second king often visits it, there is no landing-place, nor even steps cut in the steep banks to aid the ascent.

Immediately after landing I set off to look for a lodging, having been informed that I should find numerous vacant houses belonging to mandarins, amongst which I might make my choice. My men and I hunted amid the brushwood, often sinking up to our knees in mud, but could discover only seven or eight Laotian huts, the inhabitants of which form the nucleus of the population of this future stronghold, now peaceful and hospitable agriculturists, who would be deeply afflicted, and still more terrified, if ever their echoes should repeat the roar of cannon and varied sounds of war. As for the royal habitations, I could not reach them, for the whole ground, excepting a strip about fifty feet broad next the river, is a swamp; and the narrow paths are obstructed by bushes and tall grass, which had had time to grow during the six or eight months that have elapsed since the King has visited the place.

Not being able to find a lodging, some men from the village joined us, and we all set to work to cut down bamboos, with which to construct one, which was soon accomplished; and in this hut, open to every wind, we took up our abode.

I was told that a white elephant had just been taken in Laos, and had been sent off to Bangkok under the care of a mandarin.

All the inhabitants of the village, amounting perhaps to about fifty, have brought their children to me, begging for remedies; some for fevers, others for dysentery or rheumatism. I have not heard of any cases of leprosy here, as at Khao-Tchioulaü, but the children are repulsively dirty; they are covered with a coating of filth, which makes them resemble little negroes, and the greater number of them are shaking with fever.

The site of my hut is in a valley, formed by a belt of mountain-chains, running from Nephaburi and Phrabat, and connected with those of the peninsula and of Birmah. Mount Khoc is distant a kilometre from the left bank of the river, and stretches out in the form of a semicircle, afterwards joining the mountains which run eastward towards Korat, and M'Lôm, and Thibet. Facing Mount Khoc, other mountains rise abruptly from the right bank, and then extend in an easterly direction.

As soon as my dwelling was finished, which was neither a long nor a costly job, we slung up three hammocks, and then betook ourselves to prepare a place for insect-catching, the end of the rainy season being the best time for this work. We accordingly cut down a great number of trees, a hard and painful task in this climate, where the sun, drawing up the humidity from all the surrounding marshes, makes one feel as if in a stove or hothouse; but our labours have been abundantly repaid by a rich harvest of specimens. Beetles of the longicorn tribe abound here; and to-day I have filled a box with more than a thousand new or rare insects. I have even been

Drawn by M. Sabatier, from a Sketch by M. Mouhot.

LAOTIAN HOUSE.

fortunate enoguh to replace some of the more valuable kinds which were destroyed or injured by sea-water on board the 'Sir James Brooke.' The villagers come every day to bring me "beasts," as they call them, grasshoppers, scorpions, serpents, tortoises, &c., all presented to me at the end of a stick.

The sanitary condition of the place is dreadful. The rains are now less abundant, and the river has fallen more than twenty feet. They tell me that at Boatioume it is so narrow that the branches of the trees on the two banks touch and form an arch overhead. The mountains are of calcareous rock, and are covered with a fertile vegetation, but everywhere bear the traces of the water which anciently covered them. From the top you can imagine the former limits of the ocean, and see that the plain to the south was then submerged, and that all these heights formed capes or islands. I found close to their base, under a stratum of soil, banks of fossil coral and sea-shells in a good state of preservation.

The north wind now makes itself frequently felt, although the south-east and south-west winds resume their sway at times, and bring back the rain; but the heat of the nights gradually diminishes, and now, after three o'clock in the morning, I can bear a covering, and am glad to wrap myself in my burnous. My two men suffer occasionally from attacks of intermittent fever, and often complain of cold in the stomach; indeed, death lays so many snares for us here, that he who escapes may think himself lucky.

At last we breathe a pure and delicious air. It is now mid winter; since the day before yesterday a fresh north-wind has blown, and at night the thermometer has gone back to 18° centigrade. All the evening I have been walking by the river, wrapped in a warm burnous, with the hood up; and this is a pleasure I have not enjoyed since I was at Phrabat, two years ago.

One must have passed sleepless nights, suffocating with the extreme heat, in order to appreciate the comfort of sleeping under a woollen covering, and, above all, without the necessity of waging incessant war on the dreadful mosquitoes. Phrai and Deng wear their whole wardrobe both night and day, and I have seen them dressed in red flannel and with felt hats, when you might take them for Garibaldians, as far, that is to say, as their costume is concerned, for their appearance otherwise is far from warlike; however, they are not wanting in a kind of courage which has its own merit. They dance and sing round a good fire, and open their eyes with astonishment when I tell them that I have seen rivers larger than the Menam frozen over so hard that the heaviest vehicles could go upon them with safety,* and others on which whole oxen have been roasted;† and that men and animals often die of cold.

My little "Tine-Tine" says nothing, but creeps under my counterpane and sleeps at his ease; only if Phrai torments him by lifting the cover, he shows his teeth. Ungrateful being that I am, I have not yet spoken of this little companion who is so faithful and attached to me—of this pretty "King Charles," whom I brought from home. All the Siamese, and especially those who have no

* In Russia, on the Neva.

† On the Thames at London.

children, are very fond of the little creature, notwithstanding their general aversion for dogs. Theirs, however, are usually half savage. I much fear that my poor dog will come to an untimely end, and be trampled under foot by some elephant, or devoured at a mouthful by a tiger.

For the last few days we have feasted; our provisions were beginning to fail, but the fish are now coming up the river, and we take them by hundreds. Certainly they are not much larger than sardines, but in an hour we took six or eight basketfuls, and my two boys have enough to do to cut off their heads and salt them.

All the children of the neighbourhood, most of whom are still kept at the breast, come frequently to bring me insects, in exchange for a button or cigarette, for it is a common thing for them to leave their mother's breast to smoke. Were they not so dirty, they would be nice-looking; but I am afraid of touching them, lest I should again catch the itch.

The Laotian is as superstitious as the Cambodian, and perhaps more so than the Siamese. If a person falls ill of a fever, or, indeed, is ever so slightly indisposed, they believe it to be owing to a demon who has entered his body. If any matter in which they are engaged goes wrong, or an accident happens when hunting, fishing, or cutting wood, it is the fault of the demon. In their houses they carefully preserve some object, generally a simple piece of wood, or some parasitic plant, whose form they fancy bears a resemblance to some part of the human body; and this is constituted their household god, and prevents evil spirits from entering, or, at least, causes them speedily to depart.

Every day we go out on our collecting expeditions; but while we are seeking insects or birds, the sound of our voices, or the report of our guns, repeated by the mountain echoes, brings forth the wild beasts from their dens. Yesterday, after a long and fatiguing excursion, during which we had killed some birds and one or two monkeys, we were returning home quite worn out, when we reached a small clearing in the forest, and here I told my two boys* to take a little repose at the foot of a tree, while I went to hunt for insects.

Suddenly I heard a sound as of some animal gliding through the thick underwood. I looked round, at the same time loading my gun, and then crept quietly back to the tree where my servants lay asleep, when I perceived a large and beautiful leopard taking his spring to clear the brushwood, and pounce upon one of them as he lay all unconscious. I fired, the shot striking the animal in the right shoulder. He gave a tremendous leap, and rolled over among the bushes, which much embarrassed his movements. However, he was but wounded, and still dangerous, if my second ball did not kill, or at least cripple him. I fired again, and hit him between the shoulders; the ball lodged in the heart, and he fell dead almost instantaneously. The terror of my two poor fol-

* The word "boy" is generally used by me to denote a male servant.

Drawn by M. Bocourt, from a Sketch by M. Mouhot

M. MOUHOT AND HIS SERVANTS SURPRISED BY A LEOPARD.

lowers, suddenly awakened by the report of my gun so close to their ears, was only equalled by their pleasure when they saw the creature extended lifeless before them.

Another year has flown, a year chequered for me, as for others, with joy, anxiety, and trouble; and to-day my thoughts turn especially to the few who are dear to me. From more than one loving heart arise, I feel sure, on this day, good wishes for the poor traveller, and from no one more warmly than from you, my dear father. You long for my return; so writes my brother in his last letter, forwarded to me from Bangkok. But I am only commencing my new campaign; would it be like a good soldier to leave on the eve of the engagement? I am at the gates of the infernal regions, for so the Laotians and Siamese designate this forest, and I have no spell to terrify the demons which inhabit it, neither tiger's teeth nor stunted stag-horn; nothing but my faith in and love for God. If I must die here, where so many other wanderers have left their bones, I shall be ready when my hour comes.

The profound stillness of this forest, and its luxuriant tropical vegetation, are indescribable, and at this midnight hour impress me deeply. The sky is serene, the air fresh, and the moon's rays only penetrate here and there, through the foliage, in patches, which appear on the ground like pieces of white paper dispersed by the wind. Nothing breaks the silence but a few dead leaves rustling to the earth, the murmur of a brook which flows over its pebbly bed at my feet, and the frogs answering each other on either side, and whose croaking resembles the hoarse barking of a dog. Now and then I can distinguish the flapping of the bats, attracted by the flame of the torch which is fastened to a branch of the tree under which my tiger-skin is spread; or, at longer intervals, the cry of some panther calling to its mate, and responded to from the tree-tops by the growling of the chimpanzees, whose rest the sound has disturbed.

With a sabre in one hand and a torch in the other, Phrai pursues the fishes in the stream, and he and his shadow reflected on the rocks and water, as he stands there making sudden darts, and crying out "hit" or "missed," might easily be mistaken by the natives for demons.

I cannot shake off a feeling of sadness which a few hours of sleep and a long chase to-morrow will probably dissipate; yet, at the moment, I cannot forbear asking myself, how will this year end for me? Shall I accomplish all I have in view? shall I preserve that health without which I can do nothing? and can I surmount all the difficulties which oppose themselves to me, and of which not the least is the difficulty of finding any means of conveyance?

And you, my dear father, be not too anxious as to my fate, but preserve that tranquillity, hope, and love of God, which alone can make men strong and great: with this help and support, our reunion will not be long delayed. Courage then, and hope! our perseverance and efforts will be recompensed. And thou, invisible link, which, in spite of distance, unites hearts, bear to all those dear to me a thousand embraces, and fill them with all those thoughts which at all times give me strength, and supply joy and consolation in my saddest and most dreary hours. To all, then, a happy new year! and may I bring back safe and sound my poor young followers, who have been such faithful and devoted companions; and who, although already rather weakened by fever and incipient dysentery, are still full of gaiety and energy, and as much attached to me as ever.

Five or six leagues north of Khao-Khoc is Mount Sake, and two miles farther all habitations cease, and there is complete solitude as far as Boatioume. The banks become more and more picturesque; here are calcareous rocks, covered in places with a ferruginous crust, and whence flow streams endowed with petrifying properties, while hills, rising abruptly to a great height, contain grottoes ornamented by stalactites; there, are beds of sand, islands on which sport in the sun a crowd of iguanas; everywhere, a rich vegetation, mingled with tufts of bamboo, in which fight and squabble the chimpanzees, on whom Phrai exercises his skill, and which afford him a delicious repast.

We embarked in a very light pirogue, and, during the first day, passed the boats from Petchaboune, which had left Khao-Khoc the night before; for the current is still rapid, even though the water is so low that in many places you have to drag the boat over the sand, and poles have to be used instead of oars.

Tigers, which are rare at Khao-Khoc, are more common in the environs of Boatioume, where they destroy many of the cattle.

CEMETERY AT BANGKOK.

Drawn by M. Catenacci, from a Photograph.

CHAPTER XVII.

Town of Chaiapume — Journey to the Town of Korat — The Province of Korat — Temple of Penom-Wat — Return to Chaiapume — Poukiéau — Monang-Moune-Wa — Nam-Kane — Louang Prabang, Capital of West Laos.

On the 28th February, 1861, I arrived at the town of Chaiapume, and presented myself before the governor to request his permission to hire some elephants or oxen to enable me to continue my journey. I showed him my French passport, and also gave him the letter from Khrom Luang, and another from the Governor of Korat; but all in vain. He replied that, if I wanted oxen or elephants, there were plenty in the forest. I might easily have done without the assistance of this functionary, and procured animals from people in the village; but they would have made me pay two or three times the ordinary price, and my purse was too slenderly filled to allow of my submitting to this extortion, which would probably be repeated at every station.

The only thing left me to do, therefore, was to retrace my steps, and, leaving one of my servants at Korat with my baggage, to return to Bangkok and claim aid from the consul, the ministers, or the king himself; for there is a treaty between the Governments of Siam and France, concluded by M. de Montigny, which obliges the king to afford assistance and protection to the French, and especially to missionaries and naturalists. It was a sad loss of time for me, and might occasion me serious inconvenience; for, if I were delayed, the rainy season might surprise me in the midst of the forests before I could reach a healthier region, and the consequences might be fatal. However, I was forced to submit, and I returned to Bangkok.

It cost me some time and trouble, and I found it needful to make some valuable presents before I succeeded in my object; but at last I obtained more stringent letters to the governors of the provinces of Laos, and left Bangkok once more, after having experienced for a fortnight the kind hospitality of my friend Dr. Campbell, one of the best men I ever met with: his goodness, friendliness, and British frankness, won my heart and my esteem.

After all this loss of time and great expense I went again to Korat, where I was well received by the governor; and he gave me, in addition to my other letters, one for the mandarins of all provinces under his jurisdiction, commanding them to furnish me with as many oxen and elephants as I might require. The greater part of the inhabitants, with Phrai at their head, came out to meet

Drawn by M. Catenacci, from a Photograph.

BUILDING ERECTED AT THE FUNERAL OF THE QUEEN OF SIAM.

me, and several gave me presents—sacks of rice, fish, fruits, or tobacco, all in abundance.

Speaking to me of his journey to Korat, Dr. House, the most enterprising of the American missionaries at Bangkok, and the only white man who has penetrated so far for many years, told me that he found everything disappointing. I could have said the same, if, like him, I had started with any illusions; but I had a good idea of the forest, which I had already passed at several points, as at Phrabat, Khao Khoc, and Kenne Khoé, and amidst whose deleterious shades I had already spent one night. Nor did I expect to find towns amidst its thick and almost impenetrable masses of foliage, through which one can distinguish nothing beyond a distance of a few feet.

I have lately again passed ten successive nights in this forest. During our journey through it, all the Chinese in the caravan, happy to find themselves still among the living, at every halting-place hastened to draw from their baskets an abundance of provisions wherewith to make a comfortable repast: then choosing, for want of an altar, some large tree, they laid out their dishes, lighted their matches, burned a quantity of gilt paper, and, kneeling down, murmured their prayers. Both on entering and leaving the forest they erected a shed of leaves and sticks interwoven, and raised upon four bamboo stakes, intended as a sort of chapel, in which they placed a number of offerings, in order, as they said, to drive away demons and save them from death.

As for the Laotians, I have found them, although superstitious, very courageous, especially those who traverse this forest eight or ten times a year. Some of them even venture to awake the "King of Fire" by bringing down game or shooting at robbers: yet death, even in the best season, carries off one or two out of every ten who travel here. I think the number of those who fall victims to this terrible journey must be considerable in the rainy season, when every torrent overflows its bounds; the whole soil is soaked, the pathways nothing but bogs, and the rice-grounds covered with several feet of water. After five or six days' walking through all this, with feet in the mud, the body in a profuse perspiration, and breathing a fetid atmosphere, hot as a stove and reeking with putrid miasma, what wonder that many sink and die?

Two Chinese in our caravan arrived at Korat in a frightful state of fever. One I was able to save by administering quinine in good time, but the other, who appeared the strongest, was dead almost as soon as I heard of his being ill.

We halted at five o'clock in the evening and encamped on a little hill, where, in the absence of grass, our poor oxen could only appease their hunger with leaves from the shrubs. The river, which flows down from these hills, is the same which runs near Korat, and on the opposite bank was encamped another caravan with more than 200 oxen,

In a gorge of the mountain, and on the almost inaccessible heights, I found a small tribe of Karians who formerly inhabited the environs of Patawi, and who, for the sake of preserving their independence, live here in seclusion; for the dread of fever prevents the Siamese from penetrating to their haunts. They have neither temples nor priests; they raise magnificent crops of rice, and cultivate several kinds of bananas, which are only found among tribes of the same origin. Many of the inhabitants of the neighbouring districts appear to be ignorant of their very existence. It is true they are of migratory habits; others say that they pay a tribute in gum-lac, but the Governor of Korat and several chiefs of the province of Saraburi, seemed to me profoundly ignorant on the subject.

The following morning, an hour before sunrise, after having counted the oxen dead from fatigue and exhaustion, which would serve for food to the wild beasts, and repacked our goods, we resumed our march. Towards eleven o'clock, having quitted Dong Phya Phai, we entered a long tract of ground filled with brushwood and tall grass and swarming with deer, and here, before long, we halted near a stream.

The next day, after making a détour of some miles to the north to find a pass, we ascended a new chain of hills running parallel to the last, and covered with blocks of sandstone; and here the vegetation was extremely luxuriant. The air was fresh and pure, and, thanks to repeated ablutions in the running streams, those of the party whose feet had suffered most at the beginning of the journey found them greatly improved.

The monkeys and hornbills began to be heard again, and I killed several pheasants and peacocks, and an eagle, on which our guides feasted. Beyond these mountains the soil becomes sandy again and vegetation scanty. We encamped once more on the banks of the river of Korat, 300 metres from a village dignified by the name of chief town of the district.

The last range of hills which we crossed still displays itself like a sombre rampart, above which tower the dome-like and pyramidal summits of others farther in the distance.

Our guides are all Laotians from the neighbourhood of Korat, and their leader is unremitting in his care and attention towards me. Every evening he prepares my place for the night, levelling the ground and cutting down branches which he covers with leaves, and I am thus raised from the earth and protected from the dew. These guides lead a hard life, tramping in all seasons along these wretched roads, having scarcely time, morning and evening, to swallow a little rice, and having but little sleep at nights, tormented by ants, and exposed to the attacks of robbers, against whom they have constantly to be on their guard.

Every day we met one or two caravans of from eighty to a hundred oxen, laden with stag and panther skins, raw silk from Laos, *langoutis* of cotton and silk, peacocks' tails, ivory, elephants' bones, and sugar; but this latter article is scarce.

The country presented much the same kind of aspect for four days after leaving the forest. We passed through several considerable villages, in one of which, Sikiéou, are kept six hundred oxen belonging to the king. The journey from Keng-Koë to Korat occupied ten days. The Chinese quarter of this latter town contains sixty or seventy houses, built with bricks dried in the sun, and surrounded by palisades nine feet high, and as strong as those of a rampart.

These precautions are very necessary, for Korat is a nest of robbers and assassins, the resort of all the scum of the Laotian and Siamese races. Bandits and vagrants, escaped from slavery or from prison, gather here like the vultures and wolves which follow armies and caravans It is not that they enjoy complete immunity, for the governor, son of Bodine, the general who conquered Battambong and the revolted provinces, is viceroy of the state, has absolute power of life and death, and is, they say, very severe, cutting off a head or a hand with little compunction. But still it is Siamese justice, "non inviola:" there are neither gendarmes nor police; the person robbed must himself arrest the offender and bring him before the judge. Even his neighbour will give no assistance in the capture.

It was necessary to look out for a dwelling, and I applied to the Chinese, hoping to find a house rather larger than the one where Phrai had settled himself with my luggage, and I had not much difficulty in doing so.

At the end of the Chinese quarter, which is the bazaar, commences the town properly so called, which is enclosed by a wall of ferruginous stone and sandstone, brought from the distant mountain—a work which I at once recognised as that of the Khmerdôm. Within is the residence of the governor and those of the other authorities, several pagodas, a caravanserai, and a number of other houses. A stream of water, eight metres wide, crosses the town and is bordered by little plantations of betel and cocoa-nut trees.

The real town of Korat does not contain more than five or six thousand inhabitants, including six hundred Chinese. The Siamese I found impertinent and disagreeable, the Chinese friendly and kind. It was the contrast between civilization and barbarism—between the mass of vices engendered by idleness, and the good qualities cultivated by habits of industry. Unfortunately, however, the money acquired by these indefatigable merchants furnishes the means of gratifying their baneful propensities, gambling and opium-smoking.

Stretched on a carpet in some shed they lie, thin and emaciated-looking, playing at cards, or else, plunged in a kind of lethargy, they surrender themselves to the influence of the seductive drug in their dark and filthy hovels, lighted only by a single lamp. Yet, in spite of their gambling, most of them grow rich, though they generally begin poor, and with goods lent to them by some countryman from his shop, and a few voyages frequently suffice to make their fortunes.

The merchants who bring silk, which, though of inferior quality, is an important article of commerce, come from Laos, Oubone, Bassac, and Jasoutone.

The entire province of Korat comprises a number of villages, and more than eleven towns, some containing as many as fifty or sixty thousand inhabitants. This little state is simply tributary, but on condition of furnishing the first and most considerable levy of men in case of war.

The tribute consists of gold or silver, and in several districts, amongst others those of Chaiapume and Poukiéan, amounts to eight ticals a head. Some pay in silk, which is weighed by the mandarins, who, as with the cardamom at Pursat, and the *langoutis* at Battambong, buy a further quantity on their own account, and at their own price.

Elephants are numerous, and a great many are brought from the north of Laos as far as Muang-Lang. I should think there must be more than a thousand of these animals in each province. Oxen and buffaloes were formerly exceedingly cheap, but the distemper, which has for some years committed great ravages among the herds, has doubled or tripled the price. They are brought southward from the extreme north of East Laos, and even from the frontiers of Tonquin.

I went to see a temple nine miles east of Korat, called Penom-Wat. It is very remarkable, although much inferior in grandeur and beauty to those of Ongcor. The second governor lent me a pony and guide, and, after crossing extensive rice plantations, under a vertical and fiery sun, we reached the spot to which my curiosity had attracted me, and which, like an oasis, could be recognised a long way off by the freshness of its cocoa-trees and its rich verdure. I did not arrive there, however, without having taken an involuntary bath. In crossing the Tekon, which is nearly four feet deep, I, in order to escape a wetting, tried to imitate Franconi, by standing on my saddle; but, unluckily, according to the custom of the country, this was fastened on by two pieces of string, and in the middle of the stream it turned and sent me head foremost into the water. But there was no worse result from the accident than my having to remain for half an hour afterwards dressed in Siamese fashion.

Penom-Wat is an interesting temple 36 metres long by 40 wide, and the plan resembles a cross with tolerable exactness. It is composed of two pavilions, with vaulted stone roofs and elegant porticoes. The roofs are from seven to eight metres in height, the gallery three metres wide in the interior, and the walls a metre thick. At each façade of the gallery are two windows with twisted bars.

This temple is built of red and grey sandstone, coarse in the grain, and in some places beginning to decay. On one of the doors is a long inscription, and above are sculptures representing nearly the same subjects as those at Ongcor and Bassette.

Drawn by M. Catenacci, from a Sketch by M. Mouhot.

RUINS AT PAN BRANG, CHAIAPUME.

In one. of the pavilions are several Buddhist idols in stone, the largest of which is 2 metres 50 centimetres high, and actually covered with rags.

You might here easily imagine yourself among the ruins of Ongcor. There is the same style of architecture, the same taste displayed, the same immense blocks polished like marble, and so beautifully fitted together, that I can only compare it to the joining and planing of so many planks.

The whole building is, without doubt, the work of the Khmerdôm, and not an imitation, and must be as old as the illustrious reigns which have left the traces of their grandeur in different parts of the empire. The exterior is not equal to the interior. Penom was the temple of the Queen, so say the Siamese; that of the King, her husband, is at Pimaïe, a district about 30 miles east of Korat.

To consult any existing maps of Indo-China for my guidance in the interior of Laos would have been a folly, no traveller, at least to my knowledge, having penetrated into east Laos, or published any authentic information respecting it. To question the natives about places more than a degree distant would have been useless. My desire was to reach Louang-Prabang by land, to visit the northern tribes dependent on that state, and then again to descend the Mekong to Cambodia. Setting out from Korat, I had but to proceed northwards as long as I found practicable roads and inhabited places; and if I could not go by a direct route to Louang-Prabang, I should only have to diverge to the east when I judged it necessary.

I was again delayed a few days at Korat before I could obtain elephants, in consequence of the absence of the viceroy; but on his return he received me in a friendly manner, and gave me a letter of introduction to the governors of the provinces under his jurisdiction. He likewise furnished me with two elephants for myself and servants, and two others for my baggage; so at last I was able to set out for Chaiapume. Before I started, the Chinese with whom I lodged gave me the following advice:—"Buy a tam-tam, and, wherever you halt, sound it. They will say, 'Here is an officer of the king;' robbers will keep aloof, and the authorities will respect you. If this does not answer, the only plan to get rid of all the difficulties which the Laotian officials will be sure to throw in your way is to have a good stick, the longer the better. Try it on the back of any mandarin who makes the least resistance and will not do what you wish. Put all delicacy aside. Laos is not like a country of the whites. Follow my advice, and you will find it good."

I was, however, much better received on my second visit to Chaiapume, and required neither tam-tam nor cane. The sight of the elephants and the order from the viceroy of Korat made the mandarin as supple as a glove, and he provided me with other elephants for a visit to some ruins existing about 3 leagues north of the town, at the foot of a mountain. The superstitious Laotians say that these ruins contain gold, but that every one who has sought for it has been struck with madness.

Two roads lead from Chaiapume to Poukiéan; the first, across the mountains, is so excessively difficult, that I decided on taking the other, which, however, is much longer. The first day we started at 1 o'clock, and reached a village named Non Jasiea, where we were overtaken by a fearful storm. We sheltered ourselves as well as we could, and arrived before night at the entrance of a forest where we slept.

For five days we were compelled to remain in the forest on account of the weather; it rained great part of the day, and throughout the night; the torrents overflowed, and the earth was nothing but a sea of mud. I never in my life passed such wretched nights, as all the time we had to remain with our wet clothes on our backs, and I cannot describe what we suffered. The snow hurricanes, so frequent in Russia, and which nearly killed me when in that country, seemed trifling miseries in comparison. My poor Phrai was seized with a dreadful fever two days before reaching Poukiéan, and I myself felt very ill.

The passage of the mountains was easy, and the ascent very gradual; blocks of stone obstruct the road in various parts, but our oxen and elephants made their way without much difficulty. I had bought a horse for myself at Korat.

The vegetation, though not thick, is beautiful: the trees, many of which are resinous, are slender, the stems being seldom more than a foot or two in diameter, and often 25, 30, and even 40 metres in height. Under their shade are to be seen great numbers of deer, and tigers are not uncommonly met with. In the mountains are many elephants and rhinoceros. We found immense beds of stone, and in some places saw small brick buildings containing idols. During the journey one of my chests was thrown to the ground by the movements of the elephant, and broken to pieces, as, unfortunately, were all the contents, consisting of instruments, and bottles of spirit of wine containing serpents and fishes.

Poukiéan is a smaller village than Chaiapume. I met with a friendly reception from the governor, who had just returned from Korat, and had heard of my intended journey. Poverty and misery reign here; we cannot find even a fish to purchase; nothing but rice; and as soon as my faithful Phrai is on his legs again we shall leave the place.

Tine-Tine attracts the most attention. The people do not, as we pass, cry out first, "Look at the white stranger," but "A little dog!" and every one runs to see this curiosity. My turn comes afterwards.

In these mountains the Laotians make offerings to the local genii of sticks and stones.

The same chain of hills which, from the banks of the Menam, in the province of Saraburi, extends on one side to the southern extremity of the peninsula, on the other encircles Cambodia like a belt, runs along the shores of the gulf, and forms a hundred islands; stretches

Drawn by M. Bocourt, from a Sketch by M. Mouhot

ELEPHANTS BATHING.

directly northwards, continually increasing in size, and spreading its ramifications towards the east, where they form a hundred narrow valleys, the streams flowing through which empty themselves into the Mekong.

The rains had commenced on my second entrance into Dong Phya Phai, and I was greeted by a perfect deluge, which continued with intervals of two or three days; but this did not stop me, although I had to pass through a country still more to be dreaded than this forest, and where no one goes willingly.

In all this mountainous region elephants are the only means of transport. Every village possesses some, several as many as fifty or a hundred. Without this intelligent animal no communication would be possible during seven months of the year, while, with his assistance, there is scarcely a place to which you cannot penetrate.

The elephant ought to be seen on these roads, which I can only call devil's pathways, and are nothing but ravines, ruts two or three feet deep, full of mud; sometimes sliding with his feet close together on the wet clay of the steep slopes, sometimes half buried in mire, an instant afterwards mounted on sharp rocks, where one would think a Blondin alone could stand; striding across enormous trunks of fallen trees, crushing down the smaller trees and bamboos which oppose his progress, or lying down flat on his stomach that the cornacs (drivers) may the easier place the saddle on his back; a hundred times a day making his way, without injuring them, between trees where there is barely room to pass; sounding with his trunk the depth of the water in the streams or marshes; constantly kneeling down and rising again, and never making a false step. It is necessary, I repeat, to see him at work like this in his own country, to form any idea of his intelligence, docility, and strength, or how all those wonderful joints of his are adapted to their work—fully to understand that this colossus is no rough specimen of nature's handiwork, but a creature of especial amiability and sagacity, designed for the service of man.

We must not, however, exaggerate his merits. Probably the saddles used by the Laotians are capable of great improvement; but I must admit that the load of three small oxen, that is to say, about 250 or 300 pounds, is all that I ever saw the largest elephants carry easily, and 18 miles is the longest distance they can accomplish with an ordinary load. Ten or twelve miles are the usual day's work. With four, five, or sometimes seven elephants, I travelled over all the mountain country from the borders of Laos to Louang-Prabang, a distance of nearly 500 miles.

All this eastern portion, with the exception of a few villages filled with "black-bellied savages"—so called from the manner in which they tattoo themselves—is inhabited by the same race, the "white-bellied Laotians," who call themselves Laos, and are known by this name to all the Siamese, Chinese, and surrounding nations.

Drawn by M. Bocourt, from a Sketch by M. Mouhot.

CARAVAN OF ELEPHANTS CROSSING THE MOUNTAINS OF LAOS.

The black-bellied or western Laotians are called by their eastern brethren by the same name which, in Siam and Cambodia, is bestowed on the Annamites, Zuène, Lao-Zuène. The only thing that distinguishes them is, that they tattoo the under part of the body, principally the thighs, and frequently wear the hair long and knotted on the top of their heads. Their language is nearly the same, and differs little from the Siamese and Eastern Laos, except in the pronunciation, and in certain expressions no longer in use among the former.

I soon found that, but for the letter from the governor of Korat, I should have met everywhere with the same reception as at Chaiapume; however, this missive was very positively worded. Wherever I went, the authorities were ordered to furnish me with elephants, and supply me with all necessary provisions, as if I were a king's envoy. I was much amused to see these petty provincial chiefs executing the orders of my servants, and evidently in dread lest, following the Siamese custom, I should use the stick.

One of my men, to give himself importance, had tied one of these bugbears to the arms which he carried, and the sight of it alone sufficed, with the sound of the tam-tam, to inspire fear, whilst small presents judiciously distributed, and a little money to the cornacs, procured me the sympathy of the people.

Most of the villages are situated about a day's journey from one another, but frequently you have to travel for three or four days without seeing a single habitation, and then you have no alternative but to sleep in the jungle. This might be pleasant in the dry season, but, during the rains, nothing can give an idea of the sufferings of travellers at night, under a miserable shelter of leaves hastily spread over a rough framework of branches, assaulted by myriads of mosquitoes attracted by the light of the fires and torches, by legions of ox-flies, which, after sunset, attack human beings as well as elephants, and by fleas so minute as to be almost invisible, which assemble about you in swarms, and whose bites are excessively painful, and raise enormous blisters.

To these enemies add the leeches, which, after the least rain, come out of the ground, scent a man twenty feet off, and hasten to suck his blood with wonderful avidity. To coat your legs with a layer of lime when travelling is the only way to prevent them covering your whole body.

I had left Bangkok on the 12th of April, and on the 16th of May I reached Leuye, the chief town of a district belonging to two provinces, Petchaboune and Lôme. It is situated in a narrow valley, like all the towns and villages through which I have passed since I left Chaiapume.

This is the district of Siam richest in minerals; one of its mountains contains immense beds of magnetic iron of a remarkably good quality. Others yield antimony, argentiferous copper, and tin. The iron only is worked, and this population, half agriculturists, half artisans, furnish spades and cutlasses to all the surrounding pro-

Drawn by M. Thérond, from a Photograph.

"PARK" OF ELEPHANTS, EXTERNAL VIEW.

vinces, even beyond Korat. Yet they have neither foundries nor steam-engines, and it is curious to see how little it costs an iron-worker to establish himself in a hole about a yard and a half square hollowed out close to the mountain.

They pile up and smelt the mineral with charcoal: the liquified iron deposits itself in the bottom of the cavity, and there hollows out a bed, whence they withdraw it when the operation is completed, and carry it home. There, in another cavity they make a fire, which a child keeps alive by means of a couple of bellows, which are simply two trunks of hollow trees buried in the ground, and upon which play alternately two stopples surrounded by cotton. These are fixed to a small board, and have long sticks for handles, to which are attached two bamboo hollow canes which conduct the air into the cavity.

In several localities I discovered auriferous sand, but only in small quantity. In some of the villages the inhabitants employ their leisure time in searching for gold, but they told me that they hardly gained by this work sufficient to pay for the rice they ate.

In this journey I have passed through sixty villages, numbering from twenty to fifty houses each; and six small towns, with a population of from four to six hundred inhabitants. I have made a map of all this part of the country.

Since leaving Korat I have crossed five large rivers which fall into the Mekon, the bed of which is more or less full according to the season. The first of these, 35 metres wide, is called the Menam Chie, lat. 15° 45′; second, the Menam Leuye, 90 metres wide, lat. 18° 3′; third, the Menam Ouan, at Kenne-Tao, 100 metres in width, lat. 18° 35′; fourth, the Nam Pouye, 60 metres, lat. 19°; fifth, the Nam-Houn, 80 or 100 metres wide, lat. 20°.

The Chie is navigable, as far up as the latitude of Korat, from May to December; the Leuye, the Ouan, and the Houn are only navigable for a very short distance on account of their numerous rapids; neither is there any water-communication between the Menam and the Mekon in Laos or Cambodia, the mountains which separate them forming insurmountable obstacles to cutting canals.

The Laotians much resemble the Siamese: a different pronunciation and slow manner of speech being all that distinguishes their language. The women wear petticoats, and keep their hair long, which, when combed, gives the younger ones a more interesting appearance than those have who live on the banks of the Menam; but, at an advanced age, with their unkempt locks thrown negligently over one temple, and their immense goîtres, which they admire, they are repulsively ugly.

Little commerce is carried on in this part of Laos. The Chinese inhabiting Siam do not come as far, owing to the enormous expense of transporting all their merchandise on elephants. Nearly every year a caravan arrives from Yunnan and Quangsee, composed of about

Vol. II, p. 134.

LAOTIAN GIRLS.

Drawn by M. Bocourt, from a Photograph.

a hundred persons and several hundred mules. Some go to Kenne Thao, others to M. Nâne and Chieng Maï. They arrive in February, and leave in March or April.

The mulberry does not thrive in these mountains; but in some localities this tree is cultivated for the sake of furnishing food to a particular insect which lives upon its leaves, and from which is obtained the lague or Chinese varnish.

All the gum-benzoin which is sold at Bangkok comes from the northern extremity of the state of Louang Prabang, and from a district tributary both to Cochin China and Siam, and peopled rather by Tonquinites than Laotians.

On the 24th of June I arrived at Paklaïe, lat. 19° 16′ 58″, the first small town on my northward route. It is situated on the Mekon, and is a charming place; the inhabitants seem well off; the houses elegant and spacious,—larger, indeed, than I have seen before in this country; and everything betokens a degree of prosperity which I have also remarked wherever I have stopped since. The Mekon at this place is much larger than the Menam at Bangkok, and forces its way between the lofty mountains with a noise resembling the roaring of the sea and the impetuosity of a torrent, seeming scarcely able to keep within its bed. There are many rapids between Paklaïe and Louang Prabang, which is ten or fifteen days' painful travelling.

I was tired of my long journey on elephants, and was

anxious to hire a boat here, but the chief and some of the inhabitants, fearing that I might meet with some accident, advised me to continue my route by land. I therefore proceeded as far as Thadua, ninety miles farther north, and during eight days passed through much the same style of country as before, changing one valley for another, and crossing mountains which became more and more elevated, and being more than ever annoyed by the leeches. We were, however, no longer compelled to sleep in the jungle, for every evening we reached some hamlet or village, where we found shelter either in a pagoda or caravanserai.

As among the Grisons or the mountains of the Valais, the whole population, from Dong Phya Phai to this district, who drink the water of the mountain rivulets, are disfigured by immense goîtres; but the men are not so subject to them as the women, who rarely escape.

I have only passed through one village where any serious ravages are committed by the tigers. There is one danger, which may be serious, incident to travelling with elephants in a region like this. Usually, among the caravan there are one or two females, followed by their young, who run about from one side to another, playing or browsing. Now and then one of them stumbles and falls into a ravine, and immediately the whole troop jump down after him to draw him out.

In a letter which I wrote from Cambodia I described the Mekon river as imposing, but monotonous and unpicturesque; but in this part of the country it presents a very different appearance. Where it is narrowest the width is above 1000 metres, and it everywhere runs between lofty mountains, down whose sides flow torrents, all bringing their tribute. There is almost an excess of grandeur. The eye rests constantly on these mountain slopes, clothed in the richest and thickest verdure.

On the 25th of July I reached Louang Prabang, a delightful little town, covering a square mile of ground, and containing a population, not, as Mgr. Pallegoix says in his work on Siam, of 80,000, but of 7000 or 8000 only. The situation is very pleasant. The mountains which, above and below this town, enclose the Mekon, form here a kind of circular valley or amphitheatre, nine miles in diameter, and which, there can be no doubt, was anciently a lake. It was a charming picture, reminding one of the beautiful lakes of Como and Geneva. Were it not for the constant blaze of a tropical sun, or if the mid-day heat were tempered by a gentle breeze, the place would be a little paradise.

The town is built on both banks of the stream, though the greater number of the houses are built on the left bank. The most considerable part of the town surrounds an isolated mount, more than a hundred metres in height, at the top of which is a pagoda.

Were they not restrained by fear of the Siamese, and their horror of the jungles so prolific of death, this principality would soon fall into the hands of the Annamites, who now dare not advance nearer than seven days' journey off. A beautiful stream, 100 metres wide, unites with the great river to the north-east of the town, and leads to some Laotian and savage villages bearing the name of *Fie.* These are no other than the tribes called *Penoms* by the Cambodians, *Khu* by the Siamese, and *Moï* by the Annamites,—all words simply signifying "savages."

The whole chain of mountains which extends from the north of Tonquin to the south of Cochin China, about 100 miles north of Saigon, is inhabited by this primitive people, divided into tribes speaking different dialects, but whose manners and customs are the same. All the villages in the immediate neighbourhood are tributary; those nearest to the town supply workmen for buildings erected for the king and princes, and these are heavily taxed. Others pay their tribute in rice.

Their habitations are in the thickest parts of the forests, where they only can find a path. Their cultivated grounds are to be seen on the tops and sides of the mountains; in fact, they employ the same means as wild animals to escape from their enemies, and to preserve that liberty and independence which are to them, as to all God's creatures, their supreme good.

Yesterday, and the day previous, I was presented to the princes who govern this little state, and who bear the title of kings. I know not why, but they displayed for my benefit all they could devise of pomp and splendour.

The Laotians of Leuye appear to me more industrious than the Siamese, and, above all, possess a much more adventurous and mercantile spirit; and although, both physically and morally, there are great points of resemblance, yet there exist shades of difference which distinguish them at once, and are apparent in their dialect, or rather patois, and in their manners, which are more simple and affable. They are all much alike in features; the women have round faces, small noses, large almond-shaped eyes, thick hair, the mouth large and strongly-marked; but the men do not exhibit so great a diversity of race as they do in Siam.

Alas! what a journey my fragile collection of specimens, so difficult to gather together, has still to take, and what various accidents may befall them! Those who in museums contemplate the works of Nature do not think of all the perseverance, trouble, and anxiety required before they are safely brought home.

The Laotians have not the curiosity of the Siamese, and ask me fewer questions. I find them more intelligent than either the latter race or the Cambodians, and among the villagers especially there is a curious mixture of cunning and simplicity. They do not as yet seem to me to merit their reputation for hospitality,—a virtue which appeared to be much more practised in Siam. I should never have obtained any means of conveyance without the letter from the Viceroy of Korat, and my experience has been that they are less respectful, but at the same time less importunate, than the Siamese.

The ground between Leuye and Kenne Thao is hilly, but traversed without difficulty. The formations are calcareous rocks, sandstone, slaty sandstone, and lime mixed with clay; the sandstone in long beds, not in blocks. In the streams I found stones, not boulders, but with sharp angles.

The Chinese and Indians alone traffic here; it requires a day's journey to conclude the smallest bargain, and a whole village is assembled to make sure that the money is not spurious. On my route here I have not met a single Siamese, but in every village have seen Birmans, Kariens, and people from Western Laos. I have found men in Lao-Pouene moulded like athletes and of herculean strength, and thought that the King of Siam might raise in this province a fine regiment of grenadiers. In all the villages I have visited, the inhabitants, including even the priests, set to work to collect insects for me, glad to receive in return a few copper buttons, glass beads, or a little red cloth.

At Paklaïe, which I have already mentioned as a pretty town, I had the pleasure of again seeing the beautiful stream, which now seems to me like an old friend: I have so long drunk of its waters, it has so long either cradled me on its bosom or tried my patience, at one time flowing majestically among the mountains, at another muddy and yellow as the Arno at Florence.

The road between Kenne Thao and Paklaïe is dreadful. You have to force your way along a narrow path, through a thick jungle, and sometimes there is no path at all, or else it is obstructed by bamboos and branches which interlace and often catch hold of your saddle. Every moment you are in danger of being hurt by them; our hands and faces were covered with scratches, and my clothes torn to pieces.

Muang-Moune-Wa.—This place is surrounded by mountains. I am very feverish and tremble with cold, although the thermometer shows 80 degrees of heat. I am getting tired of these people, a race of children, heartless and unenergetic. I sigh and look everywhere for a man, and cannot find one; here all tremble at the stick, and the enervating climate makes them incredibly apathetic.

15th August, 1861.—Nam Kane. A splendid night; the moon shines with extraordinary brilliancy, silvering the surface of this lovely river, bordered by high mountains, looking like a grand and gloomy rampart. The chirp of the crickets alone breaks the stillness. In my little cottage all is calm and tranquil; the view from my window is charming, but I cannot appreciate or enjoy it. I am sad and anxious; I long for my native land, for a little life; to be always alone weighs on my spirits.

Louang Prabang, 29th August, 1861.—My third servant, Song, whom I had engaged at Pakpriau, begged me to allow him to return to Bangkok in the suite of the Prince of Louang Prabang, who was going there to pay tribute. I did all I could to induce him to remain with me, but he seemed to have made up his mind to go; so I paid him his wages, and gave him a letter authorising him to receive a further sum at Bangkok for the time occupied by his return journey.

Same date. Song is gone. How changeable we are! He was always complaining of cold or had some other grievance, and I cared less for him than for my other servants—but then I had not had him long. Yesterday, however, when he asked permission to go, I was vexed. Either he has really suffered much here from illness, or has not been happy with me; perhaps both. I hired a boat to take him to the town, and my good Phrai accompanied him there this morning, and recommended him from me to a mandarin whom I knew. I gave him all that was necessary for his journey, even if it lasts three months, and on his arrival at Bangkok he will receive his money. On taking leave he prostrated himself before me; I took hold of his hands and raised him up, and then he burst into tears. And I, in my turn, when I had bid him farewell, felt my eyes fill, nor do I know when I shall be quite calm, for I have before me, day and night, the poor lad, ill in the woods, among indifferent or cruel people. He has a great dread of fever, and, if he had been taken ill here and died, I should have reproached myself for keeping him; and yet, if it were to come over again, I almost fancy I would not yield to his desire to leave me. He was confided to me by the good Father Larmandy. May God protect the poor boy, and preserve him from all sickness and accidents during his journey!

Vol. II p. 143.

RECEPTION OF M. MOUHOT BY THE KINGS OF LAOS.

Drawn by M. Janet Lange, from a Sketch by M. Mouhot

I reached Louang Prabang on the 25th of July. On the 3rd of August I was presented to the King and to his cousin. On the 9th of August I left Louang Prabang and travelled eastwards.

26th.—The thermometer rose to 92° Fahr. This is the maximum I have noted this month, 71° being the minimum.

CHAPTER XVIII.

THE EAST OF LOUANG PRABANG — NOTES OF TRAVELS — OBSERVATIONS FROM BANGKOK TO LAOS — END OF THE JOURNAL — DEATH OF THE TRAVELLER.

THE dress of the Laotians differs little from that of the Siamese. The people wear the *langouti* and a little red cotton waistcoat, or often nothing at all. Both men and women go barefoot: their head-dresses are like the Siamese. The women are generally better-looking than those of the latter nation: they wear a single short petticoat of cotton, and sometimes a piece of silk over the breast. Their hair, which is black, they twist into a knot at the back of the head. The houses are built of bamboos and leaves interwoven and raised upon stakes, and underneath is a shelter for domestic animals, such as oxen, pigs, fowls, &c.

The dwellings are, in the strictest sense, unfurnished, having neither tables nor beds, nor, with few exceptions, even vessels of earth or porcelain. They eat their rice made into balls out of their hands, or from little baskets plaited with cane, some of which are far from unartistic.

The crossbow and *sarbacane* are the arms used in hunting, as well as a kind of lance made of bamboo, and

Drawn by M. Janet Lange from a Sketch by M. Mouhot

LAOTIAN WOMAN.

sometimes, but more rarely, the gun, with which they are very skilful.

In the hamlet of Na-Lê, where I had the pleasure of killing a female tiger, which with its partner was committing great ravages in the neighbourhood, the chief hunter of the village got up a rhinoceros-hunt in my honour. I had not met with this animal in all my wanderings through the forests. The manner in which he is hunted by the Laotians is curious on account of its simplicity and the skill they display. Our party consisted of eight, including myself. I and my servants were armed with guns, and at the end of mine was a sharp bayonet. The Laotians had bamboos with iron blades something between a bayonet and a poignard. The weapon of the chief was the horn of a sword-fish, long, sharp, strong, and supple, and not likely to break.

Thus armed, we set off into the thickest part of the forest, with all the windings of which our leader was well acquainted, and could tell with tolerable certainty where we should find our expected prey. After penetrating nearly two miles into the forest, we suddenly heard the crackling of branches and rustling of the dry leaves. The chief went on in advance, signing to us to keep a little way behind, but to have our arms in readiness. Soon our leader uttered a shrill cry as a token that the animal was near; he then commenced striking against each other two bamboo canes, and the men set up wild yells to provoke the animal to quit his retreat.

A few minutes only elapsed before he rushed towards

us, furious at having been disturbed. He was a rhinoceros of the largest size, and opened a most enormous mouth. Without any signs of fear, but, on the contrary, of great exultation, as though sure of his prey, the intrepid hunter advanced, lance in hand, and then stood still, waiting for the creature's assault. I must say I trembled for him, and I loaded my gun with two balls; but when the rhinoceros came within reach and opened his immense jaws to seize his enemy, the hunter thrust the lance into him to a depth of some feet, and calmly retired to where we were posted.

The animal uttered fearful cries and rolled over on his back in dreadful convulsions, while all the men shouted with delight. In a few minutes more we drew nearer to him; he was vomiting pools of blood. I shook the chief's hand in testimony of my satisfaction at his courage and skill. He told me that to myself was reserved the honour of finishing the animal, which I did by piercing his throat with my bayonet, and he almost immediately yielded up his last sigh. The hunter then drew out his lance and presented it to me as a souvenir; and in return I gave him a magnificent European poignard.

Oubon and Bassac lie W.N.W. from M. Pimaï. It takes eight days in the rainy season to travel from this last town to Oubon, two more to reach Bassac. To return occupies at least double that period, the current being excessively strong.

The Ménam-Moune at Pimaï is 75 metres wide in the dry season; in the rainy season it is from 6 to 7 metres

Drawn by M. Janet Lange, from a Sketch by M. Mouhot.

A CHIEF ATTACKING A RHINOCEROS IN THE FOREST OF LAOS.

in depth. There are in this district iron, lignites, and trunks of petrified trees lying on the ground, which even from a very short distance look like fallen trees in a natural state.

Mgi-Poukham, inhabited by the Soués, is six days' journey from Korat in a south-easterly direction.

In the dry season the navigation of the river is impeded by sandbanks: at some points the stream is tolerably wide, but in others choked with sand.

From Korat to Pimaï, on an elephant, occupies two days: from Korat to Thaison, two; to Sisapoune, two; to Josoutone, two days; to Oubon, four days; to Bassac, four.

Direction E.N.E. from Korat; Poukiéau, N. of Chaiapume; Pouvienne, ten degrees E. of Chaiapume; Dongkaïe, N.E. by E. of Chaiapume; M. Louang Prabang, N. of Chaiapume.

From Chaiapume to Vien-Tiane is fifteen days' journey on foot towards the N. and nine degrees E. M. Lôm, N.W. of Chaiapume; Petchaboune, W.N.W. of Chaiapume; Bassac, E.S.E.

Bane Prom, a mountain situated in a valley nine miles across, is nearly 300 metres high. Bane Prom, a town. Menam Prom, a river nearly 2 metres deep and 40 wide, rises in M'Lôm, and empties itself in the Menam Chie, in the province of Koukhine. Bane-Rike, between Poukiéau and Kone-Sane, four geographical leagues from each place. Menam-Rike is a torrent which empties itself into the Prom.

The vegetation is monotonous — everywhere resinous trees, chiefly of small size. There is a complete absence of birds; insects are in great number and variety, musquitoes and ox-flies in myriads. I suffer dreadfully from them, and am covered with swellings and blisters from their bites; and they torment our beasts so much that we sometimes fear it will drive them mad. The sensibility of the skin of the elephant is extraordinary, but these creatures are very skilful in brushing off their tormentors by means of a branch held in their trunks. I do not know what would become of me without these good and docile animals, and I cannot tell which to admire most, their patïence or intelligence.

From Kone-Sane to Vien-Tiane is eight good days' journey in a north-easterly direction.

To M'Lôm, four days W.N.W.

To Petchaboune, four days W.S.W.

To Kôrat, four days E.S.E.

To Chaiapume, four days E.S.E.

To Poukiéau, four days E.S.E.

To Leuye, three days' rapid travelling N.N.E. over mountains.

From Kone-Sane to Koukhène, two days' rapid journey E.S.E.

From Koukhène to Chenobote, one day's journey S.E.

On the road from Kone-Sane to Leuye, near the former place, is a stream called Oué-Mouan, and a torrent, Oué-Kha.

Bane-Nayaan, a village, five geographical leagues off,

two days' journey, with high mountains to cross, difficult of ascent for the elephants. On the first day your course is over peaked mountains, volcanic, and like those of the Khao Khoc. The next day you meet with calcareous and volcanic hills; in the valleys sandstone, jungle, and fertile ground.

Mgi-Lôm, four days' journey west of Bane-Nayaan. From this last place to Bane-Napitone runs the stream Oué-Yan.

Menam-Fon-Khau, passed over twice, a geographical league.

In the provinces of Kone-Sane and of Leuye a great number of the inhabitants are affected with goître. Is this caused by the water from the mountains and the mineral substances with which it is impregnated? I suppose so.

From Bane-Napitone to B. Proune you have to cross high mountains. Half way up one of these is a fine view extending over a wooded plain to the north-west in the direction of Nong Khaï, and bounded at a distance of twenty-five or thirty miles by a chain of mountains; whilst in every other direction you are surrounded by hills varying in height from 300 to 900 feet. The sandstone and chalky rocks of these heights have taken most picturesque forms.

From B. Proune to B. Thiassène runs a stream five leagues long, in a north-westerly direction, and which is navigable for boats. It flows on towards Leuye, and empties itself in the Mekon at M. Sione-Kane, which is ten degrees N.N.E. of N. Thiassène. From B. Thienne to Leuye are hills easy to climb, with vegetation similar to those of Chantaboune and Brelum, forests of bamboo: the rocks are calcareous, with a small mixture of sandstone.

The Menam-Rope and Menam-Ouaie are two large rivers, deep in the rainy season, which empty themselves into the Menam-Leuye: also several torrents. Villages: Bane-Kataname, Bane-Poune, Bane-Nahane, Bane-Pathiou.

From Bane-Thienne to Nong Khane you go in an easterly direction. Bane-Poua is the first village in a four days' journey: here are forests, jungles, and a small hill. The plain is barren and desolate in appearance.

Towns and provinces of Louang Prabang in coming down: Thienne-Khane, Nong-Kaïe, Saïabouri, Outène, Lakhone-Penome, Mouke-Dahane, Emarate, and Bassac.

I am literally pillaged by these petty mandarins and chiefs of villages, and have to give away guns, sabres, lead, powder, colours, pencils, and even my paper; and then, after having received their presents, they will not put themselves out of their way to do me the smallest service. I would not wish my most deadly foe, if I had one, to undergo all the trouble and persecution of this kind which I have encountered.

The Laotian priests are continually praying in their pagodas; they make a frightful noise, chanting from morning to night. Assuredly they ought to go direct to Paradise.

Between Oué-Saïe and Thienne-Khane the villages

are: Bane-Tate, B. Oué-Sake, B. Na-Saor, B. Poun, B. Na-Poué, Nam-Khane, near B. Nmïen; near Kenne Thao, between Bane Nam-Khane and Bane-Noke, is a torrent called Nam-Kheme.

Observations taken at Kéte-Tao: Vienne-Thiane, eastward; Mg. Nane, N.N.W.; Tchieng-Maïe, N.W.; Louang Prabang, N. of Kenne Thao.

Mg. Dane-Saie, four days' journey W.S.W. of Bane-Mien; Lôme, four days' journey W.S.W. of Bane-Mien.

Villages: Bane Thène, Nha-Khâ—two roads; Nâ-Thon —two roads; Nâ-Di, Nâ-Moumone, Nâ-Ho, Bane Maïe, B. Khok.

The river Menam-Ouan runs in a north-westerly direction to within a day's journey of the Menam-Sake. A high mountain lies between them.

In Lôme the villages are: Bane Tali, B. Yao, B. Khame, B. Pouksiéau, B. Name-Bongdiéau, B. Nong-Boa, B. Na-Sane-Jenne, B. Nam-Soke, B. Ine-Uun, Dong-Saïe, Bane Vang-Bane, B. Nang-Krang, Mg. Lôme-Kao, Bane Koué-Nioune. Between M. Lôme-Maïe and Thiene-Khame are Bane Oué-Saïe, B. Rate, B. Na-Shî, B. Oué-Pote, B. Na-Sao, B. Loke, B. Na-Niaô, Thiene-Khame.

Between Kenne Thao and Bane Mien are B. Kone Khêne, B. Pake-Oué, B. Khène-Toune.

The Mekon is ten leagues east of Kenne Thao.

M. Phitchaïe eight days' journey west from Bane-Nmien.

At Bane-Nmien I found the Laotians even more ungrateful and egotistical than elsewhere; they not only will give you nothing—one has no right to expect it—but after taking presents from you, they will make you no return whatever.

The Menam-Ouan rises at Dane-Saïe, S.S.W. from Kenne Thao, and joins the Mekon E.N.E. from that town.

From Kenne Thao to Louang Prabang is a distance of seven geographical or ten ordinary leagues, and a journey of ten or eleven days, quick travelling.

Mg. Pakhaie is north of Kenne Thao. From this place to Bane-Na-Ine is one day's journey; to Bane-Moun-Tioum two days.

Near this latter place, where I have found a greater number of insects than anywhere else in my travels here, is the river Nam-Shan. It is a continual ascent to this part.

Near Bane-Na-Ine auriferous quartz occurs. The jungle here is thick.

Villages in the neighbourhood of Moun-Tioume, consisting of from fifteen to thirty huts: Bane-Hape, a league to the north; Rape-Jâ, the same distance southwards; Tate-Dine, one league to the north-east; Nam-Poune, half a league south-east.

In Bane Moun-Tioume are twenty-six houses.

Route from B. Moun-Tioume to B. Kouke-Niéou:—This last village is composed of eighty houses. There is in it an abandoned pagoda, and it is environed by woods and hills. A stream, called the Nam-Peniou, flows past it and joins the Nam-Shan. There is plenty of rice on the hills, but not in the plains.

From Bane-Kouke-Niéou* there are continual hills. We are tormented by immense numbers of leeches and ox-flies. The jungle is as thick as in Dong Phya Phai. We passed the night on the banks of a stream, the Nam-Koïe, which we had several times crossed, but could get no sleep on account of the leeches; and the following night, by the same river, we were equally pestered.

Bane-Oué-Eu is a small hamlet in the immediate vicinity of Kouke-Niéou-Paklaïe, a very pleasant town, apparently prosperous. The houses are clean and elegant.

Paklaïe is two geographical leagues distant from Muang-Moune-Wâ. The district is very mountainous, with rice-grounds on some of the slopes. We several times had to cross the Laïe, which is 35 metres wide, and rushes along like a torrent, with a great noise. There are, about here, many precipices. It was wonderful to see the elephants climb, descend, and hang on by their trunks to the rocks without ever making a false step.

I have quite an admiration and regard for these noble animals. How remarkable are their strength and intelligence! What should we have done without them amidst these vast forests and rugged mountains?

Mgi-Roun, district of M. Louang, a day's journey W.N.W. of Mgi-Moune-Wâ; there are seventy houses in it.

The villages near to Moune-Wâ are Bane-Bia, 2 miles

---

* At Kouke-Niéou I sold my horse for 13 ticals, as he could no longer climb the hills, which became more and more difficult.

westward; Bane-Name-Pi, two days' journey; Thiême-Khâne, one day; B. Nam-Kang, one day. These villages are all on the road from Mgi-Moune-Wâ to Phixaïe. This place lies W.S.W. from Muang-Moune-Wâ, and five days' journey off, and three days' journey from Nam-Pate. The country between Mgi-Moune-Wâ and Nam-Pate is mountainous; from the latter place to Phixaïe is also hilly ground, and is part of the direct line from Bangkok to Mgi-Louang.*

From Mgi-Moune-Wâ to Bane-Nakhau is a good day's journey over a mountain country, through woods of resinous trees and high grass; but the jungle predominates. Auriferous sand occurs in the Nam-Poune; also, though less rich, in the Nam-Ouhan and other streams.

Bane-Phêke and B. Nalane lie between B. Nakhan and Mgi-Nam-Poune.

Mgi-Nane is six days' journey W.N.W. of Moune-Wâ. The first day, to Mgi-Roun; second day, through woods and crossing streams, to Nan-Pi (here are black-bellied Laotians); third day, Bane-Khune; fourth day, Bane-Dhare; fifth day, B. Done; sixth day, Tuke.

3rd September.—We left Bane-Nakhau, and arrived about midday at a rice-field, where we passed the night. All the women here have goîtres, often enormous and most repulsive. Even young girls of nine or ten are to be seen with them, but rarely the men.

---

* These particulars were received by me at Moune-Wâ from inhabitants of Nam-Pate.

About Tourair there are woods and thick jungles, and the river Nam-Poune, 60 metres broad, runs near. The hills here are of moderate height. I saw some pretty young girls with intelligent faces; but before the females attain the age of eighteen or twenty their features become coarse, and they grow fat. At five-and-thirty they look like old witches.

Two rivers unite here, the Nam-Poune from the west, and the Nam-Jame from the north.

On my route from B. Nakhau to B. Na-Lê, I spent the night of the 4th of September in a hut at B. Nakone. On the 5th I reached B. Na-Lê, passing through several hamlets, Na-Moune, Na-Koua, and Na-Dua. Bane-Na-Lê contains only seven houses.

The streams are, first, the Nam-Jame, crossed and re-crossed several times; the Nam-Quême, Nam-Itou, Nam-Pâne; the Nam-Khou, near Bane-Nakone.

The road lies across high mountains, with jungles full of monkeys uttering their plaintive cries. I was told of a royal tiger at Na-Lê, which, in the space of four months, had killed two men and ten buffaloes. I had the satisfaction of killing the tigress.

5th September, 1861.—From this date M. Mouhot's observations cease; but until the 25th of October he continued to keep his meteorological register.

The last dates inscribed in his journal are the following:—

20th September.—Left B . . . . . . p.

28th.—An order was sent to B . . . ., from the council

of Louang Prabang, commanding the authorities to prevent my proceeding farther.

15th October. 58 degrees Fahr.—Set off for Louang Prabang.

16th.—. . . . .

17th.—. . . . .

18th.—Halted at H . . . .

19th.—Attacked by fever. *

29th.—Have pity on me, oh my God . . . . !

These words, written with a trembling and uncertain hand, were the last found in M. Mouhot's journal. His faithful Phrai asked him several times if he did not wish to write anything to his family, but his invariable answer was, "Wait, wait; are you afraid?" The intrepid traveller never for one moment thought that death was near; he had been spared so far, and he doubtless thought he should recover, or he might have made an effort to write again. He died November 10th, 1861, at 7 o'clock in the evening, having been previously insensible for three days, before which time, however, he had complained of great pains in his head. All the words which he uttered during the delirium of the last three days were in English, and were incomprehensible to his servants.

He was buried in the European fashion, in the presence of his two servants, who never left him. It is the custom of the country to hang up the dead bodies to the trees, and there leave them.

---

* The handwriting of this entry is evidently much affected by his state of weakness.

This account of the last illness of my dear brother I received from his friends at Bangkok, particularly Dr. Campbell, to whom his two faithful servants hastened at once to give all details. His collections and other property they took to M. d'Istria, the French consul. Dr. Campbell kindly took charge of the manuscripts, and transmitted them to his widow in London.

The family of M. Mouhot have already expressed their gratitude to those who were useful and kind to the traveller. The two good servants who remained with him to the last also merit their thanks; and, if these lines should fall into the hands of Phrai, I wish him to know how much gratitude and esteem we feel for him, and for his companion Deng. We wish them every happiness in return for their devotion to my dear brother.

C. MOUHOT.

SIAMESE MONEY.

APPENDIX.

APPENDIX.

LIST OF THE NEW SPECIES OF MAMMALS DISCOVERED BY THE LATE M. MOUHOT IN CAMBODIA AND SIAM.

By Dr. Albert Günther.

a. Monkeys.

1. *Hylobates pileatus.*

Male.—Black: back of the head, back of the body, and front hind legs greyish; forehead and circumference of the black spot on the crown paler grey: hands and tuft of long hair round the organ of generation white.

The three specimens in this state are all nearly of the same size, and appear to be adult. They only vary slightly in the size of the coronal spot, and in the extent of the white colour on the hands.

Female.—White: back brownish white, slightly waved; a large ovate spot on the crown, and a very large ovate blotch on the chest, black.

These specimens are all of one size, and appear to be adult; three have the teats well developed. They vary in the size of the black chest-spot, and in the colour of the whiskers, thus:—

a, b. White: spot on the chest moderate, reaching only half-way down the abdomen: whiskers on side of face white.

c. Brownish: spot on chest larger, reaching further down the abdomen: sides of the face black: a few black hairs on the throat.

d. Brownish: side of the face, under the chin, and the whole of the throat, chest, and belly black: teats well developed.

Young.—Uniform dirty white, without any black spot on chest or head.

All those varieties were found by M. Mouhot on a small island near Cambodia. (Described by Dr. J. E. Gray, Proc. Zool. Soc., 1861, p. 135.)

b. Carnivores.

2. *Herpestes rutilus.*

Grizzled chestnut-brown, variegated with black and white rings on the hairs: the head and limbs darker chestnut, with scarcely any hair, and very narrow white rings: lips and throat, and under part of the body, uniform duller brown; the nape with longer hairs, forming a broad short crest.

Cambodia. (Gray, Proc. Zool. Soc., 1861, p. 136.)

c. Squirrels.

3. *Sciurus Mouhotii.*

Grizzled grey brown, with pale rings: lips, chin, throat, and under side of body and inside of limbs white: the upper part of the sides with a longitudinal black streak, edged above and below with a narrow white line: tail blackish, whitish washed, hairs elongate, brown, with two broad black rings and a white tip: ears simple, rounded.

The species differs from most of the squirrels of the size, in the three streaks being on the upper part of the back, and in the dark colour between the two colours of the upper and under surface.

Cambodia. (Named by Dr. J. E. Gray, after M. Mouhot, and described in Proc. Zool. Soc., 1861, p. 137.)

4. *Sciurus splendens.*

All the specimens are bright red bay.

Var. 1.—All over dark, and very intense red bay, with a white spot on each side of the base of the tail.

Var. 2.—Top of the head and tail, like var. 1, dark and very intense red bay : side of the back, under sides of the body, and tip of the tail paler red bay, without any white spot at the base of the tail.

Var. 3.—Uniform pale bay, like the side of var. 2 : tail and middle of the back rather darker and brighter : tail without pale tip or white basal spot.

Var. 4.—Crown, middle of the back, and tail dark intense red bay : throat, chest, and under side paler red bay, like var. 2, 3 : cheeks, shoulders, and thighs, and outsides of the fore and hind legs brown, grizzled, with yellow rings on the hairs : side of the body rather greyish red.

Cambodia. (Gray, Proc. Zool. Soc., 1861, p. 137.)

5. *Sciurus siamensis.*

Bright red-brown, grizzled, with elongate black tips to the longer hairs, each of which is marked with a broad subterminal yellow band. These black hairs are more abundant and have broad pale rings on the rump, outside of the thighs, and especially on the lower part of the tail, where they nearly hide the general red colour. The terminal half of the tail bright chestnut-brown, without any black hairs or pale rings. The throat, breast, belly, lower part of sides, inner side and edge of the legs, uniform bright red-brown : ears rounded : whiskers black : feet covered with short close-pressed hairs.

(Gray, Proc. Zool. Soc., 1859, p. 478.)

d. Ruminants.

6. *Tragulus affinis.*

Similar to T. javanicus in colour, but rather smaller and much paler, and the side of the neck similar in colour to the side of the body: the belly is white, with a brown streak on each side of the central line: the head is smaller. It is larger than *T. kanchil;* very much paler; and the neck is not blacker and grizzled. A specimen of the species has been in the British Museum, as above named, for many years: it is said to have come from Singapore; but that probably was only the port of transit. It may be only a small pale local variety of *T. kanchil.*

Six specimens, adult, all exactly similar, and one young, have been collected by M. Mouhot. (Gray, Proc. Zool. Soc., 1861, p. 138.)

7. *Cervulus cambojensis.*

There are the forehead covered with hair and the horns of a Muntjack in the collection sent by M. Mouhot from Cambodia: it is very much larger than any specimen of that genus in the British Museum collection, and is probably a distinct species.

The horns are thick, nearly straight, with a short, thick recurved branch on the outer part of the front side, near the base, and one of them has a somewhat similar callosity on the hinder side on the same level. Hair of forehead very rigid, close pressed, dark brown, with narrow yellow rings. (Gray, Proc. Zool. Soc., 1861, p. 138.)

LIST OF THE NEW SPECIES OF REPTILES DISCOVERED BY THE LATE M. MOUHOT IN SIAM AND CAMBODIA.

By Dr. Albert Günther.

a. Tortoises.

1. *Geoclemys macrocephala.*

The shell oblong, rather depressed, entirely three-keeled, olive-brown: the keels subcontinued, nearly parallel; the middle one higher and more distinct behind; the lateral ones, near the upper edge of the shields, continued, ending abruptly on the hinder edge of the third lateral discal shield: the hinder lateral and central shield only marked with a slight convexity: the margin entire, yellow edged: the under side yellow, with black triangular spots: the sternum flat, very indistinctly keeled on the side.

Animal black olive, head large; crown flat, covered with a single smooth plate, purplish-brown, with two streaks from middle of the nose; the upper edging the crown, the other the upper part of the beak, and with two streaks from the hinder edge of the orbit; the lower short and interrupted, extended on the temple; the upper broader and continued over the ear, along the side of the neck; two close streaks under the nostrils to the middle of the upper jaw, and two broad streaks dilated behind, down the front of the lower jaw, and continued on the edge of the lower jaw behind: the nape and hinder part of the side of the lower jaw covered with large flat scales: the rest of the neck and legs covered with minute granular scales: the front of the forelegs covered with broad band-like scales: the toes of the fore and hind feet rather short and thick, covered above with broad band-like scales. (Gray, Proc. Zool. Soc., 1859, p. 479, pl. 21.)

2. *Cyclemys Mouhotii.*

Shell oblong, pale yellow; back flattened above, with a dark-edged keel on each side: the vertebral plates continuously keeled, and rather tubercular in front: the margin strongly dentated: nuchal shield distinct. (Gray, Ann. and Mag. Nat. Hist., 1862, x. p. 157; Günth., Rept. Brit. Ind., pl. 4, fig. D.)

3. *Trionyx ornatus.*

Back of the young animal, in spirits, brown, with large, unequal-sized, irregularly disposed black circular spots: head olive, with symmetrical small black spots on the chin, forehead, and nose: throat and sides of neck with large, unequal-sized, irregular-shaped, and nearly symmetrically disposed yellow spots: legs olive, yellow spotted in front: sternum and under side of margin yellow: sternal callosities not developed.

A single specimen has been found by M. Mouhot in Cambodia, which is now in the British Museum. (Described by Dr. J. E. Gray, Proc. Zool. Soc., 1861, p. 41, pl. 5.)

b. Lizards.

1. *Draco tæniopterus.*

Tympanum not scaly: nostrils above the face-ridge directed upwards: a low longitudinal fold on the neck: scales on the back of equal size, obscurely keeled: gular sac covered with large smooth scales, uniformly coloured: wings dark-greenish olive, with five arched black bands, not extending to the margin of the wing, some being forked at the base. (Günth., Proc. Zool. Soc., 1861, April 23, and Ind. Rept., p. 126, pl. 13, fig. E.)

2. *Acanthosaura coronata.*

The upper orbital edge serrated, without elongate spine posteriorly; a short spine on each side of the neck; a yellowish-olive band edged with black across the crown, from one orbital edge to the other; an oblique, short, yellowish band, broadly edged with brown, from below the orbit to the angle of the mouth.

This and the following species belong to the genus *Acanthosaura*, as defined by Gray (Catal. Liz. p. 240). The tympanum is distinct; a short spine between it and the dorsal crest, which is rather low; no femoral or præanal pores: a short spine behind the orbital edge, and separated from it by a deep notch: back and sides covered with small smooth scales, slightly turned towards the dorsal line, and intermixed with scattered larger ones which are keeled: belly and legs with larger keeled scales: tail slightly compressed at the base, the rest being round, and without crest; all its scales are keeled; those on the lower side being oblong, and provided with more prominent keels: throat without cross-fold, and without distinct longitudinal pouch: a slight oblique fold before the shoulder. (Günth., Proc. Zool. Soc., 1861, April 23, and Ind. Rept., p. 149, pl. 14, fig. E.)

3. *Acanthosaura capra.*

The upper orbital edge not serrated, terminating posteriorly in a long moveable horn: no spine above the tympanum or on the side of the neck: nuchal crest high, not continuous with the dorsal crest, which is rather elevated anteriorly: crown and cheek without markings.

The tympanum is distinct: no femoral or præanal pores: back and sides covered with small smooth scales, which become gradually larger and more distinctly keeled towards the belly: no large scales intermixed with the small ones; only a few appear to be a little larger than the rest: tail slightly compressed at the base, surrounded by rings of oblong, keeled scales: throat expansible; a very slight fold before the shoulder. (Günth., Ind. Rept., p. 148, pl. 14, fig. F.)

4. *Physignathus mentager.*

Dorsal crest not interrupted above the shoulder; interrupted above the hip: caudal crest as high as that on the back: no large scales on the side of the neck: sides of the throat with large convex or tubercular scales.

A high crest, composed of sabre-shaped shields, extends from the nape of the neck to the second fifth of the length of the tail, being interrupted above the hip: scales on the back and the sides of equal size, very small, with an obscure keel obliquely directed upwards; those on the belly smooth, on the lower side of the tail rather elongate; strongly keeled: tympanum distinct: throat with a cross-fold: orbital edges and sides of the neck without spines: tail transversely banded with black.

One stuffed specimen is 30 inches long, the tail taking 21. (Günth., Proc. Zool. Soc., 1861, April 23, and Ind. Rept., p. 153, pl. 15.)

5. *Tropidophorus microlepis.*

Snout rather narrow and produced: scales on the back strongly keeled, the keels not terminating in elevated spines: back of the tail with two series of moderately elevated spines, the series not being continuous with those on the back of the trunk: scales of the throat smooth, or very indistinctly keeled: tail with a series of plates below, which are much larger and broader than the scales of the belly: three large præanal scales: a single anterior frontal shield (internasal). (Günth., Proc. Zool. Soc., 1861, April 23, and Ind. Rept., p. 76, pl. 10, fig. A.)

c. SNAKES.

Simotes tæniatus.

Scales in nineteen rows. Brownish-olive, with a brown longitudinal dorsal band enclosing an olive-coloured line running along the vertebral series of scales; another brownish band along the side of the body; belly whitish, chequered with black.

One loreal shield, one anterior and two posterior oculars; eight upper labials, the third, fourth, and fifth of which enter the orbit; 155 ventral plates; anal entire; 44 pairs of subcaudals. Head with the markings characteristic of the genus: each half of the dorsal band occupies one series of scales and two halves; the lateral band runs along the fourth outer series, touching the third and fifth. (Günth., Proc. Zool. Soc., 1861, April 23, and Ind. Rept., p. 216, pl. 20, fig. A.)

d. NEWTS.

Plethodon persimilis.

Black, white-speckled, the specks closer and more abundant on the sides; the hind-toes elongate, unequal. Tail compressed.

This is the first species of Newts which has been discovered in Continental India; it is exceedingly like the *Pl. glutinosus* from North America, but the hind toes are rather longer and more slender. (Gray, Proc. Zool. Soc., 1859, p. 230, c. tab.)

LIST OF THE NEW SPECIES OF FRESH-WATER FISHES DISCOVERED BY THE LATE M. MOUHOT IN SIAM AND CAMBODIA.

BY DR. ALBERT GÜNTHER.

1. *Toxotes microlepis.*

D. $\frac{5}{13}$. A. $\frac{3}{17}$. L. lat. 42. L. transv. $\frac{6}{14}$.

In the general habit and in all the generic characters the present species completely agrees with *T. jaculator;* the snout, however, is much shorter, its length being scarcely more than the diameter of the eye, and considerably less than the width between the orbits. The diameter of the eye is one-fourth of the length of the head. The length of the base of the anal equals exactly that of the dorsal. One of the largest scales covers two-thirds of the eye.

The colour may prove to be subject to as much variation as in the other species. The specimens described are yellowish, with greenish back and yellowish caudal. There is a series of four black blotches on each side: the anterior is the smallest, and situated on the upper extremity of the præoperculum; the third is the largest, and placed opposite the dorsal spines; a narrow blackish band round the base of the caudal; a round black spot on the posterior angle of the dorsal; the anal and the ventrals are black.

(Günth., Fishes, ii. p. 68.)

2. *Eleotris siamensis.*

D. 6 | 10. A. 9. L. lat. 90.

Twenty-two longitudinal series of scales between the origin of the posterior dorsal and the anal, forty transverse ones between the anterior dorsal and the snout. The height of the body is contained six times and two-thirds in the total length, the length of the head four times. Head broad, depressed, with the snout obtuse; the lower jaw is prominent, and the maxillary extends to behind the vertical from the centre of the eye. Teeth in villiform bands. The diameter of the eye is one-seventh of the length of the head, one-half of that of the snout, and of the width of the interorbital space. A small barbel on each side of the upper jaw; the head is covered with small scales; there are about ten between the posterior angle of the orbits; the snout is naked. Dorsal and anal fins much lower than the body: one-half of the caudal is covered with thin scales; its length is contained five times and a half in the total. Brown: the lower parts whitish, minutely punctulated with brown: two oblique dark stripes on the cheek, radiating from the eye. Dorsal fins variegated with blackish, the other fins uniform blackish; a black ocellus, edged with whitish, on the upper part of the root of the caudal fin.

	Lines.
Total length	60
Height of the body	9
Length of the head	15
Diameter of the eye	2
Length of the caudal fin	11

(Günth., Fish., iii. p. 129.)

3. *Osphromenus siamensis.*

D. $\frac{7}{8}$. A. $\frac{11\text{-}12}{33\text{-}35}$. L. lat. 42. L. transv. $\frac{12}{16}$.

When we take the origin of the dorsal fin as the highest point of the upper profile, and the base of the last anal spine as the lowest of the abdomen, the depth between these two points is one-half of the total length (the caudal not included). The length of the head is three times and two-thirds in the same length. The snout is broader than long, equal to the diameter of the eye, which is one-fourth of the length of the head. The interorbital space is convex, wider than the orbit. Mouth very small, rather protractile; præorbital, with its extremity truncated and serrated: angle of the præoperculum serrated; there are two or three series of scales between the eye and the angle of the præoperculum. The dorsal fin commences nearer to the root of the caudal than to the end of the snout; it has six strong spines, which increase in length posteriorly, the last being longer than one-half the length of the head. Caudal emarginate; the anal is nearly entirely scaly, and terminates immediately before the caudal. The longest ventral ray extends beyond the extremity of the caudal, and has three or four rudimentary rays in its axil.

The colour is greenish on the back, silvery on the sides and on the belly. A black spot on the middle of the body in the vertical from the origin of the dorsal, below the lateral line; a second on the middle of the root of the caudal. The soft dorsal and caudal with brown dots; anal yellowish, with lighter spots, and sometimes with brownish dots.

This description is taken from specimens which are from three to four inches long.

(Günth., Fishes, iii. p. 385.)

4. *Osphromenus microlepis.*

D. $\frac{3}{10}$. A. $\frac{10}{39}$. L. lat. 60. L. transv. $\frac{12}{22}$.

The height of the body is one-half of the total length (without caudal), the length of the head two-sevenths; the profile of the nape is convex, that of the head rather concave. The snout is somewhat depressed, broader than long, with the lower jaw prominent; the interorbital space is convex, nearly twice as wide as the orbit, the diameter of which is one-fifth of the length of the head, and less than that of the snout. Præorbital triangular, with the lower margin serrated; there are five series of scales between the orbit and the angle of the præoperculum. The entire lower margin of the præoperculum and a part of the sub- and inter-operculum are serrated. The dorsal fin commences on the middle of the distance between the snout and the root of the caudal; its spines are moderately strong, the length of the third being more than one-half of that of the head. Caudal emarginate; more than one-half of the anal fin is scaly; it terminates immediately before the caudal. The longest ventral ray extends beyond the extremity of the caudal, and has three rudimentary rays in its axil. Immaculate: back greenish, sides and belly silvery; the soft dorsal and caudal with brownish dots.

Total length six inches.

(Günth., Fishes, iii., p. 385.)

5. *Catopra siamensis.*

D. $\frac{13}{15}$. A. $\frac{3}{9}$. L. lat. 27. L. transv. $\frac{5\frac{1}{2}}{13}$.

The height of the body is contained twice and a third in the total length, the length of the head thrice and a third; head as high as long. Snout rather shorter than the eye, the diameter of which is one-fourth of the length of the head, and equal to the width of the interorbital space. The lower jaw is scarcely longer than the upper, and the maxillary extends slightly beyond the anterior margin of the orbit. Two nostrils remote from each other, both very small. Præorbital and angle of the præoperculum slightly serrated; opercles, throat, and isthmus, entirely scaly. The dorsal fin commences above the end of the operculum, and terminates close by the caudal; its spines are very strong, and can be received in a groove; the fifth, sixth, and seventh are the longest, not quite half as long as the head; the last spine is shorter than the penultimate; the soft dorsal is elevated and scaly at the base. The second anal spine is exceedingly strong, rather stronger and longer than the third, and not quite half as long as the head; the soft anal is similar to the soft dorsal. Caudal fin rounded, slightly produced, one-fourth of the total length; its basal half is scaly. Pectoral rather narrow, as long as the head without snout. The ventral is inserted immediately behind the base of the pectoral; it has a strong spine, and extends to the vent.

Scales minutely ciliated: the upper part of the lateral line terminates below the last dorsal rays, the lower commences above the third anal spine.

Gill-membranes united below the throat, not attached to the isthmus, scaly. Four gills, a slit behind the fourth; pseudo-branchiæ none.

The jaws, vomer, palatines, and upper and lower pharyngeals are armed with bands of small villiform teeth. Very remarkable are two large, ovate, dentigerous plates, one at the roof, the other at the bottom of the mouth, in front of the pharyngeals; these plates are slightly concave in the middle, pavimentated with molar-like teeth, and have evidently the same function as the pharyngeal dentigerous plates of the true Pharyngognathi.

Total length 52 lines.

(Günth., Proc. Zool. Soc., 1862, June 24.)

6. *Ophiocephalus siamensis.*

D. 42. A. 27. L. lat. 65. L. transv. $\frac{5}{11}$.

Large teeth in the lower jaw, on the vomer and the palatine bones. The height of the body is contained six times and four-fifths in the total length; the length of the head three times and two-fifths; the length of the caudal six times. The width of the interorbital space is more than the extent of the snout, and two-ninths of the length of the head. Cleft of the mouth wide the maxillary not extending to the vertical from the posterior margin of the eye (in old specimens it probably reaches to below that margin). There are eleven series of scales between the eye and the angle of the præoperculum; scales on the upper surface of the head of moderate size. The pectoral extends to the origin of the anal fin, and its length is less than one-half of that of the head: the ventral is not much shorter than the pectoral; greenish-olive, with darker streaks along the series of scales; a light longitudinal band from the eye to the middle of the caudal fin; two series of alternate darker blotches, one above the light band, the other below; side of the head with three oblique brown bands; dorsal and anal fins with oblique blackish stripes; caudal with blackish spots: the lower side of the head blackish, with white spots. (Günth., Fishes, iii., p. 476.)

7. *Mastacembelus argus.*

D. $\frac{32}{60}$. A. $\frac{3}{56}$.

Præoperculum with two or three spines. The maxillary does not extend to the vertical from the anterior margin of the eye. Vertical fins continuous: brownish-black, with white bands and round white spots: a band from the occiput, along the middle of the back, passing into the white margin of the vertical fins: a second band above the eye, interrupted and lost on the side of the back: a third from the angle of the mouth, passing into a series of spots, which is continued to the caudal: another series of spots along the side of the belly; the soft dorsal with a series of six spots: pectoral black at the base and near the margin. (Günth., Fishes, iii. p. 542.)

8. *Cynoglossus xiphoideus.*

D. 120. A. 98. V. 4. L. lat. 135.

Three lateral lines on the left side, the upper and lower separated from the middle by twenty or twenty-one longitudinal series of scales: a single line on the right side. Two nostrils: one between the posterior parts of the eyes, the other in front of the lower eye. Eyes separated by a concave space, the width of which is more than that of the orbit; the upper eye considerably in advance of the lower: lips not fringed. The length of the snout is contained twice and a third in that of the head, the angle of the mouth being behind the vertical from the posterior margin of the eye, and nearer to the gill-opening than to the end of the snout. The rostral hook terminates below the front margin of the eye. The height of the body is contained four times and two-thirds in the total length, the length of the head five times and a half. The height of the dorsal and anal fins is two-sevenths of that of the body. Uniform brownish-grey. (Günth., Fish., iv. p. 495.)

ON AN APPARENTLY UNDESCRIBED SPIDER FROM COCHIN CHINA.

BY DR. ALBERT GÜNTHER.

Cyphagogus Mouhotii.

Cephalothorax subovate, covered with fine, short, dense hairs, with a transverse groove between cephalic and thoracic portion, and with a deep impression in the middle of the upper surface of the latter.

Eyes eight, unequal in size, disposed thus ·.: : .·; the four middle occupy a slight protuberance in front of the cephalothorax, whilst the lateral are the smallest, and situated on the side of its anterior part.

Falces articulated vertically, rather compressed, with a non-denticulated claw of moderate size at their extremity; the claw is received in a sheath at the lower end of the falces, the edges of the sheath being provided with some horny spines of unequal size. Maxillæ flat; the outer margins of both together form a card-like figure; their lower extremity is hairy; sternal lip between the maxillæ, elongate elliptical. Sternum ovate, covered with rather coarse hairs. Palpi of moderate length: the terminal joint is rather longer than the two preceding together, and armed with a minute non-pectinated claw.

Legs rather robust, tapering, very unequal in length, the two anterior being nearly equally long, but much longer than the two posterior: the fourth is longer than the third: each is armed with a pair of minute claws.

Abdomen club-shaped, anteriorly produced into a very long, thin, cylindrical process, which is twice bent, so that its basal half is leaning backwards on the back of the abdomen, whilst its terminal half is directed upwards and forwards, terminating in a slight cuneiform swelling: this singular appendage is covered with a leathery, fine hairy skin, like the lower parts of the abdomen. The cephalothorax being united with the abdomen at no great distance from the spinners, the anterior portion of the abdomen, with its appendage, is situated vertically above the thorax. The abdomen is nearly smooth above, and covered with very fine hairs below; it terminates in an obtuse point directed upwards.

Six spinners in a quadrangular group immediately before the vent: the anterior and posterior pair are of moderate size: the third pair is very short, and situated between the posterior spinners.

Two branchial opercula: tracheal opercula absent.

Dimensions.

	Lines.
Length of cephalothorax	4
,, abdomen to the first bend of the appendage	12
,, appendage from its first bend	10
,, falces	$1\frac{1}{3}$
,, palpus	$4\frac{1}{3}$
,, terminal joint of palpus	$1\frac{2}{3}$
,, first leg	16
,, second leg	16_3
,, third leg	9
,, fourth leg	$10\frac{1}{2}$

Colour brownish yellow: extremities of the legs and of abdominal appendage and sternum blackish brown: upper parts of the abdomen yellow: two black bands round the femur of the first leg.

A single female specimen of this spider was obtained by the late M. Mouhot in the Lao Mountains of Cochin China. Its form is so extraordinary that we have not hesitated to refer it to a new genus, *Cyphagogus.*

DESCRIPTION BY M. LE COMTE DE CASTELNAU OF A NEW AND GIGANTIC CARABIDEOUS INSECT DISCOVERED BY M. MOUHOT IN LAOS.

(Communicated by the Count to the 'Revue et Magasin de Zoologie.' 1862. No. 8. Paris.)

Among the magnificent insects that M. Mouhot collected during the few months of his stay in Laos, the first place is claimed by the beautiful Carabus which forms the subject of this paper, and which I have named *Mouhotia gloriosa* after my unfortunate countryman.

This splendid insect is black, with a large border of flame-colour at the sides of the thorax and of the elytra; this is covered with longitudinal striæ, formed by a double row of punctures. The thorax is hollowed behind, smooth on the top, with the lateral border a brilliant coppery-red; it presents a small longitudinal stria in the middle of its disk, and the anterior angles are very prominent.

It much resembles Pasimachus and Emydopterus, but is distinguished from them; firstly, by the maxillary palpi, of which the last joint is broad, flat, angular on the inner side, and rounded at the end, this joint being a little longer than the one before it; secondly, by the labrum, which is wide, short, and indented on the exterior side; and thirdly, by the labial

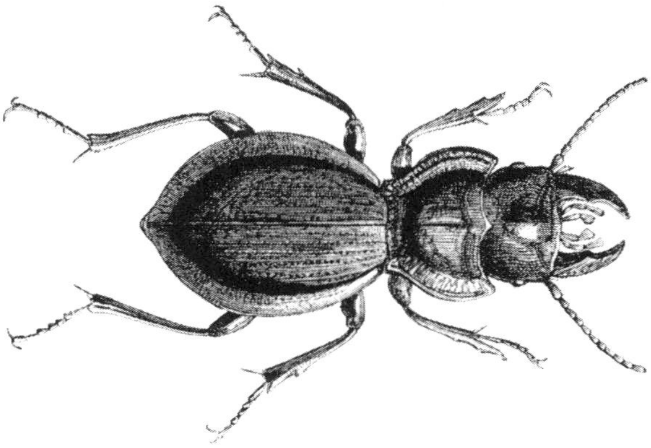

palpi, which have their last joint in the same form as the maxillary, but longer and hatchet-shaped. The mandibles are very strong, moderately arched, striated transversely, and with a strong tooth on the inner side; the jaws are also striated and obtuse at the ends. The head is similar to that of Pasimachus, the thorax is heart-shaped, the elytra oval, with angles towards the joints not strongly marked, convex, and a little serrated behind; the claws are powerful, with a strong tooth on the outer side of the middle of the tibiæ of the centre pair.

This insect is one of the most magnificent Carabidæ known, and is nearly two inches in length. The collection in the British Museum contains a fine specimen of it.

DESCRIPTIONS OF TWO NEW SPECIES OF LAND-SHELLS DISCOVERED BY M. MOUHOT IN THE INTERIOR OF CAMBODIA.

Helix cambojiensis.

Shell sinistral, deeply umbilicated, conoidly globose, rather inflated; upper portion of the whorls of a rich-toned transparent chestnut colour, edged at the satural margin with purple

black; lower portion of the whorls white, turning to a delicate straw-colour by the overlying of a shining, transparent, horny epidermis, encircled below the periphery and around the umbilicus with two very decided, broad, rich purple black bands; whorls six, corrugately puckered throughout at the satural margin, the first four whorls very densely granosely wrinkle-striated in the direction of the lines of growth, the striæ gradually disappearing on the fifth whorl; aperture lunar-orbicular; lips simple, reflected partly round the umbilicus.

Out of two thousand species of *Helix* at present known, the only one of the same type as *H. Mouhoti* is the large *H. Brookei*, collected by Mr. Arthur Adams, in company with Sir Edward Belcher, on the mountains of Borneo, during the voyage of the

'Samarang,' and described by Mr. Arthur Adams in the 'Zoology' of that expedition. *H. Mouhoti*, of which Mr. Stevens has received a few specimens in various stages of growth, is even larger and more inflated than *H. Brookei*. In adult specimens the last whorl measures 6½ inches in circumference, 3 inches in diameter, and the shell is about 2 inches high. It differs from *H. Brookei* in being conspicuously, but not broadly, umbilicated, and in the mature lip not being in the least degree reflected at the margin. The lip itself (not the margin) is reflected at its junction with the body-whorl, partly round the umbilicus, as in the *Nanina* form of the genus. But the most striking feature of the species is the colouring. In *H. Brookei* the lower half of the whorls is of a uniform dark chestnut-colour; in *H. Mouhoti* it is pure white, turned to a bright straw colour by the overlying of a shining horny epidermis, encircled immediately below the periphery by a broad, rich, purple-black band, somewhat like the bands of the large Philippine *Bulimus Reevei*, but even broader and more defined on the white ground. The region of the umbilicus is also deeply and as definitely stained with the same purple-black colour. As in *H. Brookei*, all the specimens of *H. Mouhoti* are sinistral, or what is more commonly called reversed.

Bulimus cambojiensis.

This shell is either sinistral or dextral, cylindrically ovate, thick, stout and pupoid in the spire, bluish-white, tinged with a watery fawn-colour, and clouded throughout with oblique zigzag flames of the same colour, darker, but very undefined and washy; whorls seven, smooth, rather bulbous, faintly impressed concavely below the suture; aperture ovate, of rather moderate dimensions, overlaid in a very conspicuous manner across the body-whorl, and over a very thickly reflected lip, with a callous, opaque, milk-white deposit, which in the interior is stained with a beautifully iridescent violet-rose. This fine species, of which

Mr. Stevens has received several specimens, measuring nearly 3 inches in length by 1½ inch in width, is a most characteristic example of a type of the Malayan province of the genus, represented by the old *Bulimus citrinus* of Brugnière; and it has been named after its well-authenticated place of habitation, because the species is, in all probability, confined to that locality. The islands adjacent to Cambodia have been pretty well ransacked; and we have nothing like it in species either from them or from the contiguous mainland of Siam on the west, or Cochin China on the east. This particular type of the genus appears, however, abundantly at the Moluccas, in *B. citrinus;* and at Mindanao, the southernmost of the Philippine Islands, in *B. maculiferus.* Like these two species, *B. cambojiensis* occurs with the shell convoluted either to the right or to the left. The shell is both larger and stouter than that of *B. citrinus,* differently painted, and especially characterized by its mouth of iridescent violet-rose, or what is now fashionably termed " Solferino " colour.

These descriptions are from the pen of Lovell Reeve, Esq., F.L.S., &c., and were communicated by him to 'The Annals and Magazine of Natural History.' See vol. vi. p. 203.

The annexed plate contains representations of several other new and interesting species of land shells discovered by M. Mouhot, and named by Dr. Pfeiffer, but which have yet to be described.

New Land Shells discovered by M. Mouhot.

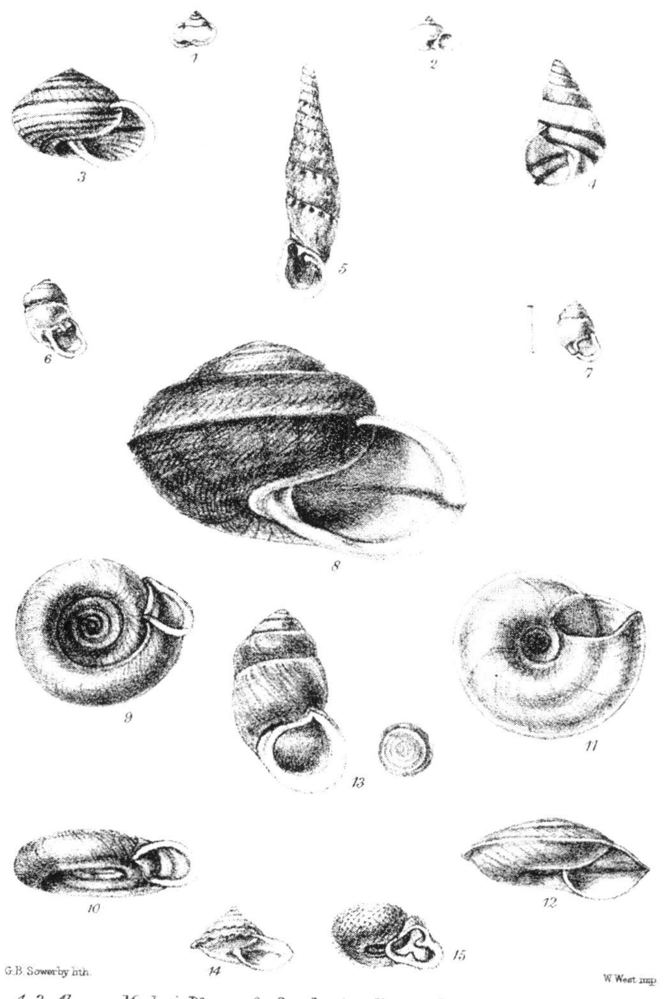

G.B. Sowerby lith. W West imp.

1. 2. *Alycæus Mouhoti*, Pfr.
3. *Helix deliciosa*, Pfr.
4. *Bulimus Römeri*, Pfr.
5. *Clausilia Mouhoti*, Pfr.
6. *Streptaxis pellucens*, Pfr.
7. *Pupina Mouhoti*, Pfr.
8. *Helix illustris*, Pfr.
9. 10. *Helix Laomontana*, Pfr.
11. 12. *Helix beligna*, Pfr.
13. *Hybocistis Mouhoti*, Pfr.
14. *Trochatella Mouhoti*, Pfr.
15. *Helix horrida*, Pfr.

ATMOSPHERICAL OBSERVATIONS.

January.—The month of January at Bangkok is generally the coolest in the whole year. The thermometer generally ranges from 58° to 60° Fahr. in the morning. The wind is sometimes N. or N.E., and at others S.S.W. or S. The rainy season ends in the latter part of October; the water has fallen in the rivers, which have not overflowed since the middle of December; therefore at this time of the year one can walk along the banks, which are pleasant. The paths are visible and in a good state for travellers, and there is less danger, even in the interior of the country, of being attacked by jungle fever. There is often fog in the morning, but yet it is not unhealthy. The weather has been fine all the month, excepting one or two rainy days towards the middle.

February.—During this month the wind frequently blows from the N.E. or E., though sometimes from S.S.W. The weather is fresh, agreeable, and healthy. It is the month which the Buddhist pilgrims choose to visit Phrabat, where they imagine they can trace the prints of Buddha's feet. It is the best time for crossing the jungles and the plains, for the banks are all raised high above the water and the earth is perfectly dry. If the wind blows from the S. for a few days, as it sometimes does, the heat becomes overwhelming for the time. There are also occasionally, as in January, two or three rainy days towards the middle of the month.

March.—This month is hotter and drier than the two preceding ones; there is less freshness. The wind blows generally from the E.N.E., S., or S.S.W., and often with great violence during the day: the Siamese call it Som Won (wind of the shuttlecock), of which game they are very fond, and one hears everywhere their noise mingled with cries of admiration from the people. Violent storms, accompanied by rain and thunder, generally mark the equinox; after that the weather becomes hot and dry. The thermometer sometimes rises as high as 93 in the middle of the day, but the nights are still pleasant.

April.—April is the hottest month of the year. The first part is generally dry, with E. or S. winds, but changes about the middle to N.E. and S.W. In the latter part of the month the excessive heat is tempered by some refreshing rains. Although the sun is very powerful during the day, the nights at Bangkok are cool. This month is not so healthy for Europeans as the three which precede it, and dysentery makes great ravages.

May.—This month is considered one of the most rainy of the year, though sometimes July and September are more so. The rain rarely lasts all day, and there are sometimes intervals of two or three fine days. In this month the people prepare their ground and sow their rice.

June.—During the whole of this month the wind blows constantly either from the S., W., or S.W. The jungles at this season are fatal to travellers, especially to Europeans, who would do wisely to avoid them and to pass this the rainy season at Bangkok, which is one of the healthiest of the tropical towns.

July.—In July sweet and refreshing breezes blow from the W. and S., but more rain falls than in June. There are sometimes very hot days, when the thermometer rises very high, but still in Siam this month is considered tolerably healthy.

August.—The same as July.

September.—This is a month of almost incessant rain, and it is very rare to have two or three consecutive fine days.

October.—Everything is inundated, some of the streets of Bangkok are transformed into canals, and the rivers everywhere overflow their banks. The first part of this month is as rainy as the preceding one.

November.—The Siamese now complain of the cold, but the Europeans rejoice in it, for the N.E. wind begins to blow. There are still some rainy days at the beginning of the month, and some hot ones. These transitions of temperature give rise to colds and catarrhs. At the end of the month the wind changes to the S.W.

December.—This is the best month to commence travelling on the rivers. Occasionally there is thunder and rain, but altogether it is considered a healthy month.

METEOROLOGICAL REGISTER kept during the month of October 1861, and up to the sixth day after M. MOUHOT was attacked by fever.

Louang Prabang (Laos).

Dates.	Fahr. 8 A.M.	Reaumur.	Fahr. 3 P.M.	Reaumur.	Fahr. 8 P.M.	Reaumur.
1	73	18	84	..	80	..
2	72	..	85	..	78	..
3	73	18	81	22⅓	76	20
4	75	..	80	22	75¼	20
5	73	18	81	24¾	75¼	20¼
6	75½	20	79	20	75	20
7	73	19	77	20½	74	..
8	72	18½	83	23¼	72¼	18½
9	73	19	79	20	74	19
10	74	19½	83	23	74	19
11	72	18	83½	23¼	74	19
12	72	18¼	79½	21½	72	18
13	70	15½	78	21	70	17½
14	63	14½	79	21½	65	15
15	60	13	72	18	60	15
16	60	13	83½	23½	70	17
17	64	14½	83½	22	70	15
18	64	14½	86	23½	70	18
19	69	17	85	24	71½	17½
20	70	15½	89	25	74	19½
21	73	19	90	26	74	19
22	71	18	86	23½	71	18
23	73	19	87	25	70	18
24	68	16½	88	25	..	..

TALE.

TRANSLATED FROM THE CHINESE BY M. HENRI MOUHOT.

In a Chinese village lived two cousins, both orphans: the eldest, who was called Moû, was cunning and egotistical; the other, on the contrary, was goodness and simplicity itself; he was called A-lo-Sine. The time for ploughing the fields arrived: A-lo-Sine possessed a buffalo, while Moû had only a dog. An idea struck him, and he went to his cousin and said, "I bring you my dog; give me your buffalo: my dog will plough your field, which is not very large, and you will see that you will have very fine rice."

A-lo-Sine consented, and worked so well with the dog that his rice was first-rate, while the field ploughed by the buffalo produced hardly anything.

Moû, then, full of spite, went by night into his cousin's field, and set fire to it: A-lo-Sine saw the flames, and, unable to repress his despair, uttered piercing cries, and rolled in the field.

Some apes, who were marauding in a neighbouring field, witnessed this spectacle, and said to each other, "That must be a god, since the fire does not hurt him." They accordingly drew near him, took him by the feet and arms, and carried him to the top of a mountain, where they laid him down, plunged in a deep sleep. The monkeys then piled up rice and delicious fruits, and bowls of gold and silver of extraordinary beauty and value, and then left him to return to the fields.

At last he awoke, and thought no more of his misfortune, seeing around him so many treasures: he gathered them all up, and returned to his hut, full of joy.

Moû, seeing him so happy, followed him, and, at the sight of the gold, "Heavens!" cried he; "my cousin as rich as a prince: give me something."

"No," replied A-lo-Sine, "I will not; for you are wicked, and you set fire to my field."

Moû then went to his own field, and set fire to that also, and imitated all that his cousin had done: he wept, cried, and, like him, threw himself into the flames. Five monkeys, one of them a young one, who were feasting close by, drew near him, curious to see what he was about. "He is a god," said they, also; "the flames have spared him. Let us carry him away." No sooner said than done. Each monkey seized one an arm, the other a leg, and they set off.

They reached a neighbouring wood; but there the little monkey began to cry out, "I want to help to carry him also." "But there is nothing of him to hold by," said the mother. The little monkey, however, continued to cry, and at last seized Moû's long tress of hair, and put himself at the head of the procession.

But this hurt Moû, and he tried to disengage his hair. The young monkey began to cry again. "Ah, you are angry; stay there, then," said all the others, and they threw him into a prickly bush.

Moû had great trouble in extricating himself from his disagreeable position; and it was nearly evening when he reached home, all covered with blood.

"Well, cousin, have you also some gold and silver?" said A-lo-Sine, on seeing him. "Ah! I am thoroughly punished for the harm I did you," replied Moû. "I bring back nothing but needles: call the women to take them out of me."

TALE.

TRANSLATED FROM THE CHINESE BY M. HENRI MOUHOT.

THERE lived formerly in a Chinese village an old couple who had no children; and one day the husband put himself in a violent passion with his wife for never having had any, and even beat her. The poor old woman rushed out of the house, crying, and ran a long way. A priest of Buddha met her accidentally, and asked her what had happened to her. "My husband was angry to-day, and beat me, because we had no children," replied she. "Listen," said the priest; "I will make you happy! Dig in this earth and knead it" (it was clay). The woman obeyed, and the priest then sat down, and with his fingers moulded nine little figures. "The first," said he, "will have long ears and very quick hearing; the second, a piercing sight; the third, a skin so hard that he will not feel any blow; the fourth will stand fire without hurt; the fifth will have an enormous head, as hard as iron; the sixth, legs long enough to cross the deepest stream; the seventh, feet as large as those of an elephant, for walking in mire; the eighth, an immense stomach; and the ninth, a nose as long as a pipe, from which jets of water will issue at command. Now," continued the priest, "go home, and every year eat one of these children." The old woman bowed several times, professing her gratitude and happiness; then she returned home; but in her joy, instead of contenting herself with one child, she eat up all nine at once. Her stomach, which had begun to swell at once, grew every month bigger and bigger, and became frightful. The husband was beside himself with joy, and was very kind to his wife.

At last the day of delivery arrived: the father received the first child, and ran to wash him in the stream; but there came a second. "Another!" cried the father, and ran again to the river. Returning, he found a third, then a fourth. He opened his eyes and cried, "Really this is quite enough: what can we give them to eat?" But the whole nine made their appearance on the same day.

All were prodigies: they grew rapidly; never cried; eat enormously, and began to run about in two months. But the old man did not know what to call them all; and one day he complained to his wife that he could not distinguish them one from another, got in another passion, and struck her again. The old woman ran away, crying, again, and went to find the priest who had helped her before. "Why do you cry now?" said he. "My husband has so many children now that he does not know what names to give them." "You are very foolish," replied he, "not to be able to distinguish them by the gifts they possess. Call one 'Quick-ear,' another 'Hard-head,' and so on for the others."

The old man had calmed down when his wife returned; but debts accumulated as the children grew up. At last they became strong and fearless.

One day a creditor came and asked for money. "I have none," replied the old man. He persisted in this reply, and at last turned the creditor out of the house. A few days after, this man collected several of his friends, and went again to the old man, declaring he would seize one of the children, and whip him. "Quick-ear" had heard all, and "Piercing-eye" had mounted to the top of a tree and seen all that was going on. They decided that "Hard-skin" would be the best to go, and the creditor succeeded in binding him and taking him away. But every cane broke on his back, without hurting him: at last they took an immense cudgel, but this broke in the same way; and seeing that it was lost time to beat him, they let him go home.

But a few days after, the creditor came back, determined to

kill one of the children with boiling water. "Quick-ear" heard the project, and "Invulnerable" was left at home, and consequently carried off. They threw him into a boiler full of water; and in about an hour, when they opened it, the child raised his head. "What, not yet dead!" cried the creditor, in a fury, and he made up a larger fire, but "Invulnerable" was still alive. They made it still hotter, but the next day their wood was exhausted, and they let him go free, saying that Buddha protected him. "This is very sad," said the creditor; "I cannot get my money; I cannot get my money: I will write a letter to Heaven, to beg that fire may be sent down to burn the house of my debtor." He did so accordingly; but "Quick-ear," who heard the plot, warned "Fountain-nose," who thereupon took care to water the roof. The thunderbolt fell, but glided from the roof to the ground. All the children joined their strength, and lifted it, chained it up, and placed it in the house.

"Is it possible," cried the creditor, "that they are not all dead? I must throw one of them into the sea." This time it was "Stilt-bird's" turn. The boat in which they placed him had not gone far from the shore when a storm arose and upset it, and all the men were drowned, with the exception of "Stilt-bird," who escaped, thanks to his long legs. However, his brothers feared for him, and sent "Big-head" to the shore, where he found him fishing, and having already caught so many fish that he did not know where to put them. Luckily "Big-head" had his hat, which they filled, and returned home with an immense load. "Large-feet" went to cut wood to fry it with; but "Great-stomach" eat it all up before his brothers had hardly had time to begin. "Weeping-eyes" began to cry, and an inundation ensued, in which many of the neighbours perished.

Meanwhile, all the children were out searching for food, and the mother was left at home alone. She, seeing the thunderbolt chained in a corner, unfastened it. Immediately it rose in the air, then, falling again, struck the poor woman, and killed her.

FABLE.

TRANSLATED FROM THE CHINESE BY M. HENRI MOUHOT.

FIRMNESS and presence of mind often make heroes of cowards, and rescue them from great dangers, while rashness is generally fatal.

In the midst of a thick and virgin forest, where everything seemed to slumber, an elephant began to utter doleful howlings, and a tiger replied by others still more dreadful, which froze all the other animals with terror. Monkeys, stags, and all the inhabitants of the neighbourhood, ran groaning to seek refuge at the tops of the trees, or in the depth of the woods, or in their dens. The elephant himself ran with all his speed, when on his way he met a hare, who stopped him, and said, "Why do you run thus, without aim and without reason?" "What! did you not hear the frightful roaring of the tiger? Would you advise me to stay here and be devoured?" "Stay here, and have no fear; I will answer for it that no harm happens to you," said the hare; "only sit down, that I may jump on your back." The elephant goodnaturedly approached and extended his four legs; then the hare jumped up, having first put into his mouth a piece of betel.

"Now, get up again," said he, "and you will see that all will go well." He then proceeded to give the elephant further counsel, and afterwards let out along his back a long stream of saliva, reddened by betel. Soon the tiger came up. "What are you coming to seek here?" said the hare, as the tiger stopped to look at them. "Do you not see that this elephant is not too much for me alone; and do you think I will share with you?" The tiger drew aside, behind a tree, to watch what passed. The hare then seized hold of the elephant's ear, made him roar, and seemed perfectly master of his prey, and busy at his work. "Heavens! how strong he is!" said the tiger; but still he drew near. "Wait a minute, and I will come to you," cried the hare, looking as though preparing to spring, and the tiger, struck with terror, turned and ran away. A chimpanzee, seeing him running away in such terror, burst out laughing. "What! you laugh at my misfortune?" cried the tiger. "I have just escaped from death, and you do not pity me." "How so? I should like to see the beast who frightened you; take me to him."

"What! to be devoured? no."

"Do not be afraid; I will get on your back, and will not leave you: we will fasten our tails together, if you like; and thus united we shall run no risk!" The tiger was persuaded by these words, and they both returned to the elephant. The hare seemed still busy at his work: he had chewed a new piece of betel, and had made another stream, red as blood, on the elephant's back. "You dare to come back!" cried he, in an angry tone, to the tiger. "You knew I had only just enough here for myself, and yet you want to carry away my prey from me; you deserve to be punished."

At these words the elephant uttered a piercing cry; the hare made an enormous bound on his back; and the tiger, struck with terror, rushed precipitately away at full speed, saying to the chimpanzee, "Now, you see; you laughed at my fears, and we both narrowly escaped death." But the chimpanzee did not hear; for in the tiger's precipitate retreat he had fallen off his back, struck himself against a bamboo, and died, cursing his rashness with his last sigh.

THE HARE AND THE SNAIL.

FABLE.

TRANSLATED FROM THE CHINESE BY M. HENRI MOUHOT.

FORMERLY, according to the Siamese, hares had thick ears; but a certain day one of these animals, having more legs than memory, met a snail dragging himself painfully along the ground, and in a moment of pride sought to humiliate him. "Why, little one, where are you going at this pace?" said he. "To the beautiful rice-fields of the next village." "But, my poor fellow, you will be a long time reaching them. Why did not Nature furnish you with legs like mine? Confess you envy me. How long, now, do you think it would take me to get there?"

"Perhaps longer than it would take me, though you pity me so much," replied the snail, coldly.

"You jest, do you not?"

"No."

"Well, will you bet about it?"

"Willingly."

"What will you bet?"

"Whatever you like."

"Well, then, if you win you shall nibble my ears; for you cannot eat me; and if you lose I will eat you: will that suit you?"

"Perfectly."

"Then set off; for I will give you a start."

While the hare began to browse the snail set off at his slow pace, and went to his brother, who was a little way off, and to him he communicated a pass-word, which he in turn told to another, and so on along the whole line which the betters had to travel, so that it quickly reached the end.

Soon the hare, having satisfied his hunger, and feeling strong, set off, and flew over the ground, calling to the snail, whom he believed to be close by. "Ohé!" answered he, from a long way off. "Oh, he is already far on the way," cried the hare, who set off again like an arrow. In a few minutes he stopped and called again: "Ohé," answered a voice still farther on. "Really, he goes very quickly," thought the hare, and he set off again. A quarter of an hour after, he stopped, quite out of breath. "Now," said he, "I may rest; I must be far in advance; but I will call and see. "Ohé! snail." "Ohé!" replied a voice a long way on. "Oh! I must be quick; I shall lose my bet," murmured the hare. He ran, and ran, and at last stopped, quite exhausted, only a few yards from the fields. "Snail," cried he, faintly: "what! you are returning from the place? Unfortunate that I am, I have lost my bet;" and he made vain efforts to get up and escape, but, alas! his strength failed him, and the snail pitilessly gnawed his ears.

Since that day the hare always avoids damp places, for fear of meeting one of the creatures who punished him for his pride.

TALE.

TRANSLATED FROM THE CHINESE BY M. HENRI MOUHOT.

THERE lived formerly in a small town in China a singular couple, of a description still met with, for the Chinese progress very slowly. The husband was noted for his folly, and the wife for her cunning. "Always remember," she used constantly to say to her husband when he went out, "that all people with long noses, in the form of an eagle's beak, and bending downwards, are good-for-nothings, beggars, cheats, and, worse still, bad paymasters, coiners of false money, false-swearers, and will go to hell; while people with small turned-up noses are good, and will go straight to heaven. Therefore, that you may not lose, sell only to these last; for, I repeat to you, the others are bad."

Every day the husband went out, and passed from street to street, examining the passers-by, but never addressing any but those who had their heads raised to look at something, so that he very seldom sold anything.

One day, when he was observing noses as usual, he saw a man reading a placard which was placed very high. "That man will go straight to heaven," thought he; "his nose is so much turned up. Will you buy some clothes, good man?" said he. "Clothes! you see I have some." "But you appear to me the most honest man I ever saw" ("I never saw such a nose," he added to himself); "and I should like to sell you a whole suit; my wife makes them herself." "Well, what is the price?" "Of my wife?" "No; of the clothes." "Two kóóu" (about ten francs). "But why do you come into this retired place to sell your clothes, when there are so many people elsewhere?" "Oh! I went to those places; but all the people had long, bent, and eagle-shaped noses, you see! and I only sell to snub-nosed people." "I do not understand you; why will you not sell to people with long noses?" "My wife who is a very clever woman, told me that all people with long, eagle-shaped noses are knaves." "Really, your wife is very sharp, and I understand you now. Well, my friend, I will buy your clothes; but as I have no money with me, I will pay you to-morrow. You have only to come to my house; I live near here. You will see a hurdle covered with eggs, a flag at the end of a mast, and a little plantation of betel." "Very well; that will do."

The merchant went home to his wife, and told her he had sold to a man with a snub nose. "Where is the money?" said she. "I have not got it yet, but I shall be sure to have it to-morrow. I am to go where I see a hurdle covered with eggs, a flag on a mast, and a little betel plantation." The next day the wife said, "Go for your money." He went, but could not find the house; and after long searching he came home again. "Have you the money?" said the wife. "No, I could not find the house." "Well, I will go myself to look for it. If I am not back in an hour, you will know that I am drowned." After an hour, as his wife did not return, the man took the sieve with which he usually sifted his rice, and set off to the river, which he began to try to empty with it. A passer-by asked him what he was doing. "I am emptying the river," replied he; "for my wife is drowned, and she had on her best yellow bonnet." "Nonsense!" said the other; "I just met her walking with a man who had a snub nose."

THE DAMIER, OR CAPE PIGEON.

Procellaria Capensis.

DURING a long voyage, when for months you have seen nothing but water and sky, the smallest novelty which appears and promises variety for the eye and the mind, though only for a few minutes, is joyfully welcome. Sometimes it may be a stormy petrel, flying like a swallow, skimming through the air in a hundred different directions, and seeming to play in that element; sometimes a ring-tail, which, with its piercing cry like that of a hawk, appears a messenger from the sun to bid the bold navigator welcome to the tropics, hovers for a few minutes over the ship, and then flies off with a jerk and disappears.

Sometimes are to be seen numerous blowers, who pass and repass the ship with bounds; or perhaps a whale, which almost stupefies you with the noise he makes as he displaces the water in rising to the surface to breathe: at another time it is some hungry shark, who, following in the wake of the ship, lets himself be caught by the bait thrown out to him, and which, when hoisted with great difficulty on deck, lashes it with his tail and looks formidable even after death; and this is a good take for the sailors, who divide the spoil and feast on it.

But of all the creatures dear and familiar to sailors, none rejoices him more than the faithful companion who, more than 3000 miles before he doubles the Cape of Good Hope or Cape Horn, appears to his sight, swims in the water, grazes a thousand times the hull or the rigging, pleases his eye by its particoloured plumage, and announces to him calm and tempest.

This bird, called by the French "*Damier*," by the English the *Cape Pigeon*, and "*Peintada*" by the Portuguese, is the Cape Petrel, or *Procellaria capensis* of naturalists.

Gifted with great powers of flight, though less than other petrels, from morn till night, and often even a part of the latter when the moon is full, it is seen in the wake or alongside of the ship, describing in its flight, in which scarcely any movement is apparent, a thousand evolutions, sometimes touching the great waves which seem ready to overwhelm it, the moment after reappearing far above them, always wheeling about and careless of the storm.

The sight of this flight and of all these evolutions is most pleasing, and one involuntarily thinks of a graceful skater flying over the ice at his utmost speed, and seeking to attract admiration.

The whole life of this bird is perpetual movement, a constant chase after a scarce and insignificant prey. Unlike the swallow, who has his hours of pleasure and of amorous warbling, and nights of sleep in his warm nest, the Cape pigeon, pressed by hunger and by his ravenous appetite, only rests for a few minutes at a time at rare intervals during the day, in order to recruit his strength, and at night, rocked by the stormy wave, must find but little sleep.

Neither does the Cape pigeon know the delight of a peaceful retreat in a favourite spot sheltered by thick foliage or long reeds; and while most birds confine themselves to a limited district, where they are almost certain to be found at the same season, and to which they invariably return at the disappearance of the frosts which have chased them away for a time, this one, a sailor by nature, has for its domain an immense empire, namely the greatest part of the Atlantic, Pacific, and Indian oceans, and has to brave night and day, at one time an icy wind, and at another the rays of a burning sun.

But in a state of liberty nothing living is often unhappy, and the foreseeing Providence, who knows how to satisfy the wants of his creatures, also knows how to create joys for them, where we see nothing but trouble and misery. In like manner the industrious workman and the hardy traveller experience, perhaps, of all men the most lively joys; to them repose would be the greatest suffering.

Although inseparable companions of the sailor, it is not certainly for the pleasure of his society, nor for that afforded by the sight of the ship, that the petrels follow it, but for the certainty of finding in the scraps thrown overboard, as well as in the number of shells in the wake of the ship, food more abundant than he would discover elsewhere in the water. Nothing can equal their voracity but the quickness and vivacity with which they catch sight of the smallest prey and seize it even amidst a stormy sea. From a great distance, and long before the albatross, and the other descriptions of petrels which are often to be seen with the Cape pigeons, have remarked it, they see and pounce on it, and have generally swallowed it before the jealous rivals who follow them have been able to overtake them. The sense of smell does not here come in aid of that of sight, for they often pounce on a piece of wood or something of that description which falls from a vessel, and only abandon it when convinced by the touch that it is not fit for food. Their greediness is such that they will often let themselves be taken in dozens with hooks; no sooner are they on deck than they disgorge a thick liquid the colour of linseed oil.

When these birds rest on the sea and let themselves be tossed about by the waves, their appearance, dimensions, form, and colour of plumage strongly resemble our domestic pigeons, and hence the English seamen, struck with the similarity, have given them the name of Cape pigeons. Their size varies; the largest measuring more than 18 inches English from the beak to the tip of the tail, and rather more than a foot in circumference.

They are generally seen in great numbers only in stormy weather and in rather high latitudes. In the winter season—that is, during our June, July, and August—they follow the ships constantly between 23° S. lat. and 31° and 103° E. long.

Is it not a wonderful thing and worthy of admiration that the instinct with which this bold little navigator is endowed guides him safely through this vast space, where there is nothing to serve him as a landmark, enables him to rejoin his comrades if accidentally separated from them, and teaches him every year when the warm season returns to recognise and find the island or the solitary rock where he was born, and where in his turn he will bring up his young ones; while man, with his maps, his books, his nautical instruments, and in spite of all his long experience, has such difficulty in finding his way across the ocean? And yet we think that our intelligence raises us above the animals. This is what confounds and overwhelms the scholar when he seeks to fathom the great mysteries of creation.

THE ALBATROSS.

A wise and bountiful Providence has taken care to people the most distant and desert parts of the globe, whether covered with eternal snow or impenetrable forests. In the waters of the ocean are, as well as in our fields and woods, creatures which rejoice the eyes of man and provide for his wants. Of all these creatures none are more charming and pleasing than the birds; endowed either with melodious voices or brilliant plumage, or with some other charm or quality, such as vivacity, quickness and grace of movement, and power of flight; all have attractions for us; and even in our museums, in spite of their faded plumage and often altered forms, they are still objects of admiration, not only to the learned naturalist, but to men who care little for other beautiful sights.

But if leaving the cabinet we visit Nature herself, penetrate into the heart of the forests, climb the rocks, or visit the shores and the ocean, then our admiration grows stronger and more deep.

Of all birds there is none which exercises a greater influence over the mind of man, or causes greater astonishment, than the albatross, so celebrated by voyagers from the earliest times. The albatross! The word recalls to the navigator a thousand souvenirs; as the name of some bloody battle in which he has taken part, or of some general who has led him to victory, awakens those of the soldier. It recalls to the memory of the sailor the principal incidents of an existence passed between calm and tempest; he feels himself transported in thought to the time when the first albatross was signalled, and passengers and sailors turned their gaze eagerly towards the spot where, like a proud man cf war, cradled by the rolling waves, advanced the powerful sailer against whom the storm rages in vain, and who, far from avoiding, seems to court it.

To this first souvenir succeed many others; there is the dead calm, which in the tropics has often detained his vessel inactive for weeks, as though chained under the burning sky, where the eye seeks in vain for a cloud, and the only sound that meets the ear is the heavy flapping of the sails against the masts as the ship rocks; a calm often more to be feared and more dangerous than the most terrible tempest, for it renders the crew inactive, impatient, and bad-tempered. But the first sight of the albatross indicates a coming change and wind to be expected. There is also the memory of painful and too sudden transitions from equatorial heat to the cold of high latitudes; that also of hours of dreadful anxiety when the storm broke out in all its violence, of the contest between winds and waves, and of the albatross hovering over the latter, as though chosen an umpire between these two formidable antagonists. The albatross inhabits the southern hemisphere of the Atlantic Ocean from the 25° or 26° of latitude, also both Pacifics, but is rarely seen farther north, and has never been known beyond the tropics; it is in the seas which bathe the three southern capes that they are seen in the greatest numbers.

It often happens, however, when the winter is mild and the weather fine, that very few are seen until you reach the 40°. They lay their eggs on some deserted southern shore; the female lays only one, and feeds her little one for nine months without leaving it, so much need has it of its mother's help.

There is much difficulty in the classification of the palmipeds, which exhibit a great number of varieties.

The beak of the albatross is long and very strong; the upper jaw furrowed at the side and much curved; the lower one sharp, smooth, and truncated at the end; the nostrils, formed by two tubes opening outwards, are lateral and placed in a groove.

The tarsi are short, but very thick, and ending in three front toes much palmated; the wings are long and narrow.

There are probably four distinct species of albatrosses.

1st. The wandering albatross, *Diomedea exulans*, which measures ten feet with the wings spread; it has a white head, the wings and belly being spotted with white, grey, and chestnut brown; the beak is the colour of horn. This species varies much in size, and still more in colour and plumage, which is more or less mixed with grey or brown, and sometimes even entirely white; this depends doubtless on the season, the sex, and the age.

2nd. The epauletted albatross, *Diomedea epomophera*, which is smaller than the common albatross. His head, neck, body, back, and rump are snowy white, while the feathers of his wings are perfectly black, with the exception of a large white lozenge-shaped spot on each; the beak is yellowish. Some naturalists believe these to be only the young of the ordinary kind.

3rd. The yellow-beaked albatross, *Diomedea chlororhyncos*. This species I have myself taken with a hook; his head, belly, and neck are brilliantly white, his back and the plumage of the wings a deep brown grey, the beak yellow, and the feet bluish grey; the rump is white, and as well as the underpart of the tail is bordered by a wide black line.

4th. The sooty albatross, *Diomedea spadicea* of Forster, which is the size of the common albatross, and of a uniform deep chestnut-colour.

CAMBODIAN VOCABULARY.

A.

Abandon (to) .. .. Lẽng, chol.
Abhor (to) .. .. Sââp.
Approach (to) .. .. Dâl.
Abstinence .. .. } Tam.
Abstain (to) .. .. }
Accept (to) .. .. Iotuol.
Accompany (to) .. .. Iam.
Accomplish (to) .. .. Ihúruéch hoì.
Accustom oneself (to) .. .. .. Ihlap.
Accuse (to) .. .. Shõdéng.
Acid .. .. Ehu.
Admire (to) .. .. Ehhugăl.
Adore (to) .. .. Ihoui bãngeom.
Adultery .. .. Bap phit propon Ki.
Afflict (to) .. .. Lruey chot chaw chot.
Age .. .. Acõschhnam.
Announce (to) .. .. Srăp, pram.
Appease (to) .. .. On.
Appetite .. .. Comléan Klileán.
After .. .. Ẽcroí.
Arid .. .. Sngnot, comynot.
Arm .. .. Crùóng predăp.
Army .. .. Iăp.
Arrive (to) .. .. Dâl.
Assembly .. .. Chumnam.

Assemble (to) .. .. .. Chumnam Kenéa.
Audacity .. .. } Ihean.
Audacious .. .. }
August .. .. Mahu.
Also .. .. Dėl.
Altar .. .. Balang, as-prĕn.
Agile .. .. Chuery.
Air .. .. Acos.
Add (to) .. .. Thêm.
Aloes .. .. Jadam.
Alum .. .. Saĕpchu.
Amuse oneself (to) .. .. Ling.
Ancient .. .. Chus.
Ass .. .. Satliá.
Angel .. .. Firĕuda.
Angle .. .. Chrung.
Animal .. .. Săt.
Avarice .. .. Comnaut.
Advocate .. .. Sma Kedey.
Abortive (to be) .. .. Relutcōn.
Arm .. .. Phlu.
Aim .. .. Vong.
Ashes .. .. Phe.
Ask (to) .. .. Som.
Above .. .. Lù ê lù.
And .. .. Non.
Awake (to) .. .. Dăs.
Arrow .. .. Prúeup.
Agreeable .. .. Totuol.
Appearance .. .. Cŏmnăp.
According to .. .. .. Tam.
Always .. .. Ruéy (iún ruey reáp darăpton muc).
Anger .. .. Conhong.
Amongst .. .. Erang.

Across .. .. Totùng.
Already .. .. Hoi.

B.

Bitter .. .. Loving.
Before .. .. Mum.
Bathe (to) .. .. Ngut tin.
Breath .. .. Dâng hina.
Bold .. .. Tahéan.
Broom .. .. Bombãs.
Bamboo .. .. Resey.
Banana .. .. Chá.
Banquet .. .. Car si.
Beard .. .. Puk mŏt.
Boat .. .. Iui.
Build (to) .. .. Sâhy, thú phtĕn.
Beat (to) .. .. Véag.
Beautiful .. .. Sââ.
Benediction .. .. Prăe pór.
Beast .. .. Sat.
Blue .. .. Khín.
Beef .. .. Cũ.
Bushel .. .. Ihang-Iao.
Box .. .. Hêp.
Bottle .. .. Săr phdŏe.
Button .. .. Leu.
Branch .. .. Mie.
Brick .. .. Ot.
Break (to) .. .. Rei.
Burn (to) .. .. Dot.
Buffalo .. .. Crebey.
Black .. .. Khnaun.

Bone .. .. Cheóng.
Bread .. .. Nam.
Basket .. .. Conchir.
Blade .. .. Lompeng.
Book .. .. Sombot.
Bed .. .. Domnéc.
But .. .. Pê.
Bad .. .. Bap, chomngú.
Breast .. .. Dă.
Beg (to) .. .. Som teau.
Better .. .. Cheang, lus.
Bite (to) .. .. Kham.
Be born (to) .. .. Cót.
Bee .. .. Khmum.
Bark (to) .. .. Sru.
Buy (to) .. .. Iink.
Business .. .. Domnor.
Bow .. .. Ehme.
Batatas .. .. Eomlong.
Bridge .. .. Spreau.
Behind .. .. Croi, ê croi.
Back .. .. Hhnang.
Be (to) .. .. Non-mêan, Chèn.
Big .. .. Phom.
Broil (to) . .. . Hang.
Bird .. .. Sat liar.
Blood .. .. Chheàm.
Blow (to) .. .. Phlõm.
Betray (to) .. .. Kebăt.
Bark .. .. Sombok.
Brother (elder) .. .. Bâng.
Brother (younger) .. .. Phŏôn.

C.

Come (to)	Moc Dăl.
Cottage	Catôm.
Corpse	Khmoch.
Cage	Irung.
Case	Hêp.
Calk (to)	Bàt.
Calm oneself (to)	On.
Cambodia	Sroch Khmêr.
Cambodian	Khmêr.
Country	Neal.
Canal	Preê.
Comb	Suét.
Cask	Thâng.
Cardamom	Crevanh.
Cause	Het dòm.
Cold (a)	Câăc.
Cup	Chan.
Conduce (to)	Tôm.
Cloth	Souipăt.
Cough	Câăc.
Commotion	Revàl.
Cut (to)	Cat.
Conquer (to)	Chhnĕa.
Conquered	Chănh.
Clothing	Ao.
Carriage	Retĕ.
Centipede	Kaêp.
Circle	Vong.
Coffin	Mochhus.
Chain	Chervăi.
Choir	Sach.
Change (to)	Prê.

Coal .. .. Khîung.
Chastity .. .. Sel.
Cat .. .. Chhma.
Chief .. .. Mechàs, héay.
Chinese .. .. Swê chèn.
Cholera .. .. Rŏmbâl.
Clear .. .. Thla.
Clock .. .. Condong.
Cocoa-nut .. .. Dong.
Combat (to) .. .. Chebang.
Commencement .. .. Dòm.
Count (to) .. .. Răp.
Consent (to) .. .. Prom.
Console (to) .. .. Tŭo Săo.
Clay .. .. Deyót.
Crowd .. .. Fông, cânbân.
Crow .. .. Khoêi.
Cord .. .. Khse.
Coast .. .. Khaeng.
Cotton .. .. Crebas.
Colour .. .. Sombar.
Cut .. .. Cap, cat.
Crown .. .. Mocŏt.
Call (to) .. .. Han.
Clean .. .. Saat.
Cry (to) .. .. Tŏui.
Carry (to) .. .. Chun, Rĕc sêng.
Clean (to) .. .. Nos leáng.
Cloud .. .. Sapŏc.
Chew (to) .. .. Bièm.
Cold .. .. Rengia.
Cricket .. .. Chungret.
Clock .. .. Novea.
Custom .. .. Chebăp, Tomlăp.

Create (to) .. .. Bângeat.
Cry .. .. Sâmléng.
Cry (to) .. .. Srêc.
Cook (to) .. .. Dam.
Copper .. .. Spŏn.
Cymbal .. .. Lông, Khmŏ.
Crab .. .. Pomgeong.
Church (temple) .. .. Preă-Vihear.
Carry away (to) .. .. Roc ton.
Coat (to) .. .. Leap.
Child .. .. Coming.

D.

Descend (to) .. .. Chô.
Desire (to) .. .. Sângvat, Châng.
Destroy (to) .. .. Pombat.
Debt .. .. Bomnàl.
Diviner .. .. Achar.
Daybreak .. .. Prealum, Preahean.
Delicate .. .. Ton.
Different .. .. Titey.
Difficult .. .. Cra.
Disciple .. .. Cŏn Sŏs.
Dearth .. .. Âmnât.
Dispute (to) .. .. Chhlŏ prokêe.
Doubt .. .. Moutûl.
Dysentery .. .. Chomngú mual.
Do (to) .. .. Thu.
Dung .. .. Ach.
Dress (to) .. .. Prăeae.
Damp .. .. Som.
Drunk .. .. Sreving.
Day .. .. Thugay.

Deliver (to) .. .. Preeol.
Doctor .. .. Cruthnam, pet.
Despise (to) .. .. Măcngeáy.
Deride (to) .. .. Sôch, châm-ôn.
Die (to) .. .. Slăp.
Dwarf .. .. Tua.
During .. .. Compung.
Dust .. .. Ehuli.
Dare (to) .. .. Héan.
Dote (to) .. .. Trūl.
Dove .. .. Rùs.
Dig (to) .. .. Hal.
Drum .. .. Seôr.
Delay (to) .. .. Ângvéng.
Dye (to) .. .. Cherlŏc.
Darkness .. .. Tângcap.
Draw (to) .. .. Téanh.
Deceive (to) .. .. Bŏn chhăt.
Dear .. .. Thlay.
Dew .. .. Ânsóm.
Deaf .. .. Câ.
Dream .. .. Sâp.
Dog .. .. Chkê.
Door .. .. Shóĕ.
Drink (to) .. .. Elinear.
Duck .. .. Iea.
Dream (to) .. .. Zăl Săp.

E.

Exchange (to) .. .. Dôr.
Efface (to) .. .. Lap.
Equal .. .. Smó.
Elephant .. .. Tamrey.

Endure (to)	Ắt, ôn.
Engage (to)	Pobuol.
Enemy	Satron-Khmang.
Enter (to)	Chôl.
Envy (to)	Cherneu.
Envy	Cherneu.
Example	Kébuon.
Exhort (to)	Boutun méan.
End	Chông.
Evening	Lŏngéach.
Easy	Ngeáy.
End	Long-âs.
Eye	Phnée.
Egg	Pong-sut.
Ear	Erechiéc.
Equal	Mytrey.
Eat (to)	Si, pisa, chhăn, soi.
Even	Smó, dock.
Everywhere	Săp ăulú.
Eagle	Antri.
Earth	Dey, Preă thorni.

F.

Face	Mŭc.
Feeble	Comsoi.
Family	Crua.
Famine	Âmnăt.
Fatigue	Nuèy.
Fault	Tus.
Female	Nhi.
Ferocious	Sahan.
Fire	Phlâng.

Fever .. .. Cran.
Figure .. .. Muc.
Flower .. .. Phŏm.
Faith .. .. Chommia.
Forest .. .. Prey.
Fresh .. .. Rehoi.
Front .. .. Thngos.
Fruit .. .. Phle.
Float (to) .. .. Ândēt.
Freeze (to) .. .. Câc.
Fat .. .. Thop.
Frog .. .. Ong Kêp.
Food .. .. Ahur Sâbiĕng.
Friend .. .. Keló.
Formerly .. .. Pidom.
Firewood .. .. Os.
Finger .. .. Day.
Fast .. .. Buos.
Fast (to) .. .. Si buos.
Free .. .. Neaĕ Cheá.
Far .. .. Chhngai.
Falsehood .. .. Câhâc.
Frightful .. .. Noiai.
Forget (to) .. .. Chŭs bât côrna.
Fly .. .. Rug.
Fishing .. .. Bap.
Fish (to) .. .. Stuch trey, Dóc non.
Father .. .. A puc.
Few .. .. Eech.
Fear .. .. Khlach.
Full .. .. Peuh.
Feather .. .. Slap, mems.
Foot .. .. Chung.
Fish .. .. Eyey.

Fowl .. .. Món.
Fill (to) .. .. Bampenh.
Fool .. .. Lengong.
Follow (to) .. .. Tam, dòr tam.
Firebrand .. .. Rengûc.
Fall (to) .. .. Duol-thleăc.
Find (to) .. .. Roi ban.
Face .. .. Mac.
Flesh .. .. Sach.
Field .. .. Prê.
Figuratively .. .. Chŏt.
Fear (to) .. .. Khlàch.
Fly (to) .. .. Luèch.
Fly (to) (like a bird) .. .. .. Hòr.

G.

Gold .. .. Meas.
Gunpowder .. .. Démsón.
Go (to) .. .. Tou.
Greedy .. .. Luphu.
Good .. .. Lââ, chiá, písa.
Grind (to) .. .. Boh.
Girdle .. .. Crevat.
Garlic .. .. Ketym Sá.
Grasshopper .. .. Chungret.
Go out (to) .. .. Chenh.
Green .. .. Khién, baí tong.
Glass (a) .. .. Péng Kên, Kên.
Go to bed (to) .. .. Dec.
Grow (to) .. .. Sbec.
God .. .. Prĕa.
Give (to) .. .. Oi, chun.
Grief .. .. Chhu.

Girl .. .. Consrey.
Gun .. .. Comphlûng.
Gain (to) .. .. Ban chonménch.
Guard (to) .. .. Reăesa.
Glove .. .. Teăc.
Generous .. .. Chôt tuléay.
Ginger .. .. Khnhey.
Glutton .. .. Luphu.
Gum .. .. Chor.
Govern (to) .. .. Tac tîng.
Governor .. .. Chanfai sroč.
Grave .. .. Ânisãng.
Grain .. .. Crŏp.
Great .. .. Thôm Kepŏs.
Graft .. .. Crechâc.
Guide (to) .. .. Nóm.
Grass .. .. Smau.
Garden .. .. Chomca, chebar.
Gladness .. .. Ngeay.

H.

Hunger .. .. Comléan.
Hungry (to be) .. .. Khléan.
Helm .. .. Changcôt.
Hail .. .. Prŭl.
Habit .. .. Tomlăp.
Hatchet .. .. Puthae.
Hate (to) .. .. Săâp.
Haricot .. .. Sondêe.
Harmonious .. .. Pirŏ.
High .. .. Kepŏs.
Hour .. .. Mong, Teune.

Hideous	Acrăc, asron.
Honour (to)	Rŏp an.
Horror (to have an) of	Kepum.
Half	Chomhieng conmat, pheac condat.
Hard	Rùng.
Hell	Morok.
Hear (to)	Lú.
House	Phtêa.
Husband	Phodey.
Honey	Tác khmum.
Host	Phnhién.
Humble	Suphéap réap téap.
Here	Nĕ ênĕ.
Heavy	Thngŏn.
Hundredweight	Hap.
Holy	Arahán.
His	Rônthuc.
Hold (to)	Can.
Hole	Prŏhong.
Heat	Cadau.
Horse	Sê.
Hair	Sôc.
Heart	Bêdông.
How much	Ponman.
How	Doehmedéch ?
Horn	Sneng.
Hang (to)	Phiuor.
Hair (of animals)	Merues.
Heap (to)	Bomol.
Have (to)	Mean.
Happiness	Boran-Lays.
Hide (to)	Puvu.
He	Veá Cắt.

Heaven .. .. Mie.
Him .. .. Châng.

I.

Ignorant .. .. Khlan.
Island .. .. Că̆.
Image .. .. Comnur.
Imbecile .. .. Chicuat.
India .. .. Pon, suey.
Impost .. .. Srŏc Keling créas.
Indicate (to) .. .. Bânghanh.
Inundate (to) .. .. Lich.
Inscribe (to) .. .. Cat.
Insipid .. .. Sap.
Instant .. .. Mŏ pŏnlú.
Instruct (to) .. .. Predan, Pourieu.
Insult (to) .. .. Promat pikhèat.
Intelligence .. .. Praehuha.
Intention .. .. Chôt.
Interdict (to) .. .. Khŏt.
Interest (of money) .. .. Lar prăe.
Interpret (to) .. .. Prêpasa.
Interrogate (to) .. .. Suor, donding.
Introduce (to) .. .. Boŭchôlnòm.
Invite (to) .. .. Anchùnh.
Ill .. .. Chhu.
Illness .. .. Chumgŭ.
If .. .. Bó.
In order that .. .. Oi.
Idle .. .. Khchìl.
Idleness .. .. Comchil.

In .. .. Kenong.
Incense .. .. Comnhau.
Is .. .. Còt.
Inhabit (to) .. .. Non, công.

J.

Join (to) .. .. Phehăp.
Joy .. .. Âmnâr.
Joyous .. .. Ar, sabai, sremŏc sŏc sabai.
Judge .. .. Chmrom.
Judge (to) .. .. Cat săch Kedey.
Just .. .. Tiéng Trâng.
Jump (to) .. .. Sut.

K.

Kiss (to) .. .. Thŏp, ap.
King .. .. Luong, sdăch.
Know (to) .. .. Déng, chê.
Kill (to) .. .. Sâmlûp.
Knife .. .. Combit.
Kneel (to) .. .. Lut cháng cong.
Knee .. .. Cháng cong.

L.

Labour .. .. Phehuor.
Lake .. .. Touli Sap.
Leave (to) .. .. Lêng, chol.
Layman .. .. Crehŏs.
Lamp .. .. Chiêng Kién.

Language .. .. Pasa.
Language .. .. Ândut.
Language (of a country) .. .. Pasa.
Large .. .. Tuléay.
Lick (to) .. .. Lit.
Light .. .. Sral.
Leper .. .. Chomugu, Khlong.
Leprous .. .. Comlong, Khlong.
Letter .. .. Âcâr, sombăt.
Leaven .. .. Tambê.
Lip .. .. Pepir.
Liberty .. .. Lâmpey.
Line .. .. Poutŏt.
Line (fishing) .. .. Sontŭch.
Limpid .. .. Thla.
Lion .. .. Sóng.
Law .. .. Crŏt, viney.
Long .. .. Véng.
Let (to) .. .. Chuol.
Lean .. .. Siom.
Lead (to) .. .. Dóc, nóm.
Lie (to) .. .. Căhăc cŏmphŭs.
Leaf .. .. Slŏr.
Left .. .. Chhnéng.
Lose (to) .. .. Bâng, bât.
Little .. .. Eoch.
Ladder .. .. Chóndór.
Light (to) .. .. Och.
Lead .. .. Somnar.
Low .. .. Iéap.
Like .. .. Suró.
Lend (to) .. .. Khchey.
Lawsuit .. .. Kedey.
Lower (to) .. .. Lontéep.

Learn (to) .. .. Lù, rién.
Look at (to) .. .. Múl.
Laugh (to) .. .. Soch.
Learned .. .. Méac, prach.
Lord .. .. Âmmechûs, mechăs.
Like .. .. Smó, doch.
Love (to) .. .. Srelant.
Life .. .. Aios.
Live (to) .. .. Rős.

M.

Malay .. .. Churéa.
Male .. .. Chnmul.
Malediction .. .. Bŏndasa.
Misfortune .. .. Ândarai, piér, lombac.
Mandarin .. .. Maman.
Mango .. .. Soai.
Manner .. .. Iĕang.
Marsh .. .. Bóng, trepang.
Marry (to) .. .. Souipĕa apea pipéa.
Mark .. .. Sâmcól.
Morning .. .. Prűc.
Medicine .. .. Thnamsangcon.
Meditate (to) .. .. Niŭ, rompúng chon chieng.
Mingle (to) .. .. Leay.
Member .. .. Thnac thang.
Mercury .. .. Bârât.
Mother .. .. Mẹdai, mê.
Merit .. .. Bŏn.
Marvellous .. .. Chôm lû.
Measure (to) .. .. Vàl.
Midnight .. .. Atréat.

Mirror .. .. Conchâe.
Model .. .. Kebuon.
Month .. .. Khe.
Monastery .. .. Vât.
Mountain .. .. Phnom.
Mount (to) .. .. Lòng.
Musquito .. .. Mus.
Mutton .. .. Chiêm.
Murmur .. .. Khsâp, Khsién.
Music .. .. Phlêng.
Mat .. .. Còntil.
Mad .. .. Chimat.
Man .. .. Menus.
Milk .. .. Tiù dă.
Moon .. .. Khê (prĕa-Chăn).
Miser .. .. Comnaut.
Much .. .. Chrón.
Mouth .. .. Môt.
Mud .. .. Phoc.
Mills .. .. Bôs, tomboa.
Money .. .. Srae.
More .. .. Lus, Cheang.
Meat .. .. Săch.

N.

Net .. .. Uon.
Narrow .. .. Chang-iѐt.
Nail .. .. Dêc ail.
Neck .. .. Kho.
Now .. .. Êlounĕ.
Noon .. .. Hmgay trâng.
Not .. .. Com.

Nine	Thmey.
Nose	Chermo.
Nest	Somboi.
Name	Ehhnaô, neàm.
No	Ei.
Nourish	Anchein.
New	Crăp.
Naked	Srat.
Night	Yap.
Nail	Creehâi.
Near	Chut.
Needle	Mòchul.
Native Priest	Meăc, nìng prĕa sâng.

O.

Obey (to)	Sdăp, doi Toudap.
Observe (to)	Mal.
Obtain (to)	Ban.
Offend (to)	Ehú tuč.
Offer (to)	Chun.
Onion	Ketym.
Ounce	Eomlong.
Opposite	Eo-tung.
Orange	Croch.
Order (to)	Bângcáp.
Open (to)	Bòc.
One	Muey.
Old man .. .. }	Chăs.
Old .. .. }	
Other	Sitey-tiĕt, e tiét.
Oil	Preńg.
Oar	Cheo.

Often .. .. Chrondâng, chron créa.
Owl .. .. Eitui.
Of .. .. Si âmpi.
Overflow .. .. Compŏi.
Oath .. .. Sâmbât.

P.

Pride .. .. Comnoi.
Pagoda .. .. G. vihéar.
Pair .. .. Cû.
Palace .. .. Vang, Preă-montir.
Palm-tree .. .. Dóm tenot.
Peacock .. .. Canghoc.
Paper .. .. Credas.
Paradise .. .. Sthan suor, phimean.
Pardon (to) .. .. Ât tus.
Priest .. .. Sâng Kreach.
Porringer .. .. Chan.
Perceive (to) .. .. Khŭuh.
Pray (to) .. .. Phéavĕanea, sot thor.
Prayer .. .. Ehór pheavinia.
Prison .. .. Erung.
Price .. .. Tomlay.
Profit .. .. Chomniuh.
Profound .. .. Chron.
Promise (to) .. .. Sãmŏt.
Prompt .. .. Ranăs.
Prostrate oneself (to) .. .. .. Crap.
Punish (to) .. .. Toctus.
Partake (to) .. .. Chec.
Pass (to) .. .. Huvs.
Poor .. .. Pibac.

Pay (to)	Sâng.
Paint (to)	Cuor.
Pelican	Eung.
Pierce (to)	Ehlu, thleay.
People	Reas.
Perhaps	Proman.
Pound (to)	Bǒc.
Pipe	Khsier.
Prickly	Hór, măt.
Place	Dăc, tuò.
Pity (to)	Anót, anot.
Please (to)	Sǎp.
Pleasure	Âmnâr sôc sabai.
Plank	Cadar.
Plant (to)	Dam.
Poison	Ehnam pal.
Pepper	Mŏreih.
Polished	Reling.
Pork	Chrue.
Pursue (to)	Ehuli.
Pomegranate	Tetum.
Pupil	Crôm Sôs.
Pincers	Eăngeap.
Power	Amnach.
Preach (to)	Eisna.
Prepare (to)	Riép.
Plane (to)	Chhus.
Perspiration	Rhûs.
Perspire (to)	Bêe nhús.
Perforated	Thlu, dăch.
Preserve (to)	Eue reaisa.
Pine-apple	Monós.
Perceive (to)	Klrúuh.
Print (to)	Bǎ pum.

Play (to) .. .. Líng.
Place .. .. Tach.
Pound (weight) .. .. Neal.
Put (to) .. .. Dăc, tuo.
Piece .. .. Comnap.

Q.

Queen .. .. Khsatrey.
Question (to) .. .. Dondeng.
Quit (to) .. .. Léng, léa.
Quick .. .. Chhăp.

R.

Reason .. .. Sack Kedey.
Row (to) .. .. Cheo.
Rank .. .. Chuor.
Raze (to) .. .. Côr.
Rat .. .. Condor.
Ray .. .. Reăcsemey.
Recently .. .. Âmbauh.
Receive (to) .. .. Totuol.
Recompense .. .. Rongvoú.
Rent .. .. Viéch.
Rule (to) .. .. Soi réach.
Regret (to) .. .. Sdai.
Religion .. .. Sassena.
Repent (to) .. .. Chhu chăt.
Reply (to) .. .. Chhlói.
Respect (to) .. .. Cat Khlach.

Remain (to) .. .. Non.
Restore (to) .. .. Saîg viuh.
Rouse (to) .. .. Dàs.
Revolt (to) .. .. Kebằt.
Rich .. .. Câằc.
Riches .. .. Sombat tròp.
River .. .. Prêe, stùng.
Rice .. .. Iron. Ângeâ. Bai.
Roast .. .. Thang.
Red .. .. Crehâm.
Route .. .. Thlon.
Roof .. .. Tambâl.
Rain .. .. Phliéng.
Run .. .. Rằt.
Rain (to) .. .. Phliéng.
Rotten .. .. Laoy.
River .. .. Touli.
Ripe .. .. Eam.
Read .. .. Sot.
Rainbow .. .. Anthua.
Ring .. .. Anchién.
Relation .. .. Bang phoon, sach uheat.

S.

Spit (to) .. .. Sdâ Pruvs.
Strengthen (to) .. .. Chuol.
Spider .. .. Ling peáng.
Sit down (to) .. .. Ângmi.
Sharp .. .. Sruéch.
Sharpen (to) .. .. Sâmbiéng.
Smell .. .. Eum Keloń.

Shadow .. .. Molâp.
Storm .. .. Phiu.
Straw .. .. Chambońg.
Speak (to) .. .. Sredey—Nieáy.
Sweep (to) .. .. Bas.
Stick .. .. Iâmbâng.
Shine (to) .. .. Phlú.
Seal .. .. Ira.
Slander (to) .. .. Chombon.
Soul .. .. Prea lúng.
Smelling .. .. Amnach, p. bâzmey.
Set out (to) .. .. Eau.
Stone .. .. Ehmâ.
Sweet .. .. Saân.
Straight .. .. Erańg.
Squirrel .. .. Comprŏc.
Still .. .. Etiér.
Swell (to) .. .. Hŏm.
Send (to) .. .. Pró, phnô.
Shoulder .. .. Sma.
Sword .. .. Sâmsér.
Stuff .. .. Sompat.
Star .. .. Pheai.
Study (to) .. .. Rień.
Split (to) .. .. Su.
Son .. .. Cou Pros.
Strong .. .. Khlang.
Strike (to) .. .. Meay.
Son-in-law .. .. Côu prusa.
Swallow .. .. Trechiéc cam.
Shame .. .. Khmas.
Swear (to) .. .. Sebât.
Shine (to) .. .. Phlu.
Slander (to) .. .. Sredey dám.

Sea .. .. Sremăt.
Sparrow .. .. Chap.
Show (to) .. .. Bânghanh.
Soft .. .. Som.
Swim (to) .. .. Hêl.
Snow .. .. Ap.
Sing (to) .. .. Chrieng.
Seek (to) .. .. Roc.
Scissors .. .. Contray.
Sew (to) .. .. Dér.
Short .. .. Keley.
See (to) .. .. Sâmléng.
Shore .. .. Mót compong.
Stream .. .. Stûng.
Sand .. .. Khsach.
Sabre .. .. Dan.
Sacrifice .. .. Buchéa.
Seize (to) .. .. Toc, chap.
Season .. .. Câughê.
Salary .. .. Chhnuol.
Sob (to) .. .. Tuéuh.
Satiety .. .. Châet.
Sauce .. .. Sômlâ.
Savoury .. .. Pisa.
Seal .. .. Era.
Seal (to) .. .. Prelâc âmbêl.
Saw .. .. Anar.
Saw (to) .. .. Ar.
Scribe .. .. Smién.
Sculptor .. .. Chhleăc.
Shake (to) .. .. Ângruom.
Succour (to) .. .. Chuey.
Secretary .. .. Smień.
Sow (to) .. .. Prô, sap.

Serpent .. .. Pôs.
Sieve .. .. Chuey.
Sex .. .. Ângiochéat.
Silent .. .. Sngiém.
Silk .. .. Pré.
Soldier .. .. Pôl, tahéan.
Sun .. .. Ehngay.
Sound (to) .. .. Phsâm.
Sulphur .. .. Eeá.
Suffer (to) .. .. Spoń thor.
Soil (to) .. .. Chhú, ât.
Suspicion .. .. Montúl.
Statue .. .. Rup.
Stimulate .. .. Âutóng.
Succession .. .. Mârdăc.
Sugar .. .. Seâr.
Suffice (to) .. .. Lemon.
Supplicate (to) .. .. Ângvâr.
Support (to) .. .. Ǎt.
Suspend (to) .. .. Phiuor.
Stoop (to) .. .. Pontĕep Khluon Êng.
Soon .. .. Chhăp.
Silent (to be) .. .. Non sugiém.
Steep (to) .. .. Trom.
Sell (to) .. .. Lŏc.
Stomach .. .. Khiâl.
Smooth (to) .. .. Smó, reling.
Say .. .. Sredey.
Small pox .. .. Ot.
Shed (to) .. .. Chăk.
Saucepan .. .. Chhang, keteă.

T.

Take (to)	Yoi.
Tail	Cŏntui.
Think (to)	Niŭ, rompûng chŏuchúng.
Thus	Hêt nê.
Then	Eŭp.
To-day	Ehngay nĕ.
Thin	Siom.
Trade	Ehneúh prô.
Thunder	Routèa.
Taste (to)	Shlŏc.
Tear (to)	Reliĕr.
To-morrow	Sŏă.
Tooth	Ehmeúh.
Teach (to)	Predan.
Together	Kenéa.
Thick	Crăs.
Thorn	Soŭla.
Tin	Somnăr Pahang.
Trust (to)	Dêc.
Take care (to)	Réacsa.
Tipsy	Chăêt, srevońg.
Tobacco	Ehnăm chŏc.
Table	Tang.
Try	Prońg.
Tax	Pŏn, suey.
Testimony	Bŏntál.
Tempest	Phin.
Temple	Preă viheár.
Time	Cal, pileá, vileá.
Thibet	Preă, sumér.

Tiger .. .. Khla.
Thee .. .. Êng, preă, sedêng.
Thunder .. .. Phiôr, roŭteă.
Torch .. .. Chôulô.
Torrent .. .. Stung.
Tortoise .. .. Ândoc.
Touch (to) .. .. Pŏl.
Tower .. .. Preă-sat.
Turn (to) .. .. Vil.
Translate (to) .. .. Prê.
Traffic .. .. Chomnuénh.
Transcribe (to) .. .. Châmlâng.
Tremble (to) .. .. Nhór.
Trumpet .. .. Erê.
Throne .. .. Cŏl.
Too much .. .. Pic.
Troop .. .. Fông, cân-bân.
Tile .. .. Kebúońg.
Turbulent .. .. Repus.
Town .. .. Pŏnteéy.
True .. .. Prăcăt ; Arăng.
Thing .. .. Rebâs.
Travel (to) .. .. Dór.
Toad .. .. King cok.
Twin .. .. Cŏn Phlô.
There .. .. Ênŏ, nŏ.
Tear .. .. Eŭć Phneé.

U.

Undergo (to) .. .. Mãrdăc.
Uproar .. .. Vôr.
Ulcer .. .. Bŏs.

Universe	Lu key.
Unite (to)	Phsăm.
Urine	Tuc uŏum.
Usage	Tomlóp.
Use (to)	Pro.
Useful	Preioch.
Utility	Preioch.
Understand (to)	Yŏl.
Useless	Ât preíoch.
Upright	Chhor.
Untie (to)	Srai.
Under	Crom, ê crom.
Ungrateful	Smŏr.
Ugly	Airâc.

V.

Very	Năs.
Vague	Relŏc.
Vessel	Sâmpon, capol.
Vaunt (to)	Uot.
Vase	Chan.
Vein	Sesay.
Venom	Pŭs.
Virtue	Cousâl, bŏn.
Victory	Chhneă.
Virgin	Prommăchărey.
Village	Phum.
Violent	Khlang.
Violet	Sâmbôr soag.
Violin	Chăpey.
Visit (to)	Suor.
Vow	Bâmmăn.

Vow (to) .. .. Bân bâmmăn.
Veil .. .. Sounoiéa.
Veil (to) .. .. Bang.
Voice .. .. Sâmleńg.
Vomit (to) .. .. Cunot.
Voracious .. .. Lupha.
Vice .. .. Bap, tus.
Vegetable .. .. Poule pongea.

W.

When .. .. Calna.
Who .. .. Nana.
What .. .. Oy ? Sat ay ?
Wake (to) .. .. Phuheăc.
Wisdom .. .. Samphi.
Winding .. .. Chhăp.
Work .. .. Car.
Work (to) .. .. Thú car.
Watch (to) .. .. Retrit tetrut.
Wind .. .. Khiâl.
Worm .. .. Chŏulin dûngeon.
Well (a) .. .. Andońg.
Word .. .. Peac.
Why .. .. Debâtay.
We .. .. Túng.
Work .. .. Chĕang.
Water (to) .. .. Sroch.
Wait (to) .. .. Ohâm.
Wash (to) .. .. Pongeon.
Water-closet .. .. Leáng.
When .. .. Căl, calêna, compung.
Wicked .. .. Bap, Chomugí.

Walk (to) .. .. Dór.
World .. .. Long.
Word .. .. Peác.
Wall .. .. Comphiñg.
Water .. .. Tŭć.
Write (to) .. .. Săcer.
Wife .. .. Propôn.
Wake (to) .. .. Dăs.
Wave .. .. Touli.
Wager .. .. Phnŏl.
War .. .. Sŏc.
Wine .. .. Sra.
Wish (to) .. .. Châng.
Warm .. .. Cadan.
Warm (to) .. .. Prap.
White .. .. Sâ.
Wound .. .. Rebuos.
Wood .. .. Srey.
Where .. .. Êna.
Woman .. .. Srey.
Widower .. .. Pomaí.

Y.

Yes .. .. Chŭs, bât, côrna.
Year .. .. Chhnam.
Yellow .. .. Lúóng.
Young .. .. Coming.
Yesterday .. .. Mŏsăl.

Z.

Zeal .. .. Chhú chaăl.
Zinc .. .. Sămnăr pang Krey.

NAMES OF THE NUMBERS.

1	Muey.	30	Sumsăp.
2	Pir.	40	Sêsŏp.
3	Bey.	50	Hosăp.
4	Buon.	60	Hocsăp.
5	Prăm.	70	Chêtsăp.
6	Prămmuey.	80	Pêtsŏp.
7	Prămpil.	90	Cansăp.
8	Prămbey.	100	Mŏ roi.
9	Prambuon.	200	Pir roi.
10	Dăp.	300	Bey roi.
11	Mŏtŏn Dăp.	400	Buon roi.
12	Pirtŏn dăp.	500	Prăm roi.
13	Beytŏn dăp.	600	Prămmuey roi. &c.
14	Buontŏn dăp.		
15	Prămtŏn dăp.		
16	Prămmueytŏn dăp.	1,000	Mŏ pŏn.
17	Prămpiltŏn dăp.	2,000	Pir pŏn. &c.
18	Prămbeytŏn dăp.		
19	Prămbuontŏn dăp.	10,000	Mŏ mŭn.
20	Mŏphey, or Bien Phey.	100,000	Mŏ sên.
21	Mŏphey muey, or Phey muey.	1,000,000	Mŏ cŏt.
		10,000,000	Mŏ béan.
22	Mŏphey pir, or Phey pir.	100,000,000	Mŏ a Kho.
23	Mŏphey bey, or Phey bey. &c.	1,000,000,000	Mŏ puni.

CARDINAL POINTS.

North	Ê chŭng, Tùs udãr.
South	Ê thbong, Tus ê bor.
East	Ê cát, Tus ê cát.
West	Ê lich, Tus ê chém.

SEASONS.

Rainy Season ..	Cânghê or redon phliéng.
Hot or Dry Season	Cânghê or redon cadan.
Winter	Cânghê or redon rengèa.

THE DAYS OF THE WEEK.

Sunday .. .. .. Atǖt.	Thursday .. .. Prĕa-hŏs.
Monday .. .. .. Chan.	Friday .. .. .. Sŏc.
Tuesday .. .. .. Âng Kéar.	Saturday .. .. .. San.
Wednesday .. .. Pût.	

THE NAMES OF THE MONTHS.

1. March .. .. .. Chêt.	7. September .. Asôch.
2. April .. .. Pisac.	8. October .. .. Cârdŏc.
3. May .. .. Chis.	9. November .. Méac Khsér.
4. June .. .. Asat.	10. December .. Bŏs.
5. July .. .. Srap.	11. January .. Méac thŏm.
6. August .. .. .. Phetrebot.	12. February .. Phãl cun.

CYCLE OF TWELVE YEARS.

1. Pig .. .. .. Côr.	7. Serpent .. .. Méa Sanh.
2. Rat .. .. .. Chût.	8. Horse .. .. Méa mê.
3. Ox .. .. .. Chhlom.	9. Goat .. .. Méa mê.
4. Tiger .. .. .. Khal.	10. Monkey .. .. Voê.
5. Hare .. .. .. Thâ.	11. Cock .. .. Roca.
6. Dragon .. .. Rung.	12. Dog .. .. .. Chô.

PRONUNCIATION OF THE CAMBODIAN VOWELS.

a, ă, ã; é, ê; i; o, ó; u, ú.

a. This is pronounced like the English word, "Palm."

ă. This is pronounced short; as, "Mat."

ã. This is something between the *a* and the *o*; it is pronounced like a very open *o*.

é. This is pronounced like our close *e;* as, "Men."
ê. This is pronounced like our open *e;* as, "He."
i. This is pronounced also like our *e*.
o. This is pronounced like our *o;* as, "Go."
ó. This is pronounced like *eu* in "Liqueur."
u. Like *ou*, in "You."
ú. This is pronounced like *u*.

DIPHTHONGS.

Ai, ei, oi, ôi, ói. This is pronounced with a single emission of sound.

Ay, ey, oy, óy, ui, úi. This is pronounced with two emissions of sound, as, a-ï, e-ï, o-ï, u-ï, u-ï.

Cha, ché, chi, cho, chu. This is pronounced as Tia, tié, tii, tio, tiu; with a single emission of sound.

Chha, chhé, chhi, chho, chhu. This is pronounced as Thcha, thché (etc.), with a strong aspiration.

Kha, khe, khi, kho, khu. This is pronounced as Ka, ke, ki (etc.), with a strong aspiration.

Nha, nhe, nhi, nho, nhu. This is pronounced as Nia, Nie (etc.), with a single emission of sound.

Pha, phe, phi, pho, phu. This is pronounced as pa, pe, pi (etc.)., with an aspiration.

Nga, nge, ngi, ngo, ngu. This is pronounced hard.

Tha, thé, thi, tho, thu. Hard, and with an aspiration.

THE LORD'S PRAYER IN CAMBODIAN.

O' Preă dâ công lu mic, apuc Túng Khnhŏm oi: Túng Khnhŏm ângvâr Preă-âng, som oi ûs neăc phâng têng núng cot sesór preă néam Preă-ang: som oi preă-nocor Preă-âng ban Tûng Khnhŏm. Som ai rebal méan non dey thú tam preă hartey Preă-âng dock lú mic. Ahar Túng Khnhŏm săp thngay som ai Túng Khnhŏm ban thngai nê: hoï som pros bap Túng Khnhŏm dock iung Khnhŏm ắt tus neăc êna mian tus núng Túng Khnhŏm: hoï som pum ai Túng Khnhŏm doi comnach: tê aî Túng Khnhŏm ban ruéch âmpi ândărai teăng puâng. Amén!

LETTERS FROM M. MOUHOT.

TO SAMUEL STEVENS, ESQ.

[To be communicated to the Royal Geographical Society.]

Brelum, among the Savage Stiêns, lat. N. 11° 46′ 30″, long. W. 103° 3′, merid. of Paris, 15th October, 1859.

DEAR MR. STEVENS,

I profit by a favourable opportunity which has just presented itself to write you a few hasty lines to let you know that I am alive. For the last two months I have been living with the savage Stiêns amidst their immense forests, the latitude being precisely as I have stated above, and here I have passed the season most favourable for collecting insects and land shells. In spite of the letter given to me by the King of Cambodia, ordering all the chiefs of the Srok Khmer, or Cambodian villages, to furnish me with the means of transport on my journey, I experienced much difficulty, as frequently neither buffaloes nor carts were to be found in the hamlets through which I passed. My journey took me a month to accomplish, which is about three times as long as it would have taken me on foot.

On the 21st July, after having descended the great arm of the Mekon from Pinhalú, a village about nine miles from the capital, and in lat. 11° 46′ 30″ N. and long. 103° 3 W. merid. of Paris, as far as Penom Peuh, a commercial town filled with Chinese, and situated at the conflux of two streams, I ascended the great Cambodian River, the water of which is still low, as all through the country the rainy season is two months later than usual. The Mekon is studded with islands, of which many are eight or nine miles long and more than a mile broad; such is the large and beautiful island of Ko-Sutin, where I arrived after five days' journey. I estimate the width of the river to be about three miles. Pelicans are found on its waters, often in flocks of more than fifty, and storks, sea swallows, and other aquatic birds, abound in the shallow parts of the river. The general aspect of this mighty river is, however, rather sombre than gay, although doubtless there is something imposing in the rapidity of its waters, which run like a torrent. Few boats are to be seen on it, and its banks are almost barren (the forests being more than a mile distant), and, being constantly undermined by the water, fall down at the least shock, and this is generally all that you can see or hear. The Menam is much more gay and animated.

The rapids and cataracts commence about thirty or forty leagues north of Ko-Sutin, on the confines of Laos, and it is there necessary to leave the large boats and take to canoes, which as well as the luggage are often obliged to be carried on men's backs.

The current of the Mekon is so strong that at certain times of the year you can go little more than a league a day, and the rowers often seek for fire in the evening at the very place where they cooked their rice in the morning. I ascended it in a small boat with three rowers, but at every bend of the river we had the greatest trouble to make any progress, and were frequently obliged to hold on by the rushes to prevent our being carried away by the current. Eight days after leaving Pinhalú I reached Pemptiélan, a large Cambodian village, where I found it necessary to take to land travelling.

There still remained 150 miles to travel in carts, all in an easterly direction. I was well received by the mandarin at the head of affairs in this part of the country, and was able to set out again in two days.

The first day our conveyances upset, and I feared that we should be unable to proceed; there were continually dreadful bogs, quagmires, and marshes, in which the carts sank up to the axletrees and the buffaloes to their bellies. Fortunately on the following day the road improved, but for three weeks all that was visible was a few scattered rice-fields round the villages, and we had to make our way through a marshy plain, covered with thick and dark woods, which reminded one of the enchanted forest of Tasso, and it is easy to understand that the imagination of a pagan race peoples these gloomy solitudes with evil spirits. Twenty times in an hour the men who accompanied us were obliged to raise the large branches and cut down the trunks which obstructed our passage, and sometimes we had to make a new path for ourselves.

The Cambodians were all much surprised at seeing us journeying towards the Stiêns at the worst time of the year, for in that country the rainy season had commenced, and even those who live nearest dare not venture there; and had I not brought with me from Siam my two young servants, I could not for any money have found a single individual to accompany me. Even they felt great repugnance to proceed—for in Siam, Cambodia bears a terrible reputation for unhealthiness, and unhappily both for them and for myself they were attacked with fever in the forests, since which, instead of receiving any help from them, I have had two patients to nurse.

Passing through a village peopled by a barbarous race of Annamites, I ran great risk of being taken prisoner by them, and being sent to finish my researches in a dungeon. Last year the carriages belonging to a French missionary were completely rifled, and the men sent with ropes round their necks to Cochin China. I loaded all my guns, and gave one to each of my men:

our firm appearance, no doubt, frightened them, for we were not attacked.

In spite of the heat, the fatigue, and privations inseparable from such a journey, I arrived among the Stiêns in perfectly good health as far as I was concerned, and here I found a settlement of Catholic missionaries from Cochin China. It would have been impossible to go further, for I could neither find means of transport nor provisions, for at this time of the year the poor savages have consumed all their rice, and have nothing to live upon but herbs, a little maize, and what they can catch in the chase. I therefore accepted the hospitality offered to me with much kindness by a good priest. In a few weeks the rainy season will be over, the nights will become cold, and for several months insects will be found, and after that will come the turn of the birds, with which I shall exclusively occupy myself.

My departure from here will depend upon circumstances; perhaps I shall myself be the bearer of this letter to Pinhalú, perhaps I may be detained here some months by the bad state of the roads and the impossibility of procuring vehicles during the rice-harvest.

If you ask who are this strange people, living retired on the table-lands and mountains of Cambodia, which they appear never to have quitted, and differing entirely in manners, language, and features from the Annamites, Cambodians, and Laotians, my answer is that I believe them to be the aborigines of the country, and that they have been driven into these districts by the repeated inroads of the Thibetians, from whom they evidently descend, as is proved by the resemblance of features, religion, and character.

The whole country from the eastern side of the mountains of Cochin China as far as 103° long., and from 11° lat. to Laos, is inhabited by savage tribes, all known under one name, which signifies "inhabitants of the heights." They have no attachment to the soil, and frequently change their abode; most of the villages are in a state of continual hostility with each other, but they do not attack in troops, but seek to surprise each other, and the prisoners are sold as slaves to the Laotians.

Their only weapon is the cross-bow, which they use with extraordinary skill, but rarely at a distance of more than twenty paces. Poisoned arrows are used only for hunting the larger animals, such as elephants, rhinoceros, buffaloes, and wild oxen, and with these the smallest scratch causes death, if the poison is fresh: the strongest animal does not go more than fifty paces before it falls; they then cut out the wounded part, half roast it without skinning or cutting it up, after which they summon the whole village by sound of trumpet to partake of it. The most perfect equality and fraternity reign in these little communities, and the Communists would here find their theories reduced to practice and producing nothing but misery.

The strongest European would find it difficult to bend the bow which the Stiên, weak and frail as he appears, bends without effort, doubtless by long practice.

They are not unacquainted with agriculture, but grow rice and plant gourds, melons, bananas, and other fruit-trees; their rice-fields are kept with the greatest care, but nearly all the hard work is done by the women. They seldom go out in the rainy season on account of the leeches, which abound in the woods to such a degree as to render them almost unapproachable; they remain in their fields, where they construct small huts of bamboo, but as soon as the harvest is over and the dry season returns they are continually out fishing or hunting. They never go out without their baskets on their backs, and carrying their bows and a large knife-blade in a bamboo handle. They forge nearly all their instruments from ore which they procure from Annam and Cambodia. Although they know how to make earthen vessels, they generally cook their rice and herbs in bamboo. Their only clothing is a strip of cloth passed between the thighs and rolled round the waist. The women weave these scarfs, which are long and rather pretty, and which when well made often sell for as much as an ox. They are fond of ornaments, and always have their feet, arms, and fingers covered with rings made of thick brass wire; they wear necklaces of glass beads, and their ears are pierced with an enormous hole, through which they hang the bone of an animal, or a piece of ivory sometimes more than three inches in circumference. They wear their hair long in the Annamite fashion, and knot it up with a comb made of bamboo; some pass through it a kind of arrow made of brass wire, and ornamented by a pheasant's crest.

Their features are handsome and sometimes regular, and many wear thick mustachios and imperials.

Quite alone and independent amidst their forests, they scarcely recognise any authority but that of the chief of the village, whose dignity is generally hereditary. For the last year or two the King of Cambodia has occasionally sent the mandarin who lives nearest the Stiêns to their first villages, in order to distribute marks of honour to their chiefs, hoping little by little to subdue them, and to get from them slaves and ivory, and already he receives a small tribute every year. His emissaries, however, scarcely dare pass the limits of the kingdom, so fearful are they of the arrows of the savages and of the fevers which reign in their forests.

The Stiên is gentle and hospitable, and possesses neither the stupid pride of the Cambodian, nor the refined cruelty and corruption of the Annamite. He is the "good fellow" of the forest, simple and even generous; his faults are those common to all Asiatics, namely, cunning, an extraordinary power of dissimulation, and idleness; his great passion is hunting, and he leaves work to the women, but, unlike the Cambodians, robbery is very rare among them.

They believe in a supreme being, but only invoke the evil spirit to induce him to leave them in peace. They bury the dead near their dwellings. They do not believe in metempsychosis, but think that animals have also souls which live after their death, and continue to haunt the places they frequented in their lives. Their superstitions are numerous; the cry of an owl, or the sight of a crow, just as they are about to set off on a journey, they consider a bad augury, which is sufficient to turn them from their plans.

When any one is ill they say it is the demon tormenting him, and keep up night and day a frightful uproar round him, which only ceases when one of the bystanders falls as in a fit, crying out, "He has passed into me, he is stifling me." They then question the new patient as to the remedies which must be employed to cure the sick man, and as to what the demon demands to abandon his prey. Sometimes it is an ox, a pig, too often a human victim; in the latter case they pitilessly seize on some poor slave, and immolate him without remorse.

They imagine that all white people inhabit secluded corners of the earth in the midst of the sea, and often ask if there are any women in our country. When and how I can return to Cambodia and Siam I am ignorant, and I dare not think of the difficulty I shall experience among the rude and stupid Cambodians in transporting my treasures. What heartbreaking jolts my boxes of insects will receive! What palpitations I shall feel each time some rough fellow takes them to place on the oxen, elephants, or his own back! Poor soldiers of science! these are our trophies, and in the eyes of some people find as much merit as a piece of silk fastened to a pole; and what pains, patience, and solicitude is necessary to procure them! therefore I believe my anxiety as to my collections will be understood by the lovers of nature.

Pinhalú, 20th December, 1859.

P.S.—I arrived last evening at Pinhalú, in perfect health, and am now about to go northward to visit the famous ruins of Ongcor and then return to Bangkok, so I have little time to give you any details as to what I despatch from Komput and Singapore. I am not quite satisfied; for birds are scarce here, and I have but a small number; besides, my boxes as I feared have been much knocked about; I sent them off to Komput on men's backs. On my return to Bangkok I will send you some good maps of this almost unknown country.

To Samuel Stevens, Esq.

[To be communicated to the Geographical Society of London.]

Khao Samoune, Province of Pechaburi (Siam).
Lat. N. 13° 4', long. 100°. 15th June, 1860.

In my last letter, of March, 1859, I told you about two active volcanoes that I discovered in the Gulf of Siam, one in the little isle of Koman, lat. 12° 30′ 29″ N., and long. 101° 50′ 2″ W., mer. of Greenwich, and of the probable existence of others whose workings were latent and slow. Since then I have travelled through Cambodia, from north to south and from east to west, gone up the Mekon as far as the frontier of Laos, visited one of the savage tribes which live between these two countries and Cochin China, then crossed the great lake Touli Sap, explored the provinces of Ongcor and Battambong, which are full of splendid ruins, one of which in particular, the temple of Ongcor, is almost perfect, and, perhaps, unequalled in the world. I then passed from the Mekon to the Menam, and returned to Bangkok.

A low table-land, of which the gradual slope takes a week to ascend, separates the two rivers.

A chain of mountains, of which the highest peak is 6274 English feet above the level of the sea, extends to the S.W., joins the ranges of Chantaboun, Pursak, and Thung Yai, which are from 4000 to 5000 feet high, and reaches nearly to Komput and Hatienne; while to the north another small chain, joining the greater one of Korat, runs eastward, throws some ramifications into the provinces of Battambong and Ongcor Borege, which is 40 miles farther north, and bears the name of the mountains of Somrai.

Not being in direct communication with the Archæological Society, I wish to call your attention to the marvellous remains at Ongcor of the civilization of a great people.

The country is rich in woods and mines, and although thinly populated, produces enough cotton for the use of Cochin China, while the great lake, which abounds in fish, furnishes an immense quantity of this article also to China. Iron of a superior quality is also abundant, and the Kouis, an ancient tribe of a primitive race, living east of the Mekon, who speak the same language as the Stiêns, work it very industriously. There are also many other mines, rich in gold, lead, and copper, in the chains to the east and west; that of Pursak produces the beautiful cardamom, which, when transplanted, gives fine stems but no fruit.

Unluckily most of these mountains are frightfully unhealthy, and no one but those who have lived there from infancy can remain long among them with impunity.

In the island of Phu-Quor or Koh Trou, which belongs to Cochin China, and which is very near to Komput, there are rich mines of cannel coal. I was not able to get there, the war having rendered the people hostile and cruel to all white men; but my attention having been drawn to it by some ornaments worked in this mineral by the islanders, I procured two specimens, which I send you.

There are several extinct volcanoes in Pechaburi, four of

which I have ascertained to form part of the numerous detached and conical hills which are probably all ancient craters belonging to the great chain Khao Deng, which occupies all the northern part of the centre of the Malayan peninsula, and is inhabited by the Kariens, a primitive and independent people, who, like the Stiêns and other tribes, have doubtless been driven back to the mountains by the encroachments of the Siamese, and where the inclemency of the climate protects them against all attacks from their neighbours. The mountains are known in the country as the Na-Khou, Khao, Panom Knot, Khao Tamonne, and Khao Samroum. The last two are 1700 and 1900 feet above the level of the sea, and only a few leagues distant from each other. All these craters appear to have been originally upheaved ("craters of elevation" M. de Buch styles them) from the bottom of the water, at a period when all this part of the country, as far as the great chain, which I have not yet been able to visit, was under the sea.

Besides an immense volcanic cone, in part fallen in, and where the ground resounds under one's feet, each of the mounts has several lateral mouths and a number of fissures and chimneys, or passages, which bear evident traces of subterranean fires. They are entirely composed of trachy̆tic rocks, scoria, lava, felspar, &c.

The Siamese have made temples of the largest of these caverns, which are of great depth and breadth, and extremely picturesque. One of the caverns of Samroum is quite inaccessible. Having descended to the depth of 20 feet by a chimney 2 feet wide at its mouth, and shut in between rocks, I found myself at the entrance of a deep cavern, but there all my efforts to proceed farther were defeated; a few steps from the entrance my torch suddenly went out, my breathing was checked, and I in vain fired my gun several times in order to disperse the foul air.

To M. Charles Mouhot (his Brother).

Bangkok, 13th October, 1860.

To you, my dear brother, I address my last letter before quitting Bangkok for my long journey to Laos. I have waited till the last moment for the steamer which ought to bring me letters from Europe, but unfortunately I am obliged to set out without receiving any answers to those which I sent in May, on my return from Cambodia. I fear that, once in the interior of the country, I shall have no means of sending letters; arm yourself, therefore, with patience, dear brother, and do not think me neglectful if you do not receive any; but be sure that I, alone in those profound solitudes, shall suffer more than you, from my ignorance of everything concerning those dear to me; and during the eighteen or twenty months which the journey will probably occupy I shall not see a European face nor hear a word which can recall to me my beloved country.

I have done everything in my power to obtain letters and passports from the French and Siamese authorities here, but all have been nearly useless. I have obtained nothing but a letter from the King's brother, who has the superintendence of the provinces north of Laos, and with that I trust to be able to get on. The good Dr. Campbell has supplied me with medicines of all kinds, and as I am nearly acclimatized, and have with me devoted followers—one particularly, Phrai, who would die for me—you may be easy on my account. Besides, and I really know not why, I have hitherto been much liked by the missionaries and natives, and I am sure it will be the same there. Fever does not kill all travellers. I have traversed many dangerous districts in my journey to Cambodia, and I am safe. Let us trust in God, my brother, that I shall be as fortunate in this expedition, and that we shall meet again. Nothing is requisite but courage, hope, and patience. I am sober, and drink nothing but tea. My food is the same as that of the natives, dried fish and rice, and sometimes a little game which I shoot, and roast on a spit after the fashion of the natives, that is, by two bamboos stuck into the ground and another laid horizontally on them, which is turned from time to time. My amusements are hunting, arranging my collections, my drawings, to which I devote a great deal of time, and of which some are not bad, as you may judge by those sent to the Geographical Society of London, and my journal; with those I pass many pleasant hours. Besides, you know how I love nature, and am only really happy in the woods with my gun, and that when there, if I know you all to be happy, I have nothing to wish for. I often think of our good old father, but as long as you are with him I feel easy about him; you will make him bear my absence patiently, repeat often to him how I love him, and how happy I shall be when I can tell him about my long journeys. And you, my brother, love and cherish your two dear children, my little nephews; inculcate in them the love of nature, and teach them to think that virtue is recompensed even here, and a good conscience ennobles more than patents of nobility, or orders in the button-hole; bring up your little ones in the love of God, and of all that is good and great. Think and talk sometimes with Jenny of the poor traveller. Adieu, my brother!

TO MADAME CHARLES MOUHOT (HIS SISTER-IN-LAW).

Khao Khoc, 21st December, 1861.

AN unexpected opportunity presents itself, my dear Jenny, to send you a few words before proceeding farther. A new year is about to commence: may you, my dear little sister, experience in its course only joy and satisfaction; may your interesting little family cause you unmixed happiness; in a word, I desire every possible good for you. As for myself, I ask nothing but the happiness of seeing you all again. Think occasionally of the poor traveller whom every day removes farther and farther from civilization, and who for eighteen months or perhaps two years is about to live alone in a strange place, where I shall not have even the consolation of meeting those good missionaries as at Brelum and in Cambodia.

You know my manner of life, so I shall not repeat it. The heat and the musquitoes make a real hell of this place. Those who praise it must have hard heads and skins, or else must be comfortably lodged, and surrounded by an army of slaves. They know nothing but its enjoyments. If there is one pleasant hour in the morning and another in the evening, one must think oneself lucky, for often there is no peace night or day. My pleasures are, first, liberty, that precious thing without which man cannot be happy, and for which so many have fought and will fight still; then, seeing so much that is beautiful, grand, and new, and which no one has seen before me. From these I draw my contentment. Thank God! my health is as good as when I left you, although three years have passed over me.

Soon I shall be in Laos, and then, what strange things I shall see daily! what curious beings I shall meet, to whom I shall be equally an object of curiosity! I shall have delightful days, then, perhaps, sad ones, if my servants have the fever, which happens at intervals. If only to enliven these solitudes, I could have you here, my dear Jenny, or if I could sing like you, or even like a nightingale! Sometimes I do make use of my falsetto voice, and hum the beautiful airs of Béranger, and feel strengthened by the sublime odes of that great man of genius.

Two or three thin volumes—I say thin, for the white ants have eaten the greater part of them—and a few old newspapers (new to me) compose my library; but I have blank paper, which I fill as I best can; it is an amusement, at least; and if it turn out of no other use than to serve to amuse you all, I shall be satisfied, for I am not ambitious. I dream as I smoke my pipe, for I must confess that I smoke more than ever.

Well! the musquitoes and thorns will still be my companions for a long time. It is my own choice, and I shall never complain as long as God grants to all of you the joy and happiness I wish for you.

How I shall accomplish the long journey before me I know not; probably with oxen and elephants; but if even I have to go on foot I care not, so that I reach there, for I have determined to drive away even the devil, should I meet him here.

To M. Charles Mouhot.

Khao Khoc, near Pakpriau (Siam), 23rd Dec. 1860.

My dear Brother,

This is the sixth letter I have written, and written on my knees; and in this heat, and tormented by musquitoes, it is an affair of as many days. Do not complain, therefore, if this is short. Khao-Khoc is a mountain nine or ten leagues north of Pakpriau, which I visited two years ago, and where I have been waiting two months for the roads to become passable, in order to reach Korat, and then Laos. I have made a fine collection of coleoptera, particularly some remarkable longicorns. I have but few shells or birds; nevertheless, the collection is precious, and, although less numerous than the one at Pechaburi, it is quite equal to it. I have been lucky enough to replace a great part of the insects that were lost in the *Sir J. Brooke.*

I remain perfectly well, but my two poor lads suffer from time to time with intermittent fever; quinine, however, generally stops it, and I hope the change of air will do them good.

The brave fellows do their work none the less cheerfully, and they love me, and are quite devoted to me.

I am only waiting for the arrival of my letters, through the medium of my good friend Dr. Campbell, to set out, because when I have once started I fear none of your letters will reach me.

I think I shall explore the Mekon, and go up as far as China, if circumstances are favourable, and trust to bring back from this journey many rare and precious things. I bought at Bangkok many articles to give to those who shall aid me, such as red and white cloth, brass wire, glass beads, needles, spectacles, &c.

28th Dec.—The night before my departure for Korat. All the good news I have received from Europe and from Bangkok has made me joyful. I have just received with your letters a mass of papers. Every one is kind to me, and that is very pleasant. My friend Malherbe has sent me some *caporal*, which I had not enjoyed for a long time; he had just received some from France, along with some pipes, and a precious extract of sarsaparilla, invaluable for cooling the blood heated by the climate, the food, and the troublesome musquitoes of which I have spoken so often. I shall require another elephant to carry all the red cloth sent to me by Mr. Adamson, and which will be invaluable in Laos, as the people delight in it. I was moved even to tears at so many marks of kindness from people who hardly know me.

To M. Charles Mouhot.

Korat, 26th January, 1861.

I have been three days at Korat, which is about 140 miles east-north-east of Pakpriau,—that is, nearly in the same longitude as Battambong.

The journey, which I performed on foot, in company with a caravan of 400 oxen carrying merchandise, lasted ten days, from four in the morning to sunset, deducting only a few hours in the middle of the day. My feet are in a bad state from crossing the mountains, but, nevertheless, I enjoyed my journey.

On these uplands, which are more than 4000 feet high, the air is pure and pleasant, the nights are fresh, and the early morning almost cold.

During these ten days I have collected but little, and my expenses have been greater than I calculated on. Within the last two years everything has doubled in price; but the governor appears honest; he paid me a visit, which cost me a pair of spectacles, some engravings, and other little things, but he has promised me conveyances, and a letter to the chief of another province, who will provide me with elephants.

My health is excellent, and I hope it will remain so; my servants are better. I am surrounded by a crowd of curious gazers, who fill up my hut.

To M. Charles Mouhot.

Saraburi (Siam), 24th February, 1861.

You will be astonished, my dear friend, to see my letter dated from Saraburi, instead of from Laos. When I reached Chaiapume, I went to the governor with my letters, and asked him to lend me elephants to enable me to continue my journey, that being the only method of travelling among these mountains; but he refused me decidedly, and consequently I have been forced to retrace my steps. Here one can do nothing without the help of the people in power.

I therefore returned to Korat, and established Phrai in a

hut which I hired of a Chinese; and went myself to Bangkok, to procure from the authorities orders to the different governors of provinces to aid me instead of throwing obstacles in my way.

From Korat I had the pleasure of travelling with an amiable mandarin of Bangkok, who had been to fetch a white elephant from Laos, and who had conceived a great friendship for me. He travelled in great style; the caravan was magnificent; we had more than sixty elephants, two of which were placed at my disposal, one for my own use, and one for my servants.

Finding myself in the good graces of this mandarin, I told him why I was going to Bangkok, and he promised to obtain for me all I wanted.

When I reached Saraburi I found all the governors of Laos and the first mandarins of Bangkok assembled there to take care of the white elephant. The Siamese, being very superstitious, and believing in metempsychosis, think that the soul of some prince or king has passed into the white elephant; they have the same belief as to white apes and albinoes, consequently they hold them all in great respect. They do not worship them, for the Siamese recognise no God, not even Buddha, but they believe that a white elephant brings luck to the country.

During the whole journey the men were busy cutting down branches to make his passage easy; two mandarins fed him with different kinds of cakes in golden dishes, and the King came out to meet him.

I owe, therefore, to the white elephant the most satisfactory letters which I have obtained, and which have cost me my best gun and nearly 300 francs in presents; but I might have had to give much more, and, as I am going to Bangkok, I can replenish my stock. As for the poor elephant, he was so much cared for and so well fed, that he died of indigestion.

It is a terrible affliction, and all the mandarins and other dignitaries collected here are in great grief about it.

To Madame Mouhot (his Wife).

Saraburi, 24th February, 1861.

My dear Annette,

You will be much surprised on receiving this letter to see it dated from Saraburi, for if you have received the one I wrote in January, you must believe me to be already in Laos. But man proposes, and God disposes. However, to reassure you, I must begin by saying that I am in perfect health, and full of strength and hope. All goes well with me.

I had in fact reached Laos. I arrived at Korat after a tedious and troublesome journey, for I had only a few oxen for my baggage, and was forced to walk myself. From there I went to Chaiapume, and here an animal of the mandarin species made himself great, and under the pretext of having no elephants refused me the means of going further, and was so rude and impolite to me that I determined at once to return and protest against the very insufficient protection which had been granted to me. Indeed, I could do nothing else, not being able to go on. The elephant which had brought me to Chaiapume took me back to Korat, and there I found a mandarin from Bangkok, who had been sent to fetch a white elephant which had been taken in Laos. I begged him to let me join his party, and he lent me two elephants, one for my servant and luggage, and one for myself. I left Phrai at Korat, with the greater part of my possessions, having hired a room for him in the house of a Chinese, and a week afterwards found myself back at Saraburi, in company with this strange divinity (who, by the way, had more black than white about him), and of the grand personage who had been sent to escort him, and who had showered on him every kind of attention during the journey. He had an escort of fifty foot soldiers and several on horseback. As for me, I wanted for nothing; at every halt the mandarin sent me ducks, fish, fruit, sweetmeats, &c., and he was also kind enough to allow me eight men as night-guards to watch round my fire. In return, I discovered for him in the mountains large quantities of copper, and even gold, which delighted him.

The whole province of Saraburi was in motion to do honour to the white elephant; the King and all his court are coming here; the ministers are here already to watch over him. I decided, therefore, to apply to the Siamese, hoping to obtain more from them than from the Europeans; and yesterday, hearing of the arrival of Khrom Luang, the King's brother, I hastened to address myself to him. He, however, had only passed through, and was gone to Prabat, to join the King. However, I found here the man I wanted, the mandarin who has most interest in Laos, and without a letter from whom it would have been difficult to proceed. I did not know him, but I went to him to ask about the Prince, and told him what I wanted. "I am your man," said he; "the Prince can only give an order for me to write a letter, such as I will give you, if you like." I accepted gladly, and promised him in return my double-barrelled gun, which I could easily replace, "if he would only furnish me with the means of travelling through Laos without expense, and would bring the Chaiapume mandarin to reason." The poor governor of Saraburi was with us, and had to remain more than an hour amidst a number of others kneeling on the bare ground, while I was seated on the mat of the mandarin, by his side, eating sweetmeats and drinking tea, while he dictated a letter in which he called the governor of Chaiapume a fool, and threatened to deprive him of his office, and of this letter I was to be the bearer; and he promised me another general one on the morrow, in which he stated that if I did not receive efficient aid it might bring on a war; and this he also repeated to all the chiefs present. My cause was gained, and I could plainly see that our affairs must be going on well in Cochin China; the echo of the cannon had its effect in Siam. However, I had promised him my gun, and evidently he wished to have it before he gave me the letters. This morning, therefore, I took it to him all cleaned and furbished up. He was delighted with it, and gave me at once the letter for Korat and Chaiapume, and to-morrow I am to have one which will carry me all through Laos without any expense but a few ticals to the cornacs. Without this, judging by what I had to pay for an elephant from Korat to Chaiapume, my purse would have been exhausted by the time I reached the north of Laos, and I should not have had the means of returning without sending to Bangkok to ask for help, which would have been a work of difficulty, and, what is worse, I should have been exposed all along the route to the insolence of these arrogant mandarins. Now, they will all humble themselves before me, taking me for some important personage sent by the Emperor Napoleon or Queen Victoria to collect butterflies, insects, and birds for them. I shall no longer travel on foot, but on elephants, and shall want for nothing. Agree, then, with me, that out of evil comes good, or rather, that God does all for the best. When at Chaiapume I found myself obliged to retrace my steps, after so many fatigues, and so great a waste of money, I was only downcast for a few minutes; God almost immediately inspired me with the idea that all would turn to my advantage, and this persuasion never left me again. Unaccountably to myself, I was gayer on my return than I had been in coming, although then I was everywhere well received and kindly treated by the people. Even after my discourteous reception at Chaiapume, all the inhabitants came to see me, to bring me little presents, and to express their regret that they could not aid me from fear of their chief. The head of the monastery took me to see some ruins similar to those in Cambodia, and gave me a tiger-skin; and all along the road I experienced the same kindness, and numbers came to me to ask for advice and various remedies.

The Chinese are all my friends. When I returned to this

town, you should have seen them all run out to see me, and those at whose houses I had stopped were full of inquiries as to my affairs, and crying out "Ah! here is the gentleman back again." The next day would be their New Year's Day, which they keep as a feast as we do Christmas. "I have come back to feast with you to-morrow," replied I; and the next day I was so loaded with cakes and other good things that I have not finished them yet.

You must arm yourself with patience, dear Annette, for I have not yet finished. I learned this morning that a French ship of war is at Paknam, I presume for the purpose of taking back the Siamese Ambassador who has been so long expected in France. The king must be delighted, for he has a great dread of any quarrel with France or England now that he has seen their power. They may very probably come here, and at the risk of losing three days I shall wait and see, for, doubtless, the officer would receive me well, and do more for me than the Consul did. After that, I shall go to Bangkok, where I shall remain only a day, in order to buy a few necessaries in which I was beginning to run short, such as camphor, shoes, cloth, and a gun, and to get a little money, 50 or 100 ticals, from M. Adamson, who will willingly advance it to me, as he promised; and above all, to receive all the dear letters from home, of which a number must be lying at Dr. Campbell's.

My useless voyage to Chaiapume diminished my resources, and it would be great pity that the want of a few hundred francs should force me to return before I have completed my journey, and before I have finished collecting what will amply repay all my expenses.

In a few days I will add a line to this letter to tell you the result of my interview with the officer, and of my journey to Bangkok. I shall hear news also from your letters; let them only be good, and I shall be happy. I must now close my letter for to-day, my dear Annette; some day you will see my journal, and read all my adventures in detail. I can write no more to-day, but only repeat my assurance that I am perfectly well, in spite of all trials, thanks to my prudence and sobriety. Show this letter or anything that is interesting in it to all friends. I speak only of my own affairs, but you know I am not changed. And yet a few words of love would doubtless be more prized by you, but were I to write a thousand I could not express half the love with which my heart is filled for you all; indeed I fear to begin, for that would have no end. I write all this on my knees; my back aches, and now I must go and seek some repose. Au revoir! I trust soon to send you still better news than this. I embrace you a thousand times from the bottom of my heart, as well as all those dear to us, and am ever

Your devoted husband,

H. MOUHOT.

TO MADAME MOUHOT.

Saraburi, 25th February, 1861.

MY VERY DEAR ANNETTE,

I reached Korat two days ago, and in four more I hope to be able to proceed northward. I have been obliged to travel on foot, not having been able to procure elephants at Saraburi; my baggage was carried by oxen. I feel perfectly well, and experience so little fatigue that on the day of my arrival here I walked about till evening.

I write you these few lines only to set your mind at ease, for — surrounded from morning till night by curious gazers who have never before seen a European—it would be difficult to enter into details, but, in truth, my journey furnished but few. I travelled with Laotians, and found them very kind; in a few days I shall be in the heart of their country, and think I shall find them superior to the Siamese. I regret that this letter will be short, but I have little to tell since I wrote last; when I am quietly settled in some little hut in the midst of a village, I can write at my ease if an opportunity presents itself.

Be easy on my account, dear Annie, and feel sure that God will not abandon me; all my confidence is in Him, and this will never deceive me. He will sustain and protect you also, and this assurance gives me strength.

Adieu, my good Annette; take great care of yourself. I embrace you tenderly, and am ever your devoted and affectionate husband,

H. Mouhot.

P.S.—I shall set off to-morrow. Yesterday I visited an old pagoda; there is another, but to which I shall not be able to go, as it would cost me 9 ticals, and take several days, and I shall be obliged to be excessively economical. Yesterday I had a visit from a mandarin, the viceroy of the province. He was very amiable, and promised me a letter, but the people are so kind that I have really no need of it, and even the disagreeable ones I manage to gain over.

Adieu, my love. Do not forget me, but do not be uneasy. May God grant to you the same tranquillity and confidence that I feel and make you as happy as I am. Do not complain of the shortness of this letter; you cannot imagine how I am pestered by gazers and idlers.

Embrace your dear mamma for me, to whom I wish good health; say everything kind to Kate, &c. Once more, adieu, and au revoir! Your devoted Henri. I shall write whenever I find an opportunity.

To Madame Charles Mouhot.

Louang Prabang (Laos), 23rd July, 1861.

Now, my dear Jenny, let us converse together. Do you know of what I often think when every one around me is asleep, and I, lying wrapped in my mosquito-curtains, let my thoughts wander back to all the members of my family? Then I seem to hear again the charming voice of my little Jenny, and to be listening once more to 'La Traviata,' 'The Death of Nelson,' or some other of the airs that I loved so much to hear you sing. I then feel regret, mingled with joy, at the souvenirs of the happy—oh, how happy!—past. Then I open the gauze curtains, light my pipe, and gaze out upon the stars, humming softly the 'Pâtre' of Béranger, or the 'Old Sergeant,' and thinking that one day I may return Corporal or Sergeant of the battalion of Naturalists.

Perhaps all this does not interest you, but you may feel sure that I do not forget you nor your children; so let me, my dear child, talk to you as we used to talk in the old times as we sat by the fire. When shall we do so again?

In another year, or perhaps two, dear Jenny, I shall think of returning to you all for some time. Shall you be very angry, my dear little sister, when I say that it will be with regret?—for I should wish to visit the whole of the mountains that I can see from my window. I say "window," but here such a luxury is unknown: I live in a shed without either doors or windows—a room open to every wind.

I would wish, I repeat, to cross the whole network of mountains which extend northward, see what lies beyond them, visit China or Thibet, and see the Calmucks or the Irkoutsk. But, alas! I cannot trust my dear insects. I say "my dear insects" as you would say "my dear children" to the king of Louang Prabang.

How does all go on at Jersey?—for I hope that you are still

there. Your children form your happiness, and you can dispense easily with travelling, or with those people commonly called "friends"—nothing is so general as the name, or so rare as the reality—and you are right; yet I consider a true friend as a real treasure. I may be wrong, for man is so constituted as always to long for what he has not, but I wish I had friends around me here; these places, now often gloomy, would please me more.

I hoped that at the king's return I should have the happiness of hearing from you; but I am told that his journey will occupy a year, and before that time I shall be away from here.

I hope, my little friend, that all is well with you. Embrace your dear children for me, and talk to them sometimes about their uncle "Barberousse," who often thinks of them in this distant land, and is collecting stories for their amusement on his return. Ask C—— what I shall bring him—a monkey, a sabre to cut off M——'s dolls' heads—no, that would give him warlike ideas, and I do not like our modern soldiers—or a tiger-skin for a carpet. I have several. And your pretty little M——, will she have an ape, a fan, some Chinese slippers (for she must have feet which would be small even in China), some marabout feathers, or a cane to keep her brothers in order?

Adieu, adieu! Au revoir! Do not forget me.

TO MADAME MOUHOT.

Laos, Louang Prabang, 27th July, 1861.

DURING my journey through the forests I enjoyed in anticipation the pleasure I should enjoy on reaching Louang Prabang, the capital of the province of Laos, in writing you good long letters containing all details of my journey; but

I reckoned without my host, and it will be several weeks before I can enjoy any repose, or carry my wishes into execution.

In the villages through which I passed no great degree of curiosity was manifested; but here, where the population is greater, I am surrounded by a compact and curious crowd, which extends even to the walls of a pagoda adjoining the caravanserai where I am lodged by the favour of his Majesty the King. Besides, I, in my turn, see people of various nations and tribes who excite my curiosity. Judge, therefore, if it be easy to collect my ideas. However, I profit by the occasion of the king's departure for Bangkok in a few days to pay his tribute, and who has offered to take charge of any letters for me, to give some signs of life to you.

You will be happy to hear that I have accomplished this troublesome journey satisfactorily, without the loss of a single man, and without any personal illness. Indeed, my health has been very good, which is more than I can say for my servants, who are so kind and devoted to me. I am even astonished at myself, having gone through the mountainous district which separates the basin of the Menam from that of the Mekon, a place much dreaded by the Siamese, and covered with virgin-forests like those of Dong Phya Phia, without having had a single touch of fever, or, indeed, any indisposition, with the exception of *migraine*, caused by the heat of the sun, and having my feet in a very bad state.

I bless God for the favour granted to me of having accomplished these perilous journeys, and trust wholly to His goodness for the future.

I am now more than 250 leagues north of the place where two years ago I first drank the waters of the Mekon. This immense stream, which is larger here than the Menam at Bangkok or the Thames below London Bridge, flows between high mountains with the rapidity of a torrent, tearing up in the rainy season the trees along the banks, and breaking with a noise like that of a stormy sea against the rocks, which form a number of frightful rapids.

I arrived here only the day before yesterday, after a journey of four months and ten days; but I stopped in several places, for I often found fields ready to cut in the rice-grounds that the mountaineers cultivate on the slopes of the mountains, and when the crops are cut down insects abound.

My collections made during the journey are very valuable and beautiful, and I have a great number of new species, both entomological and conchological, with which, if they only reach London in safety, our friends will be delighted. All the beautiful kinds that I was asked for, but which elsewhere are so rare that with great trouble I was only able to procure one or two specimens, I have now in great abundance, and also many new sorts. Here I hope to do still better.

They are all savages in this province, and I have just received a visit from two young princes remarkable for their stupidity.

I have suffered little from the heat, in spite of the season, which is easy to understand, as I have been always amidst thick forests or on mountains. In the valleys the air is heavy, and the heat overwhelming; but everywhere the nights were so fresh that my wraps were useful and almost indispensable. In a few months we shall probably want fire. I prefer this climate to that of the South; there are few mosquitoes (that plague of the tropics and especially of Siam) in comparison with other places—indeed, in some of these parts I have not found any.

Thanks to the Governor of Korat, who gave me an excellent letter to the mandarins, I have travelled at little expense; without it, I should have paid much more, and have suffered every kind of inconvenience. Everywhere I have been furnished with elephants (as many as seven in some provinces), an escort, guard, and plenty of provisions.

I had this morning an audience of the great body of State Mandarins, like the House of Peers with us. Twenty of them were assembled in a vast caravanserai, and presided over by the eldest prince. You may form some idea of the dignity of these gentlemen by the drawing which I will send to you.

My plan is to pass six or eight months of the good season in the neighbouring villages, in order to complete my collection, and next January or March I will try to go north or east, where I shall pass a few more months amidst the Laotian tribes. Probably I shall go no farther, for China would be a barrier to me on the north, and Cochin China on the east. I shall then return here, and go down the Mekon in July or August, 1862, the time when the waters are high, and shall thus reach Korat in a few weeks. I am yet uncertain whether I shall stop there, whether I shall explore the eastern part of the river, or whether I shall go to Cambodia. All my movements depend upon circumstances that may arise. I shall try to profit by all that are favourable, and that will contribute to give interest to my journey.

Do not be anxious when you think of your poor friend the traveller, for you know that up to the present time everything has prospered with him: and truly I experience a degree of contentment, strength of soul, and internal peace, which I have never known before.

[*Same Letter.*]

Louang Prabang, 8th August, 1861.

No event could have caused more sensation here than the arrival of "the long-bearded stranger." From the humblest to the greatest—for even here are distinctions of rank—every one looks on a "white" as a natural curiosity, and they are not yet satisfied with looking—nothing is talked of but the stranger. When I pass through the town in my white dress, to go to the market or to visit the pagodas or other interesting places, the people crowd round me, and look after me as long as they can catch a glimpse of me. Everywhere I go complete silence reigns, and I am treated as though I were a sovereign or prince, and the council, by order of the king, have given to me as to them power of life or death over his subjects. Poor people! why can I not raise you from the abasement into which you have fallen? I am overwhelmed with presents of all kinds in return for the slightest favour shown to these unfortunate people. They seem to me some of the most to be pitied that I have seen; even the women and children are opium-eaters: they might really be called a nation of crétins.

The heat is greater here than any I have felt; when the sun shines, and there has been no rain for several days, I find it worse than at Bangkok; still the nights are generally pleasant, and from the month of December to the end of March I am told that it is really cold.

To M. Charles Mouhot.

Louang Prabang, West Laos, 27th July, 1861.

As you will have the opportunity, my dear brother, of reading my other letters, I shall not write to you at length; but, nevertheless, I must give you some details as to my journey to Laos, although I cannot tell whether the crowd of curious gazers around me will permit me to write as I would wish; if not, you must blame them and not me.

On the 10th April I wrote you from Korat, and I think you must also have received a message which I sent to you by a good and honest Chinese, who has been very useful to me, and from whom I have received more help and kindness than from any other of the mandarins.

I was not then in good spirits, for I doubted whether I should be able to accomplish the journey for which I had already suffered so many annoyances, one of which was having to return to Korat to procure more useful letters than those which I had taken with me on starting. At last I obtained one from the Viceroy of Korat, which was the only one of service to me, and which sufficed to secure me aid and protection during my whole journey to Laos.

From Korat to Bangkok you know that I travelled in company with an animal who has a title equal to that of the greatest Siamese mandarin, and who was served by two inferior mandarins, who gave him his meals composed of cakes, biscuits, and sweetmeats out of golden dishes; and who had slaves sent before him to clear the way and cut down the brushwood and branches, for this elephant, according to the Siamese superstition and ignorance, possesses the soul of some deceased prince or king. They called him a white elephant, but in reality he had only a few spots of that colour on his body. Alas! The king and all his mandarins are now in mourning, for the object of their worship died of indigestion. Poor beast and poor king!

I have travelled a long way since I last wrote, and God has protected me. I crossed the mountains and went through the most dreaded jungles in the rainy season without losing a man, and without having suffered myself. My travelling expenses were comparatively small to what they might have been; everywhere I was furnished gratis with elephants, escorts, guards, and provisions (rice and fowls), as though I were an envoy from the king, and all this owing solely to a letter from the Viceroy of Korat.

I have made a good collection of coleoptera, and have procured a number of excessively rare and beautiful species.

I have also obtained some very rare and interesting conchological specimens. As for animals, I have but few; some monkeys and a good many serpents.

In a week I shall be settled in a new place, where I intend to spend four or five months, and by the end of the year I trust to have 4000 insects.

The Mekon is a large and beautiful stream, full of rocks, which form frightful rapids in the rainy season. I shall descend it at the season when the waters are high, and when the navigation though dangerous is easy and rapid. I can then reach Cambodia in a month if I like, but I am undecided whether or not I shall go eastward towards the 15th degree of latitude.

It seems to me, my dear brother, that my happiness would be complete if I could have good news of you all; but, alas! more than a year must elapse before I shall hear. The last letters I received were in January; yet I am resigned, since I willingly embraced this career, which has been the dream of my whole life, for you remember how in our young days, when we still had the happiness of a tender mother to guide us, and impress on us, by her example, virtuous principles, religion, and the love of mankind, we delighted to roam the woods of our dear native place, to draw from nature, and how I stuffed the birds that we took in snares or nets.

That time is long passed, my friend, but I trust in God, who will I hope watch over you. I think of you every day in my solitude, and in the long nights when we bivouac beside the fires lighted to keep off the wild beasts, a scene of which I will send you a drawing before long.

What are your dear children doing? I picture to myself all the happiness they give you and your dear Jenny; she is well I hope. Ah! my friend, protect them all with a tender affection, and endeavour by your love, your care, and your example, to render them all happy and good.

There is one subject on which I can hardly write, that of our dear old father; it would make me too sad to think he was not happy; console him for my absence, write to him often, repeat to him how much I love him, that he is always associated in my thoughts with the memory of our good and worthy mother. But I have no need to recommend all this to you: have you not ever been good to him, a worthy son? therefore I am without anxiety on this point.

I do not speak to you of any of my physical sufferings, for I hold mental ones to be the only ones worth thinking of; but you may imagine that one cannot make a four months' journey on elephants, who toss and shake one like a stormy sea, without fatigue, and that the heat, the long bad nights generally passed at the foot of some tree, and the wretched food, are all painful. But what matters all this? I am used to it, and my patience is inexhaustible. In truth, this life is happiness to me; how joyful I am when I find a new insect, or see a monkey fall from a tree! I do not therefore complain. The nights here are pleasant, and the mosquitoes not numerous.

The men of this nation are dull and apathetic and full of small vices. The women are generally better, and some of them are even pretty in spite of their yellow skins, but they have little idea of modesty. The men and women all bathe together without any clothing. But for the people, Louang Prabang would be one of the most charming places in the world: the lake of Geneva does not present scenes more beautiful than many here by the river.

After waiting for ten days I have at length been presented to the king with great pomp. The reception room was a shed such as they build in our villages on fête-days, but larger and hung with every possible colour. His Majesty was enthroned at one end of the hall, lazily reclining on a divan, having on his right hand four guards squatting down, and each holding a sabre: behind were the princes all prostrated, and farther off the senators, with their backs to the public and their faces in the dust; then in front of his Majesty was your poor brother, dressed all in white, and seated on a carpet, with teacups, basins, and spittoons in silver placed by his side, contemplating this grotesque scene, and having some trouble to preserve his gravity as he smoked his pipe. This visit cost me a gun for the king and various small presents for the princes, for one cannot travel here without being well furnished with presents for the kings, princes, and mandarins. Luckily it is not here as in Siam; the natives are willing to help me, and for a few inches of brass wire I get a beautiful longicorn or some other insect, and these are brought to me on all sides: thus I have succeeded in largely increasing my collection, but five pieces of red cloth have disappeared already.

The day after my first audience I had another from the second king, who wished also for a present. I sought among my stock, which anywhere else would cause me to be taken for a dealer in old stores, and found a magnifying glass and a pair of old-fashioned spectacles with round glasses, which make him look like a gorilla without hair, a little cake of soap (he had great need of it), a bottle of eau-de-cologne, and a bottle of brandy. This last was opened on the spot and duly appreciated. You see all this is expensive, but I am obliged to pay these good people, and the king has been kind to me, and is going to carry my letters for me. It is lucky that he does not understand French; for if at Bangkok the same system of postal curiosity was carried on as was established in Europe by the great king who betrayed La Vallière, I should be hung from the highest tree they could find, without even a warning. I afterwards distributed among the princes some engravings which I had bought at Bangkok—fine Cossack cavalry, lance in rest; some Napoleons (the First), for which I gave a penny; and some battles of Magenta, portraits of Victor Emmanuel and of Garibaldi, very white, blue, and red, and some Zouaves; also some brass-headed nails and some brandy; and it was quite pleasing to see how delighted they were, regretting only that I should go away before I had given them my whole stock.

To Samuel Stevens, Esq.

[To be communicated to the Royal Geographical Society.]

Louang Prabang, 1st August, 1861.
Lat. 20° 50', long. 102° 35' 3", merid. Greenwich.

Dear Mr. Stevens,

Being entirely cut off from all communication with Bangkok, from which I am nearly 700 miles distant, is the only reason why you have not heard from me for so long a time.

In January last I quitted the Siamese province of Saraburi, where during four months I had been making active exertions in order to enable me to penetrate into Western Laos, and to explore the basin of the Mekon. Unluckily in March I was forced, after having at great expense proceeded 350 miles, to return to Bangkok, in order to claim more assistance and protection than had hitherto been accorded to me, and a passport to counteract the difficulties continually thrown in my way by the mandarins, a class not less jealous and greedy here than in China. A letter of recommendation which had been voluntarily given to me (on my departure in October, 1860) by the Khrôme Louang Wougsâ, who is considered to be the prince best disposed towards Europeans in all Siam, and who has the superintendence of all the country which I intended to visit, turned out after all to be only a kind of letter of Bellerophon's. In spite of all my entreaties and valuable presents I obtained nothing better; still I set off again.

I have passed three times through the forest of the Dong Phya Phia, which separates Korat from the ancient Siamese provinces of the south and east. This thick jungle covers a space of thirty miles in breadth,—that is to say, the chain of mountains which separates the basin of the Mekon from that of the Menam.

After passing the mountains you reach a sandy and generally arid plain, where nothing is to be seen but resinous trees of stunted growth, bamboos, underwood, and sometimes only grass; but in some places a richer soil permits cultivation, and there fields of rice and bananas have been established. I found in this district both oligist and magnetic iron.

In the bed of a torrent I also discovered gold and copper in two different places. This district is rich and abundant in precious minerals, neglected or unknown until now, except by a small tribe of 400 or 500 Kariens, without doubt a remnant of the aborigines, who a short time ago, in order to preserve their independence, retired into almost inaccessible places, thirty or forty miles eastward of the tracts traversed by the caravans. Monkeys, panthers, elephants, and other wild beasts are the only inhabitants of this mountain, which the natives regard as the abode of death on account of its insalubrity.

Korat Ongcor Aithe of the Cambodians was formerly the bulwark of Cambodia on the north and west: a solid rampart supported by a large épaulement, the work of Khmer Dôme (the ancient Cambodians), still surrounds the town. It is at present governed by a Siamese mandarin of the first class, a kind of viceroy, but the ancient inhabitants have nearly disappeared, and it contains only about 300 Chinese or their descendants, small resident merchants, 300 other individuals who go about the country trading, and 1500 or 2000 Laotians, Cambodians, and Siamese, who, like wolves or jackals which follow an army or caravan, have come there from all parts of the kingdom, or have remained there after the wars of Laos and Cambodia, in

T 2

order to lead a life in harmony with their inclinations, attacking travellers and Chinese merchants, in fact a band of miscreants, with few exceptions destitute of all good qualities.

In the environs are two temples, which would do honour to the founders of the Cambodian edifices: one of them is in good preservation, and of this I have made a drawing. The style, architecture, and workmanship are all alike; one would say that the same artists and workmen had drawn the plans and executed them. Again you see those immense blocks, beautifully cut, joined without cement, and covered with carving and bas-reliefs.

One of these temples is situated about thirty miles from the town, and is said to have been founded by a Queen; the other, nine miles to the east, is supposed to have been built by the King her husband. Much farther east it is said that there are others containing beautiful sculptures, but I have not been able to visit them, as they are out of my route.

Want of means for the easy and advantageous removal of merchandise, causes Korat to be the central market for all the eastern part of the country. There they bring all the silk of Laos, langoutis, skins, horns, ivory, peacocks' tails, &c., which the active Chinese merchants sell again at a good profit at Bangkok, notwithstanding all the taxes they have to pay, having brought from thence cotton and other useful articles of Chinese and European manufacture for the use of the natives. Thus there passes daily through the forest of Dong Phya Phia, on the average, a caravan of from 100 to 150 oxen. With protective instead of restrictive laws, and an enlightened and civilized government, this commerce would increase threefold in a very short time.

Notwithstanding the small population of Korat, it is the chief town of a province, or rather an extensive state, containing eleven towns or boroughs, chief towns of districts, and a great number of villages, more or less populated. Fifteen days' journey brings you from Korat to Bassac on the banks of the Mekon, and in the same latitude.

My intention was to proceed northwards, only stopping in the province of Louang Prabang, and then to descend the river as far as Cambodia. I hired elephants, and five days after, having passed through several villages inhabited by the descendants of ancient Siamese colonists who had taken refuge there in time of war, passing continually through forests of resin trees thinly scattered, I arrived at Ban Prang, a village where I discovered a ruined tower, and also the remains of an ancient temple. The next place I arrived at was Chaiapoune, the principal Laotian town in the north, and the chief town of the district. Here also I found ruins; but they were inconsiderable, and seemed more like a Laotian imitation than the work of Khmer Dôme. The inscriptions on the other temples in the province of Korat resemble those of Ongcor: here I found upon a block of broken slate-stone an inscription in Laotian characters, but which is unintelligible even to the inhabitants of the country. These, with some remains of idols and towers at the foot of a mountain in the district, were the only vestiges of that ancient civilization which I discovered in the north. Everything leads me to suppose that here also were the limits which separated the kingdom of Cambodia from that of Vieng Thiane, destroyed during the last war which the Siamese raised against the Western Laotians or *white-bellies*. It was in this district that I was stopped in my travels by the authorities of the country, who treated me with great rudeness, and who forbade the people to let me have any means of transport, even after seeing my passport. I was therefore obliged to retrace my steps, deploring the expense and loss of time in the best part of the year, and which will cause me serious inconvenience.

LETTERS ADDRESSED TO M. MOUHOT.*

FROM M. GUILLOUX.

Brelum, among the Stiêns, 12th August, 1859.

DEAR M. MOUHOT,

It must be allowed that you have plenty of courage; and before knowing you, I feel a strong interest in you; indeed, I feel as though I loved you already. You will be very welcome, and must share pot-luck with me, like a brother, will you not? I trust you vill not be scandalized at any of our ways; for among the savages we live in rather an uncivilized fashion. But with good hearts all will go well.

Your servant Nhu arrived yesterday among the Stiêns at Brelum, quite tired with the journey, and with his feet in a sad state. A few days' rest, however, will restore him. He looks to me like a good fellow. You may be sure we shall take care of him, as well as of your little Chinese when he arrives.

You must never trust to the word of a Cambodian, dear M. Mouhot; they are terrible boasters.

You are two long days' journey from us, and will have to pass one night in the forest. We will try to send you one or two vehicles. These, with a good covering and a fire, will preserve you from injury from the night air. You say, too, that you are accustomed to sleep on the ground; it is well to be able to do everything.

Unluckily, my feet are very bad just now, or I should have been delighted to come and meet you. I will send the three

* Several of these letters were never received by M. Mouhot.

carriages—carriages! wretched carts rather! There will be an Annamite seminarist to lead the caravan; he is a good fellow, and clever at that kind of work. You can talk to him in Latin. Two of the carts are drawn by oxen, and one by buffaloes; but if they are not enough to bring your luggage, ask the Cambodians boldly for more, and show them your letter from the king.

Our carts will arrive one day after the return of the Cambodians; when you arrive I will explain why. I trust that will be soon. I wish you a good journey. Keep your gun loaded, for animals of all kinds abound. But you will find here warm hearts, patriotism, and, above all, no ceremony.

From M. Chas. Fontaine.

Pinhalú, Cambodia.

Dear M. Mouhot,

I think of you in your peregrinations, and I feel sure that you must meet with many obstacles and difficulties; but with patience, perseverance, and help from on high, a great deal may be done.

As for myself, I have not got rid of my atony—for such is my illness. At first I obtained some relief by means of opium as an astringent and quinine as a tonic, and by great attention to diet, living almost wholly on broth; a piece of meat, or even an egg, throws me back for a week.

M. Guilloux set off in good health on the 9th January. He tells me that you have promised to go and see his relations when you return to France.

I shall never forget, dear M. Mouhot, the pleasure that I experienced in the few days that I passed in your society; such days are so rare in our missionary life.

All is quiet just now in Cambodia; the forts or redoubts

are guarded only by a few men. Mgr. Miche is expected to return from Komput about the end of March. Shall I be so happy as to receive news of you? It would give me great pleasure, and recall that which I have already experienced in our meeting in this life. Let us hope to be re-united, no more to part, in a happier one.

Pray receive my kindest remembrances, and believe me, dear M. Mouhot,

Your true friend in the Lord,

MARIE CHS. FONTAINE.

FROM M. CHAS. FONTAINE.

Singapore, 29th May, 1860.

MY VERY DEAR FRIEND, M. MOUHOT,

Your two kind and welcome letters, one from Battambong on the 7th March, and the other from Bangkok on the 3rd May, reached me when I was about three days' distance from Singapore, where I had gone for my health, and which I reached in April, after having passed the whole month of March in Bangkok.

I must tell you that MM. Arnoux and Guilloux have been able to buy five or six little savage children, and that they now meet with a little more kindness from the natives than they did. When France shall reign in Cochin China, and the natives can shake off the yoke of the Cambodians, it is to be hoped that they will be better disposed towards religion. The king has already discovered the mistake he made in attacking the Annamites, who may fall upon him without dread of the French. Mgr. Miche thinks that the daily flight of the Cambodian soldiers will avoid new provocation, and that the war may not take place; but every one is on the *qui vive.* The king has sent a letter to ask for silence on the part of M. Miche. They are fawning curs now; but on the slightest return of good fortune, their arrogance will be redoubled.

You gave me much pleasure, dear M. Mouhot, by your promise to visit my family at Laval. If you go near there, I shall expect no less from your kindness.

I hope to see you again, either at Singapore or at Saigon, before your return to Europe. May the good God guide your steps and preserve your life in this country, where death finds so many victims! I beg it through the intercession of our common mother.

Believe in my cordial friendship.

Yours most truly, in Jesus and Mary,

M. CH. FONTAINE.

FROM M. GUILLOUX.

Among the Stiêns at Brelum, 1st October, 1860.

DEAR M. MOUHOT,

I received your welcome letter of the 4th May, and it is impossible to tell you the pleasure it gave me. I was much pleased to hear that you were still in good health. May the good God aid and bless your efforts, and send you home safe and well to your family and country!

I sympathize sincerely with you in your disappointment at not meeting at Bangkok with more kindness among those from whom you had a right to expect aid and protection, and who are paid well for that purpose. Alas! how weak we all are when we rely for aid only on men like ourselves. But you, dear M. Mouhot, do not do so; you know how to seek support from a higher source; and while you remain the submissive child of God, be sure He will not abandon you.

I went to Pinhalú last month, and brought back a young Annamite with me, but the poor fellow died.

You see I can travel; but I am not strong. I have been often ill since your departure; and M. Arnoux is going this time to undertake the journey to Cambodia. May God bring him back safe and well!

The affairs of Cochin China are very bad; debauchery and infamy are rife at Saigon. So many crimes cannot bring a blessing on the colony.

No news from China.

Adieu, dear M. Mouhot. Believe me ever one of your most faithful friends,

GUILLOUX.

FROM DR. CAMPBELL, R.N.

Bangkok, 15th Dec. 1860.

MY DEAR M. MOUHOT,

Your letters of the 30th October and 20th November were duly delivered to me on the 12th instant. I was naturally rejoiced to find you continue in good health and spirits; and I sincerely trust you will be able, on each occasion you write, to give me a like favourable account.

Since you left there has been little or no change in Bangkok, the only domestic item I have to communicate being the recent marriage of Dr. Brady's eldest daughter to one of the missionaries named M'Gilvary, who used to stay with Dr. House.

Only one European letter has arrived for you, but I enclose others from Mr. Wilson and Mr. Adamson, and, by the way, some newspapers from him and M. Malherbe. The latter will probably write to you; if so, I shall enclose his letter. The box from Europe also accompanies this letter. Luckily it has arrived in time; but I only received it yesterday. I forward you the evening mails just arrived by last vessel. I could send you all that have come to hand since you left; but as it is a voluminous paper, it would take up much space, and you might not care to wade through all of them, in spite of the stirring events in Europe. Garibaldi, you will perceive, has liberated Sicily, and all but done likewise for the Neapolitan kingdom. The King of Naples left his capital without firing a shot; but made a stand at Capua, where his Neapolitans and mercenaries made a determined though ineffectual resistance. The King of Sardinia in the mean time has invaded the Marches, and now it is believed the states of the Pope are wrested from him, Rome and the suburban villages alone being retained for him by the French army stationed at Rome. It is not believed that an attempt will be made to take Rome or Venice, as that would be encountering the two great military Continental Powers, Austria and France. And it is supposed that the aim of the King of Sardinia, in invading the states of the Church and Naples, is to prevent the too ardent Garibaldi from fulfilling his threat of no peace till the Quirinal and the palace of the Doges be emancipated. However, all this you will see by the papers herewith.

The China war is over. The combined forces advanced and took Pekin. The emperor fled; but a treaty has been signed, and a large sum as indemnity—though, I believe, not equal to the outlay—is to be given to the European belligerents.

A Dutch ship is now here with an ambassador to make a treaty.

At Bangkok we have had higher tides this season than there have been for several years. The place continues healthy.

I forward you some calomel as requested. Calomel is a good purgative, and it might be well occasionally to take one such in preference to others; but castor oil is the safest where there is any irritation of the bowels. In such cases it should alone be used; though, if you fancy there be derangement of the liver, it would be well to use the mineral.

M. Malherbe has made up his mind to stay in Bangkok. As soon as his successor comes out, he (M. M.) will live near Santa Cruz, at the house owned by Mr. Hunter.

There is a chance of the second king going to Saraburi shortly in a steamer; so, if I think newspapers would reach you before the Chinaman, I may send you some, if a mail arrives by that time. However, I shall not, you may depend upon it, forget to attend to your wishes; but I really fear, after leaving Korat, it will be difficult to send you letters. Even to Korat it will not be easy; but though you did not tell me to send thither, I will do so, if possible, within two or three months; after that date it would be precarious, and I shall not do so. However, you can often, by the governors, have an opportunity of writing to me; and if you have altered any of your plans, or think of doing so, let me know, so that I may forward news if an opportunity offers for doing so.

The articles sent are: one large box from Mr. Adamson, one small ditto from Malherbe, one ditto from England, one parcel of papers from Mr. Swainson, one ditto from myself; three letters (besides this one) are enclosed in the box from M. Malherbe, which I will seal after enclosing this. The calomel is also in the same box.

And now, wishing you a prosperous, pleasant journey, believe me,

Yours very sincerely,

Jas. Campbell.

P.S.—Remember, whenever you return, I shall expect you to come direct to my house, and make it your own.

FROM M. E. SILVESTRE.

Battambong, 26th Nov. 1860.

DEAR M. MOUHOT,

I had the honour of writing to you in September last; did you receive my letter? As I did not know the courier, and am ignorant whether his fidelity was to be depended upon, I do not wish to lose a sure occasion which presents itself of recalling myself to your remembrance.

It is now the end of the rainy season, and I think that you must have returned from your expedition. I trust it has been successful, and that you have not left your courage and good health behind you on the banks of the Mekon or in the forests of Laos.

I had promised to collect for you some "sinsei;" but the ants, true Garibaldians, have annexed them during my journey to Pinhalú, and all that I have been able to collect since are as nothing compared to what the first rains brought with them. Such as they are, I send them to you; they are few in number, but for that you must blame the ants.

I have just had a visit from M. Miche and M. Arnoux. They only remained a few days; and in spite of his wish to see Ongcor, M. Arnoux was unable to go there.

They are raising troops here, preparing arms, and getting ready to assist the Cambodians against the Annamites. The death of the King of Cambodia will perhaps put an end to these fine projects.

The mandarin who was sent by the King of Siam to carry away the stones from Ongcor, and bring them to Bangkok, has been assassinated in the "Pra Sat Ea proum," and the mandarins of Ongcor are accused of the murder; but they say that those of Battambong had a hand in it. They have, therefore, all been sent for to Bangkok for judgment, and among them the son of our late governor. You see we are not over tranquil here. The war particularly terrifies my poor Battambongians.

Mgr. Miche is going to Bangkok in January or February; perhaps you may be there.

Receive the assurance, &c.,

E. SILVESTRE.

FROM M. LARNAUDIE.*

Pakprio, 25th January, 1861.

MY DEAR FRIEND, M. MOUHOT,

I have just received the two letters which you were kind enough to write to me from Kong Khoc, containing enclosures for MM. Arnoux and Silvestre. I much regretted not finding you here, that I might have had the pleasure of seeing you once more, and of conversing with you again before your departure for Laos. I am glad to hear that you have been able to do something at Khao-Khoc in spite of the advanced season.

I wish you much success in your new sphere of action. Do you know that I sometimes envy you? Do not forget to procure some skins of the argus pheasant; I think it differs from those of the Malayan peninsula. Take great care of your health; and if you are in want of anything which can be sent to you by way of Korat, write to me for it.

The young man who will give you this is a Christian and an associate of Cheek-Ke; he is a worthy lad, and you may trust him with your collections, if you have been able to make any in going through Don Phya Phia. All the Laotians declare that in that forest there is a kind of orang-outang which they

---

* M. Larnaudie accompanied the Siamese Ambassador to Paris, as interpreter, in 1860.

call Bua, and which they say is only to be distinguished from an old man by its having no joints in its knees. Among all their fables there is probably some truth; try to find out.

Excuse this scrawl; I write on my knees.

Your sincere friend,

Larnaudie.

From M. E. Silvestre.

Battambong, 4th January, 1862.*

Dear M. Mouhot,

Imagine my surprise and joy when, a week ago, a worthy Chinese from Korat entered my house, bringing me your letter of the 8th April. Blessed be God for granting you good health and courage. With these you can go far, even to the source of the Mekon; and if you return through Cambodia, with what pleasure I shall see you again! But your letter is dated more than eight months ago, and where are you now? I trust that the rainy season induced you to descend the Menam instead of the Mekon. Should you ever return to Battambong, you will find something new there. A pretty little church now replaces the old one; it is not yet quite finished, but I trust will be so very shortly.

Since I last wrote to you, grave events have taken place in Cambodia; the mandarins and people have risen against the young king in favour of his brother. It has been less a revolt than a universal pillage; nothing has been spared. Mgr. Miche had great trouble to guard his house, with the help of a young missionary and M. Aussoleil, for all the Christians fled. For a fortnight he was subject to constant attacks, and more than once saw sabres uplifted over his head; but his firmness

---

* This date is after M. Mouhot's death.

and bravery awed the mob, and he was lucky enough to preserve his house.

Some damage was done to the Annamite church at the end of the village. M. Miche wrote letter after letter to the French commander in Cochin China, but his messengers were all murdered, or else robbed, and their boats taken away from them.

At last, out of six letters, one reached its destination, and two days after the French flag appeared in the rivers of Cambodia; and at Pinhalú, six or seven cannon-shots spread terror among the rebels for twenty-five leagues round.

The mandarins who had pillaged the village were fined, and since then the Christians in Cambodia have been respected; and a letter sealed by M. Miche is the best possible passport. All this is well, you will say, and our countrymen did their duty.

You must excuse my lengthiness; at least, it will show that you are not forgotten at Battambong, but that we preserve here a happy remembrance of your too short stay. May you return in a few months, and recruit after your fatigues.

I must conclude with offering you my good wishes on the new year, and praying God to have you always and everywhere in his holy keeping.

I am yours very sincerely,

E. Silvestre.

From M. Malherbe.

Bangkok, 25th May, 1861.

My dear Friend,

On my return from Singapore I was much astonished to hear that you had been forced to go back again, and was much pained to think of all the troubles and discomforts you must have had to endure. How much I regret not having been with you!

perhaps I might have succeeded in persuading you against making a new attempt, and have induced you rather to pass some years here with me. Your task is a glorious one; but when life is at stake, one must take care and not risk it rashly. In any case do not attempt the impossible; and if your troubles recommence, return here; you will always find a friend ready to receive you.

Your letter from Korat reached me a few days ago. I thank you for it; it gave me great pleasure. In a few days I shall set out for Europe; but I have given my orders, and you will find my house ready for you at any time of the day or night. If you do not make use of it, I shall be really angry.

Every one here is interested for you, and asks for news of you. Where are you now? Doubtless much fatigued and *ennuyé* wherever you are; yet you must be travelling through a fine country. If you want anything which it is possible to send you, have no scruples; I have given my clerks all necessary instructions, if by chance or any unforeseen circumstance—such as may easily occur on a journey—you find yourself in want of what they call here "ticals." We are friends,—dispose freely of my purse; we will divide like brothers. Do not be offended at this offer, it comes from a heart devoted to you; therefore, have no false pride. Ask, and I will help you.

The heat is dreadful just now, and every one is ill of dysentery.

Au revoir, dear M. Mouhot. Take care of yourself, and do not be discouraged by the dreadful climate. That we may have, please God, many pleasant days together yet, is the earnest wish of your real friend,

L. Malherbe.

LETTERS ADDRESSED TO THE FAMILY OF THE LATE M. MOUHOT.

From Dr. Campbell to Madame Mouhot.

Bangkok, April 7th, 1862.

My dear Madame Mouhot,

About three weeks ago I had the pleasure of forwarding a letter from your husband, and I mentioned the probability of a second one, written before the one sent, reaching me in time for this mail. This has been realized, and I enclose the letter referred to. News from Luang Prabang, up to the middle of November, have also reached Bangkok, and oh! my dear madam, what a sad duty devolves upon me in narrating certainties that have transpired since my last communication. Would that I had some relation in London to whom I could write and request him to call upon you, to divulge the painful truth that your husband—my valued friend—is, alas! now no more. It may perhaps in a measure tend to soothe your sorrow under this severe trial, to say that I never knew a person who was so universally esteemed as he was by the foreign community of this city; and that all who had the pleasure of his acquaintance deeply regret his sudden and premature loss. The last letter he wrote me was dated from Louang Prabang, on the 30th August; in it he was satisfied with his success, and altogether buoyant in spirits. He continued in the neighbourhood of the above-named city, which is the capital of north-east Laos, till the middle of October, when he returned to the city. On the 19th he has written in his journal, "Attacked with fever;" but his servant and the Laos official account of his illness make it the 18th. On the 29th he made an entry, but nothing subsequently, and departed this life on Sunday the 10th November, at 7 P.M., being twenty-eight days subsequent to the attack. His servants, after seeing him interred, commenced their journey hither, taking with them his baggage and everything he had collected. M. D'Istria, the present French Consul, has to officiate as administrator to the late M. Mouhot's estate, but has assigned to me the care of all your late husband's manuscripts and collections. These I thought of forwarding forthwith for Singapore, and thence, by the kindness of Mr. Pady, to Europe; but as I expect to leave for England on a short leave of absence by the middle of next month, I think it better to retain them till then, and convey them home myself.

On your late husband arriving here, he brought me a small parcel from Dr. Norton Shaw, Secretary to the Royal Geographical Society, Whitehall-place; and as it is only proper that the Society should be made aware of this martyr to science, I enclose two letters—the last he wrote me—for your perusal, and that they may be handed to the above-named gentleman for his information, forwarding, at the same time, the announcement of M. Mouhot's untimely death. On looking over the charts he has left behind him, I find Louang Prabang placed 3° to the north and about 1° to the east of that denoted in the map given by Bishop Pallegoix; but as it would be improper to write about his discoveries till you have received the documents, and given them to some person for publication, I shall not dilate further on that topic.

And now, my dear madam, I beg to tender you my sincere condolence under the heavy bereavement which it has pleased the Almighty to inflict upon you,

And remain yours very sincerely,

JAMES CAMPBELL.

FROM M. CH. FONTAINE, MISSIONARY AT COCHIN CHINA, TO M. CHARLES MOUHOT.

Foreign Missions, Paris, 128, Rue du Bac,
15th August, 1862.

DEAR FRIEND,

Permit me to give you this title; all the sentiments expressed in your letter authorise it. What a worthy brother you weep for! and I, what an honoured friend!

I had the pleasure of knowing M. H. Mouhot. I saw him first at Bangkok, and six or eight months after at Pinhalú, in Cambodia, where he remained with us ten days, sharing with us our house and our table, which is always open to any worthy fellow-countryman whom chance may lead to those parts. In both places all our brotherhood were charmed to make the acquaintance of so devoted a scion of learning, so polished a Frenchman, and so exemplary a Christian. All these qualities rendered him dear to the whole of the missionaries who had the pleasure of his acquaintance; and it was a real happiness to us to render him any little service possible in the performance of the troublesome task which he had imposed upon himself, of exploring countries so wild and destitute of comfort.

On his return from among the Stiêns, where he met MM. Guilloux and Arnoux, this dear friend lavished on me the greatest care, and expended for me all his medical science; for I had then been several months suffering from the malady which afterwards obliged me to return to France to recruit.

He left us to go to Battambong to M. Silvestre, and at the parting we experienced the deepest regret at losing the society of a friend who had so much cheered our solitude. From Battambong he was to return to Siam, and thence to Birmah, Bengal, and Europe. I wrote to him several times, both from Bangkok, from Pinhalú, and from Singapore, where my illness had induced me to go to consult an English physician; but M. Mouhot had changed his plans; he wished to explore Laos, a country whose climate is always so fatal to foreigners. There God saw fit to summon him to a better world. This I read with great sorrow in a Parisian newspaper; it was an extract from a London journal.

When I was abroad I heard of the death of my father, then of that of my mother, and I declare that these two announcements did not make more impression upon me than did the news of the death of a man whose equal I had not met with for twenty years; and the thought of his death, without any help but that of his servants during his illness and in his last moments, was more than enough to bring tears to my eyes as I remembered this good and benevolent friend. Be assured, dear Sir, that my feelings are shared by all the brothers who knew him. The natives themselves must have felt regret at his death; for all who knew him had only praises to repeat of his conduct towards them; and all acknowledged his gentleness and generosity—both qualities invaluable in the eyes of those people.

Permit me, then, dear Sir, to unite my regrets to your grief, and to present my respects to Madame Mouhot, together with my warmest sympathy with her in her affliction; also with your father and your wife. Receive my thanks for your having honoured me with your friendship; and be assured of my desire to be useful to you if ever it should lie in my power.

MARIE CH. FONTAINE,
Missionary at Saigon, Cochin China.

P.S.—Twelve of us are about to set out for Indo-China, and I will not fail to express to Mgr. Miche and his companions the kind feelings which you express with regard to them. On the 20th we shall sail from Marseilles in the *Hydaspe*. Write to the Seminary of Foreign Missions, whence our correspondence will be forwarded to us. My family live at Laval, and you will be always welcome there.

From Mr. Samuel Stevens to M. Charles Mouhot.

Mr. Stevens has the honour to inform M. C. Mouhot that the collection made by his late brother in the mountains of Laos is very fine, particularly the insects and shells. Among the former are a great number of beautiful and new species, one of which, a splendid Carabus, has been described in the 'Zoological Review' at Paris, under the name of Mouhotia gloriosa, in compliment to the late lamented M. Mouhot. This name is very appropriate, as it is one of the most beautiful and remarkable beetles which has been seen for years. There is also a beautiful set of Longicorns, and other insects of the order of Coleoptera, of which a great number are new to science.

The land and fresh-water shells are also very beautiful. Among the former there are twenty-five different genera; eight or ten are quite new, and some of them very remarkable. They will shortly be described by Dr. Pfeiffer and others.

I can truly say that the insects and shells equal, if they do not surpass, the most beautiful collections I have ever received; and clearly demonstrate how rich a country for the naturalist lies between Siam and Cochin China.

There is also a small collection of birds and some monkeys, small animals, reptiles, and serpents in spirits, of which some are quite new.

The collection of insects and shells made in Cambodia was also very beautiful, and contained the large and fine *Helix Cambojiensis*, one of the best and most beautiful specimens known; also, the *Bulimus Cambojiensis*, and a splendid *Buprestida*, new and unique, besides a great number of others, new to science.*

---

* M. Mouhot, in his letters to his family, always spoke with the highest esteem of Mr. Stevens, to whom they now beg to offer their thanks for the honourable manner in which he has conducted everything connected with their unfortunate relative.

FROM M. MALHERBE TO M. CHARLES MOUHOT.

Bangkok, Nov. 1862.

DEAR SIR,

On my return from Java a few days ago, I found waiting for me your kind letter, for which I thank you, although I should have wished to make your acquaintance under happier circumstances. All consolation from me, I know, would be ineffectual. The friendship I felt for your brother was not that of a stranger, but rather as though he were a member of my family; and I felt most painfully the news which met me on my return, of his death so far away: for I had been pleasing myself with the idea of his return, and long before my arrival here had given orders for his reception, and that he should be welcomed as though I were present.

One great consolation to the survivors is the feeling of how much he is regretted; here he had not a single enemy, but every one spoke of him as the best of men. I vainly tried to dissuade him from undertaking this dangerous expedition, for I had already lost a dear friend in that country. He was treacherously assassinated there by his boatmen.

I am much pleased with the frank manner in which you offer me your friendship. I thank you, and accept it with all my heart.

PAPER READ AT THE ROYAL GEOGRAPHICAL SOCIETY,

10TH MARCH, 1862.

LORD ASHBURTON, PRESIDENT.

M. MOUHOT traversed Cambodia from east to west, and also ascended the Mekon river to the frontier of Laos. He returned to the coast by crossing the water-parting between it and the basin of the Menam river, and descending to Bangkok.

The Mekon is a vast melancholy-looking river, three miles broad, covered with islands, and flowing with the rapidity of a torrent. Its shores are covered with aquatic birds, but its waters are almost deserted by canoes.* A plain covered with coarse herbage separates it from the forest by which Cambodia is overspread, and which can rarely be traversed except by cutting a way. That forest is exceedingly unhealthy.

M. Mouhot reached Brelum, a village in lat. 11° 58′, long. 107° 12′, inhabited by a secluded race of wild people, whose customs are minutely described, differing in features from the Cambodian and Laos tribes, and forming one of a series of similar groups widely distributed in the less accessible parts of Cochin China, Cambodia, and Burmah. They are believed by M. Mouhot to be the aborigines of the land. Two Catholic missionaries were resident at Brelum.

Subsequently the author visited the large Buddhist ruins of Ongcor, of which he has brought back numerous sketches. He

---

* The war in Cochin China has prevented many of the Annamite fishermen from coming down the Mekon to fish in the great lake, which is one cause of its desertion.

speaks of the mineral wealth of Cambodia—its iron, gold, lead, and copper. In the islands of Phu-Quoc or Koh Tron, belonging to Cochin China and near to Komput, there are rich mines of coal, similar to our Cannel coal, from which ornaments are made. Several extinct volcanoes exist in Pechaburi, of heights not exceeding 2000 feet above the sea-level, and there are two active ones in an island called Ko-man, lat. 12° 30′, long. 101° 50′, in the Gulf of Siam.

Dr. Hodgkin stated that, besides the two letters, portions of which had been read, and the drawings and charts, M. Mouhot had likewise sent an elaborate description of the ruins which he found at Ongcor and in its vicinity. The plans on the table would give some idea of the magnitude of these ruins. A great part of the manuscript which accompanied them described their structure and workmanship. They were constructed chiefly of granite, and many of the stones were not only of very large size, but were elaborately carved. The workmanship of some of them was described as exquisite, and the designs not so deficient in artistic taste as one might suppose. Many of them represented imaginary animals, such as serpents with many heads; others, beasts of burden—horses, elephants, and bullocks. These temples were situated in a district which was now completely imbedded in a forest very difficult of access, and were so much in ruins that trees were growing on the roofs, and many of the galleries were in a state of great decay. The base and a large portion of the elevation were constructed of a ferruginous rock, but for the upper part blocks of granite were used—so exquisitely cut as to require no mortar to fill the interstices, and carved with relievos relating to mythological subjects indicative of Buddhism. M. Mouhot had copied some of the inscriptions, which from their antiquity the natives who accompanied him were unable to read. The characters so nearly resembled the Siamese that Dr. H. had no doubt that a skilful archæologist would have very little difficulty in deciphering them. He believed that the remains in question would be found equal in value to those which had recently been explored in Central America; and he felt convinced that when the descriptions were published, M. Mouhot would be thought deserving of great respect.

Mr. Crawfurd said it was about forty years since he visited the country, but his recollection of it continued vivid to this day. Most people knew very little about Cambodia; its very name was only familiar to us in that of its product, gamboge, which word was nothing else than a corruption of Cambodia. It was one of five or six states lying between India and China, whose inhabitants had lived under a second or third-rate civilisation at all times—never equal, whether physically, morally, or intellectually, to the Chinese, or even the Hindoos. At the present time Cambodia was a poor little state, having been encroached upon by the Siamese to the north, and by Cochin China to the south. M. Mouhot had given us an account of a country that no European had ever visited before. With respect to that gentleman's belief that certain wild tribes whom he described had descended from Thibet, he (Mr. Crawfurd) believed that his ethnology was at fault. For his part, he believed these wild people to be no other than natives of the country—mere mountaineers, who had escaped from the bondage, and hence from the civilisation, of the plain. Such people existed in Hindoostan, in Siam, in the Burmese empire, in Cochin China, and in China itself—in fact, they were of no distinct origin, but simply the natives in a rude, savage, uncivilised state.

With respect to the French, he did not know on what grounds they had gone to Cambodia. They had obtained possession of one spot which was eminently fitted for a settlement. The finest river in all India, as far as European shipping was concerned, was the river at Saigon, which he had himself ascended about 14 miles, and found it navigable even for an old "seventy-four." He believed it was the intention of the French to attempt the conquest of the whole of Cochin China. If they effected it, and occupied it, they would find it a monstrous difficulty. It would prove another Algeria, with the additional disadvantage of being 15,000 miles off instead of 500, and within the torrid instead of the temperate zone. The climate was very hot, the country was covered with forests, the malaria and the heat rendered it unsuitable for the European constitution. If they made an advance upon the Cochin Chinese capital, they would find the enterprise one of great difficulty. From Saigon to the northern confines of Cochin China the distance is 1500 miles, and the capital itself could not be less than 700 or 800 miles from Saigon, situated on a small river navigable only for large boats, with a narrow mouth, and two considerable fortresses, one on each side, at its mouth. When they arrived, they would find one of the largest and most regular fortifications in the East. He believed it was the most regular, after Fort William in Bengal, and a great deal larger than Fort William. It was constructed by the French, and now they will have considerable difficulty in conquering their own work. The French had a perfect right to be in Cochin China, and their being there would do no harm, but rather good, however questionable the benefit to themselves; for their presence amounted to the substitution of a friendly and civilised power for a rude and inhospitable one.

The drawings on the table were exceedingly curious and interesting; they were admirably done, and exhibited representations of some remarkable monuments, evidently of Buddhist origin. They reminded him very much, though inferior in quality and beauty, of the monuments of the island of Java. He never heard of volcanoes when he was in Cambodia, but he had no doubt M. Mouhot's information was correct, though it appeared he did not describe them from his own personal experience. He would add a word upon the alphabets which were on the table. The Cambodians had invented a written phonetic character, which they used at the present time; therefore there could be no difficulty in understanding a Cambodian manuscript. But there were several of those now exhibited which were of more or less antiquity. One of them seemed to be the alphabet which was used by the Cambodians in their religious rites. The figure of Buddha showed that the Cambodians were worshippers of Buddha.

To M. Charles Mouhot.

Montbéliard,* 13th June, 1862.

The members of the "Société d'Émulation" at Montbéliard desire to express the deep regret which they have experienced at the premature death of their fellow-townsman M. Henri Mouhot. After a three years' journey in Cambodia and Siam, during which he devoted himself to researches which have been highly appreciated by the Geographical and Zoological Societies of London, he fell a victim at the early age of thirty-five to his love of science. His work remained unfinished, but it was gloriously commenced, and his name will not perish. The regret experienced by his friends is the greater from their conviction that had he lived he would have been still more an honour to his native town, and that the name of Mouhot would have ranked side by side with those illustrious ones which have already rendered Montbéliard famous in the department of Natural Science.

---

* Montbéliard is the birthplace of Cuvier and of Laurillard.

THE END.

LONDON: PRINTED BY WILLIAM CLOWES AND SONS, STAMFORD STREET, AND CHARING CROSS.

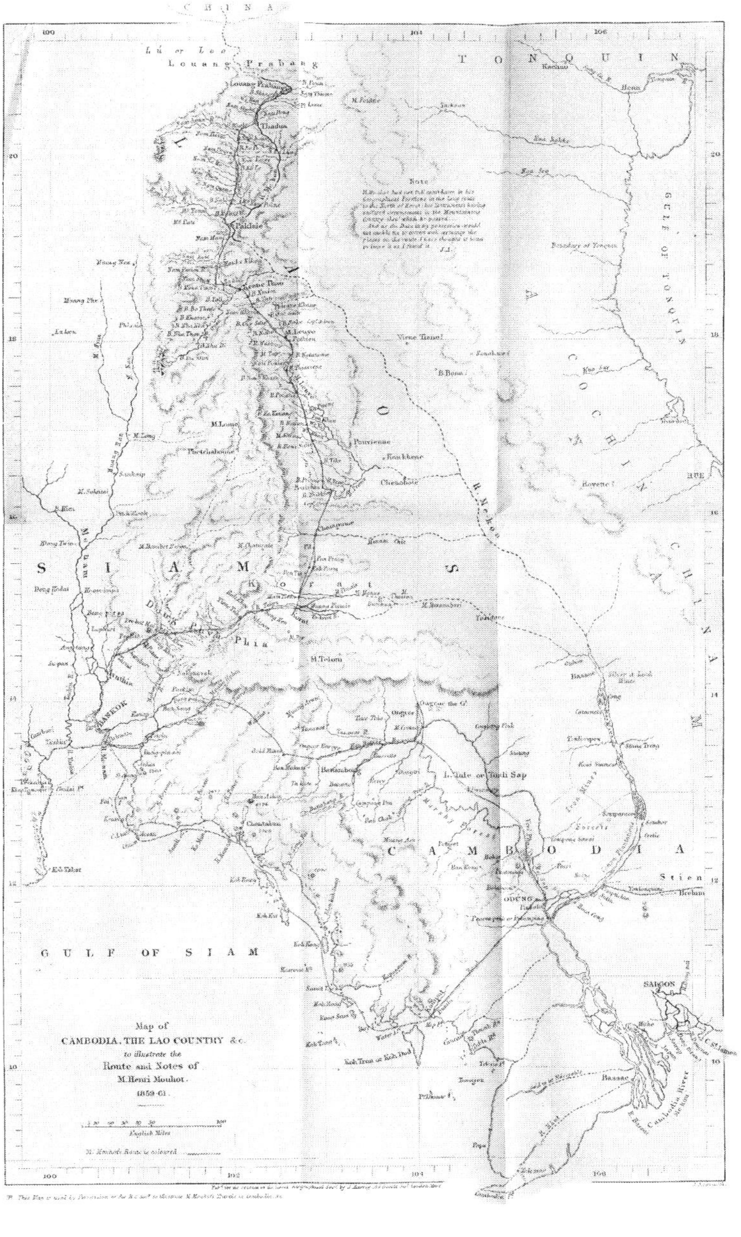

CHINA

TONQUIN

LAOS

SIAM

Korat

CAMBODIA

COCHIN CHINA

ANAM

GULF OF TONQUIN

GULF OF SIAM

BANKOK

SAIGON

Map of
CAMBODIA, THE LAO COUNTRY &c.
to illustrate the
Route and Notes of
M. Henri Mouhot.
1859-61.

English Miles

M. Mouhot's Route is coloured

ALBEMARLE STREET, LONDON.
March, 1863.

MR. MURRAY'S
GENERAL LIST OF WORKS.

ALBERT (THE PRINCE). PRINCIPAL SPEECHES AND ADDRESSES of H.R.H. THE PRINCE CONSORT; with an Introduction giving some Outlines of his Character. *10th Thousand.* Portrait. 8vo. 10*s.* 6*d.*

ABBOTT'S (REV. J.) Philip Musgrave; or, Memoirs of a Church of England Missionary in the North American Colonies. Post 8vo. 2*s.*

ABERCROMBIE'S (JOHN) Enquiries concerning the Intellectual Powers and the Investigation of Truth. *Sixteenth Edition.* Fcap. 8vo. 6*s.* 6*d.*

——— Philosophy of the Moral Feelings. *Twelfth Edition.* Fcap. 8vo. 4*s.*

——— Pathological and Practical Researches on the Diseases of the Stomach, &c. *Third Edition.* Fcap. 8vo. 6*s.*

ACLAND'S (REV. CHARLES) Popular Account of the Manners and Customs of India. Post 8vo. 2*s.*

ADOLPHUS'S (J. L.) Letters from Spain, in 1856 and 1857. Post 8vo. 10*s.* 6*d.*

ÆSOP'S FABLES. A New Translation. With Historical Preface. By Rev. THOMAS JAMES. With 100 Woodcuts, by TENNIEL and WOLF. *38th Thousand.* Post 8vo. 2*s.* 6*d.*

AGRICULTURAL (THE) JOURNAL. Of the Royal Agricultural Society of England. 8vo. *Published half-yearly.*

AIDS TO FAITH: a Series of Essays. By various Writers. Edited by WILLIAM THOMSON, D.D., Lord Archbishop of York. 8vo. 9*s.*

CONTENTS.

Rev. H. L. MANSEL—*On Miracles.*
BISHOP FITZGERALD—*Christian Evidences.*
REV. DR. McCAUL—*On Prophecy.*
Rev. F. C. COOK—*Ideology and Subscription.*
Rev. DR. McCAUL—*Mosaic Record of Creation.*
Rev. GEORGE RAWLINSON—*The Pentateuch.*
ARCHBISHOP THOMSON—*Doctrine of the Atonement.*
Rev. HAROLD BROWNE—*On Inspiration.*
BISHOP ELLICOTT—*Scripture and its Interpretation.*

AMBER-WITCH (THE). The most interesting Trial for Witchcraft ever known. Translated from the German by LADY DUFF GORDON. Post 8vo. 2*s.*

ARTHUR'S (LITTLE) History of England. By LADY CALLCOTT. *120th Thousand.* With 20 Woodcuts. Fcap. 8vo. 2*s.* 6*d.*

ATKINSON'S (MRS.) Recollections of Tartar Steppes and their Inhabitants. With Illustrations. Post 8vo. 12*s.*

AUNT IDA'S Walks and Talks; a Story Book for Children. By a LADY. Woodcuts. 16mo. 5*s.*

AUSTIN'S (JOHN) PROVINCE OF JURISPRUDENCE DETERMINED; or, Philosophy of Positive Law. *Second Edition.* 8vo. 15*s.*

——— Lectures on Jurisprudence. Being a Continuation of the "Province of Jurisprudence Determined." 2 vols. 8vo.

——— (SARAH) Fragments from German Prose Writers. With Biographical Notes. Post 8vo. 10*s.*

ADMIRALTY PUBLICATIONS; Issued by direction of the Lords Commissioners of the Admiralty:—

A MANUAL OF SCIENTIFIC ENQUIRY, for the Use of Travellers. Edited by Sir JOHN F. HERSCHEL, and Rev. ROBERT MAIN. *Third Edition.* Woodcuts. Post 8vo. 9*s.*

AIRY'S ASTRONOMICAL OBSERVATIONS MADE AT GREENWICH. 1836 to 1847. Royal 4to. 50*s.* each.

——— ASTRONOMICAL RESULTS. 1848 to 1858. 4to. 8*s.* each.

——— APPENDICES TO THE ASTRONOMICAL OBSERVATIONS.

1836.—I. Bessel's Refraction Tables.
II. Tables for converting Errors of R.A. and N.P.D. into Errors of Longitude and Ecliptic P.D. } 8*s.*

1837.—I. Logarithms of Sines and Cosines to every Ten Seconds of Time.
II. Table for converting Sidereal into Mean Solar Time. } 8*s.*

1842.—Catalogue of 1439 Stars. 8*s.*
1845.—Longitude of Valentia. 8*s.*
1847.—Twelve Years' Catalogue of Stars. 14*s.*
1851.—Maskelyne's Ledger of Stars. 6*s.*
1852.—I. Description of the Transit Circle. 5*s.*
II. Regulations of the Royal Observatory. 2*s.*
1853.—Bessel's Refraction Tables. 3*s.*
1854.—I. Description of the Zenith Tube. 3*s.*
II. Six Years' Catalogue of Stars. 10*s.*
1856.—Description of the Galvanic Apparatus at Greenwich Observatory. 8s.

——— MAGNETICAL AND METEOROLOGICAL OBSERVATIONS. 1840 to 1847. Royal 4to. 50*s.* each.

——— ASTRONOMICAL, MAGNETICAL, AND METEOROLOGICAL OBSERVATIONS, 1848 to 1860. Royal 4to. 50*s.* each.

——— ASTRONOMICAL RESULTS. 1859. 4to.

——— MAGNETICAL AND METEOROLOGICAL RESULTS. 1848 to 1859. 4to. 8*s.* each.

——— REDUCTION OF THE OBSERVATIONS OF PLANETS. 1750 to 1830. Royal 4to. 50*s.*

——————— LUNAR OBSERVATIONS. 1750 to 1830. 2 Vols. Royal 4to. 50*s.* each.

——————— 1831 to 1851. 4to. 20*s.*

BERNOULLI'S SEXCENTENARY TABLE. *London,* 1779. 4to.

BESSEL'S AUXILIARY TABLES FOR HIS METHOD OF CLEARING LUNAR DISTANCES. 8vo.

——— FUNDAMENTA ASTRONOMIÆ: *Regiomontii,* 1818. Folio. 60*s.*

BIRD'S METHOD OF CONSTRUCTING MURAL QUADRANTS. *London,* 1768. 4to. 2*s.* 6*d.*

——— METHOD OF DIVIDING ASTRONOMICAL INSTRUMENTS. *London,* 1767. 4to. 2*s.* 6*d.*

COOK, KING, AND BAYLY'S ASTRONOMICAL OBSERVATIONS. *London* 1782. 4to. 21*s.*

EIFFE'S ACCOUNT OF IMPROVEMENTS IN CHRONOMETERS. 4to. 2*s.*

ENCKE'S BERLINER JAHRBUCH, for 1830. *Berlin,* 1828. 8vo. 9*s.*

GROOMBRIDGE'S CATALOGUE OF CIRCUMPOLAR STARS. 4to. 10*s.*

HANSEN'S TABLES DE LA LUNE. 4to. 20*s.*

HARRISON'S PRINCIPLES OF HIS TIME-KEEPER. PLATES. 1797. 4to. 5*s.*

HUTTON'S TABLES OF THE PRODUCTS AND POWERS OF NUMBERS. 1781. Folio. 7*s.* 6*d.*

ADMIRALTY PUBLICATIONS—*continued.*

LAX'S TABLES FOR FINDING THE LATITUDE AND LONGITUDE. 1821. 8vo. 10*s.*

LUNAR OBSERVATIONS at GREENWICH. 1783 to 1819. Compared with the Tables, 1821. 4to. 7*s.* 6*d.*

MASKELYNE'S ACCOUNT OF THE GOING OF HARRISON'S WATCH. 1767. 4to. 2*s.* 6*d.*

MAYER'S DISTANCES of the MOON'S CENTRE from the PLANETS. 1822, 3*s.*; 1823, 4*s.* 6*d.* 1824 to 1835, 8vo. 4*s.* each.

——— THEORIA LUNÆ JUXTA SYSTEMA NEWTONIANUM. 4to. 2*s.* 6*d.*

——— TABULÆ MOTUUM SOLIS ET LUNÆ. 1770. 4to. 5*s.*

——— ASTRONOMICAL OBSERVATIONS MADE AT GOTTINGEN, from 1756 to 1761. 1826. Folio. 7*s.* 6*d.*

NAUTICAL ALMANACS, from 1767 to 1866. 8vo. 2*s.* 6*d.* each.

——— SELECTIONS FROM THE ADDITIONS up to 1812. 8vo. 5*s.* 1834-54. 8vo. 5*s.*

——— SUPPLEMENTS, 1828 to 1833, 1837 and 1838. 8vo. 2*s.* each.

——— TABLE requisite to be used with the N.A. 1781. 8vo. 5*s.*

POND'S ASTRONOMICAL OBSERVATIONS. 1811 to 1835. 4to. 21*s.* each.

RAMSDEN'S ENGINE for DIVIDING MATHEMATICAL INSTRUMENTS. 4to. 5*s.*

——— ENGINE for DIVIDING STRAIGHT LINES. 4to. 5*s.*

SABINE'S PENDULUM EXPERIMENTS to DETERMINE THE FIGURE OF THE EARTH. 1825. 4to. 40*s.*

SHEPHERD'S TABLES for CORRECTING LUNAR DISTANCES. 1772. Royal 4to. 21*s.*

——— TABLES, GENERAL, of the MOON'S DISTANCE from the SUN, and 10 STARS. 1787. Folio. 5*s.* 6*d.*

TAYLOR'S SEXAGESIMAL TABLE. 1780. 4to. 15*s.*

——— TABLES OF LOGARITHMS. 4to. 3*l.*

TIARK'S ASTRONOMICAL OBSERVATIONS for the LONGITUDE of MADEIRA. 1822. 4to. 5*s.*

——— CHRONOMETRICAL OBSERVATIONS for DIFFERENCES of LONGITUDE between DOVER, PORTSMOUTH, and FALMOUTH. 1823. 4to. 5*s.*

VENUS and JUPITER: OBSERVATIONS of, compared with the TABLES. *London*, 1822. 4to. 2*s.*

WALES' AND BAYLY'S ASTRONOMICAL OBSERVATIONS. 1777. 4to. 21*s.*

WALES' REDUCTION OF ASTRONOMICAL OBSERVATIONS MADE IN THE SOUTHERN HEMISPHERE. 1764—1771. 1788. 4to. 10*s.* 6*d.*

BABBAGE'S (CHARLES) Economy of Machinery and Manufactures. *Fourth Edition.* Fcap. 8vo. 6*s.*

——— Ninth Bridgewater Treatise. 8vo. 9*s.* 6*d.*

——— Reflections on the Decline of Science in England, and on some of its Causes. 4to. 7*s.* 6*d.*

BAIKIE'S (W. B.) Narrative of an Exploring Voyage up the Rivers Quorra and Tshadda in 1854. Map. 8vo. 16*s.*

BANKES' (GEORGE) STORY OF CORFE CASTLE, with documents relating to the Time of the Civil Wars, &c. Woodcuts. Post 8vo. 10*s.* 6*d.*

BARROW'S (Sir John) Autobiographical Memoir, including Reflections, Observations, and Reminiscences at Home and Abroad. From Early Life to Advanced Age. Portrait. 8vo. 16*s.*

——— Voyages of Discovery and Research within the Arctic Regions, from 1818 to the present time. Abridged and arranged from the Official Narratives. 8vo. 15*s.*

——— (Sir George) Ceylon; Past and Present. Map. Post 8vo. 6*s.* 6*d.*

——— (John) Naval Worthies of Queen Elizabeth's Reign, their Gallant Deeds, Daring Adventures, and Services in the infant state of the British Navy. 8vo. 14*s.*

——— Life and Voyages of Sir Francis Drake. With numerous Original Letters. Post 8vo. 2*s.*

BASSOMPIERRE'S Memoirs of his Embassy to the Court of England in 1626. Translated with Notes. 8vo. 9*s.* 6*d.*

BASTIAT'S (Frederic) Harmonies of Political Economy. Translated, with a Notice of his Life and Writings, by P. J. Stirling. 8vo. 7*s.* 6*d.*

BATES' (H. W.) Naturalist on the Amazons; Adventures during eleven years of Travel. With Social Sketches, Native Life, Habits of Animals, and Features of Nature in the Tropics. Illustrations. 2 Vols. Post 8vo.

BEES AND FLOWERS. Two Essays. By Rev. Thomas James. Reprinted from the "Quarterly Review." Fcap. 8vo. 1*s.* each.

BELL'S (Sir Charles) Mechanism and Vital Endowments of the Hand as evincing Design. *Sixth Edition.* Woodcuts. Post 8vo. 6*s.*

BENEDICT'S (Jules) Sketch of the Life and Works of Felix Mendelssohn-Bartholdy. *Second Edition.* 8vo. 2*s.* 6*d.*

BERTHA'S Journal during a Visit to her Uncle in England. Containing a Variety of Interesting and Instructive Information. *Seventh Edition.* Woodcuts. 12mo.

BIRCH'S (Samuel) History of Ancient Pottery and Porcelain: Egyptian, Assyrian, Greek, Roman, and Etruscan. With 200 Illustrations. 2 Vols. Medium 8vo. 42*s.*

BLUNT'S (Rev. J. J.) Principles for the proper understanding of the Mosaic Writings, stated and applied, together with an Incidental Argument for the truth of the Resurrection of our Lord. Being the Hulsean Lectures for 1832. Post 8vo. 6*s.* 6*d.*

——— Undesigned Coincidences in the Writings of the Old and New Testament, an Argument of their Veracity: containing the Books of Moses, Historical and Prophetical Scriptures, and the Gospels and Acts. *8th Edition.* Post 8vo. 6*s.*

——— History of the Church in the First Three Centuries. *Third Edition.* Post 8vo. 7*s.* 6*d.*

——— Parish Priest; His Duties, Acquirements and Obligations. *Third Edition.* Post 8vo. 7*s.* 6*d.*

——— Lectures on the Right Use of the Early Fathers. *Second Edition.* 8vo. 15*s.*

——— Plain Sermons Preached to a Country Congregation. *Second Edition.* 3 Vols. Post 8vo. 7*s.* 6*d.* each.

——— Literary and Clerical Essays, reprinted from the Quarterly Review. 8vo. 12*s.*

BLACKSTONE'S COMMENTARIES on the Laws of England. Adapted to the present state of the law. By R. MALCOLM KERR, LL.D. *Third Edition*, corrected to 1861. 4 Vols. 8vo. 63*s*.

——— For STUDENTS. Being those Portions which relate to the BRITISH CONSTITUTION and the RIGHTS OF PERSONS. Post 8vo. 9*s*.

BLAKISTON'S (CAPT.) Five Months on the Yang-Tsze, with a Narrative of the Expedition sent to explore its Upper Waters. Maps and 24 Illustrations. 8vo. 18*s*.

BLOMFIELD'S (REV. A.) Memoir of the late Bishop Blomfield, D.D., with Selections from his Correspondence. Portrait, 2 Vols. post 8vo.

BOOK OF COMMON PRAYER. Illustrated with Borders, Initials, Letters, and Woodcuts. A new and carefully printed edition. 8vo.

BORROW'S (GEORGE) Bible in Spain; or the Journeys, Adventures, and Imprisonments of an Englishman in an Attempt to circulate the Scriptures in the Peninsula. 3 Vols. Post 8vo. 27*s*.; or *Popular Edition*, 16mo, 3*s*. 6*d*.

——— Zincali, or the Gipsies of Spain; their Manners, Customs, Religion, and Language. 2 Vols. Post 8vo. 18*s*.; or *Popular Edition*, 16mo, 3*s*. 6*d*.

——— Lavengro; The Scholar—The Gipsy—and the Priest. Portrait. 3 Vols. Post 8vo. 30*s*.

——— Romany Rye; a Sequel to Lavengro. *Second Edition*. 2 Vols. Post 8vo. 21*s*.

——— Wild Wales: its People, Language, and Scenery. 3 Vols. Post 8vo. 30*s*.

BOSWELL'S (JAMES) Life of Samuel Johnson, LL.D. Including the Tour to the Hebrides. Edited by Mr. CROKER. Portraits. Royal 8vo. 10*s*.

BRAY'S (MRS.) Life of Thomas Stothard, R.A. With Personal Reminiscences. Illustrated with Portrait and 60 Woodcuts of his chief works. 4to.

BREWSTER'S (SIR DAVID) Martyrs of Science, or the Lives of Galileo, Tycho Brahe, and Kepler. *Fourth Edition*. Fcap. 8vo. 4*s*. 6*d*.

——— More Worlds than One. The Creed of the Philosopher and the Hope of the Christian. *Eighth Edition*. Post 8vo. 6*s*.

——— Stereoscope: its History, Theory, Construction, and Application to the Arts and to Education. Woodcuts. 12mo. 5*s*. 6*d*.

——— Kaleidoscope: its History, Theory, and Construction, with its application to the Fine and Useful Arts. *Second Edition*. Woodcuts. Post 8vo. 5*s*. 6*d*.

BRINE'S (L.) Narrative of the Rise and Progress of the Taeping Rebellion in China. Maps and Plans. Post 8vo. 10*s*. 6*d*.

BRITISH ASSOCIATION REPORTS. 8vo. York and Oxford, 1831-32, 13*s*. 6*d*. Cambridge, 1833, 12*s*. Edinburgh, 1834, 15*s*. Dublin, 1835, 13*s*. 6*d*. Bristol, 1836, 12*s*. Liverpool, 1837, 16*s*. 6*d*. Newcastle, 1838, 15*s*. Birmingham, 1839, 13*s*. 6*d*. Glasgow, 1840, 15*s*. Plymouth, 1841, 13*s*. 6*d*. Manchester, 1842, 10*s*. 6*d*. Cork, 1843, 12*s*. York, 1844, 20*s*. Cambridge, 1845, 12*s*. Southampton, 1846, 15*s*. Oxford, 1847, 18*s*. Swansea, 1848, 9*s*. Birmingham, 1849, 10*s*. Edinburgh, 1850, 15*s*. Ipswich, 1851, 16*s*. 6*d*. Belfast, 1852, 15*s*. Hull, 1853, 10*s*. 6*d*. Liverpool, 1854, 18*s*. Glasgow, 1855, 15*s*.; Cheltenham, 1856, 18*s*.; Dublin, 1857, 15*s*.; Leeds, 1858, 20*s*. Aberdeen, 1859, 15*s*. Oxford, 1860. Manchester, 1861. 15*s*.

BRITISH CLASSICS. A New Series of Standard English Authors, printed from the most correct text, and edited with elucidatory notes. Published occasionally in demy 8vo. Volumes, varying in price.

Already Published.

GOLDSMITH'S WORKS. Edited by PETER CUNNINGHAM, F.S.A. Vignettes. 4 Vols. 30*s.*

GIBBON'S DECLINE AND FALL OF THE ROMAN EMPIRE. Edited by WILLIAM SMITH, LL.D. Portrait and Maps. 8 Vols. 60*s.*

JOHNSON'S LIVES OF THE ENGLISH POETS. Edited by PETER CUNNINGHAM, F.S.A. 3 Vols. 22*s.* 6*d.*

BYRON'S POETICAL WORKS. Edited, with Notes. 6 vols. 45*s.*

In Preparation.

WORKS OF POPE. With Life, Introductions, and Notes, by REV. WHITWELL ELWIN. Portrait.

HUME'S HISTORY OF ENGLAND. Edited, with Notes.

LIFE AND WORKS OF SWIFT. Edited by JOHN FORSTER.

BROUGHAM'S (LORD) Address at the Social Science Association, Dublin. August, 1861. Revised, with Notes. 8vo. 1*s.*

BROUGHTON'S (LORD) Journey through Albania and other Provinces of Turkey in Europe and Asia, to Constantinople, 1809—10. *Third Edition.* Maps and Woodcuts. 2 Vols. 8vo. 30*s.*

——— Visits to Italy. *Third Edition.* 2 vols. Post 8vo. 18*s.*

BUBBLES FROM THE BRUNNEN OF NASSAU. By an Old MAN. *Sixth Edition.* 16mo. 5*s.*

BUNBURY'S (C. J. F.) Journal of a Residence at the Cape of Good Hope; with Excursions into the Interior, and Notes on the Natural History and Native Tribes of the Country. Woodcuts. Post 8vo. 9*s.*

BUNYAN (JOHN) and Oliver Cromwell. Select Biographies. By ROBERT SOUTHEY. Post 8vo. 2*s.*

BUONAPARTE'S (NAPOLEON) Confidential Correspondence with his Brother Joseph, sometime King of Spain. *Second Edition.* 2 vols. 8vo. 26*s.*

BURGHERSH'S (LORD) Memoir of the Operations of the Allied Armies under Prince Schwarzenberg and Marshal Blucher during the latter end of 1813—14. 8vo. 21*s.*

——— Early Campaigns of the Duke of Wellington in Portugal and Spain. 8vo. 8*s.* 6*d.*

BURGON'S (Rev. J. W.) Memoir of Patrick Fraser Tytler. *Second Edition.* Post 8vo. 9*s.*

——— Letters from Rome, written to Friends at Home. Illustrations. Post 8vo. 12*s.*

BURN'S (LIEUT.-COL.) French and English Dictionary of Naval and Military Technical Terms. *Fourth Edition.* Crown 8vo. 15*s.*

BURNS' (ROBERT) Life. By JOHN GIBSON LOCKHART. Fifth *Edition.* Fcap. 8vo. 3*s.*

BURR'S (G. D.) Instructions in Practical Surveying, Topographical Plan Drawing, and on sketching ground without Instruments. *Third Edition.* Woodcuts. Post 8vo. 7*s.* 6*d.*

BUTTMAN'S LEXILOGUS; a Critical Examination of the Meaning of numerous Greek Words, chiefly in Homer and Hesiod. Translated by Rev. J. R. FISHLAKE. *Fifth Edition.* 8vo. 12*s.*

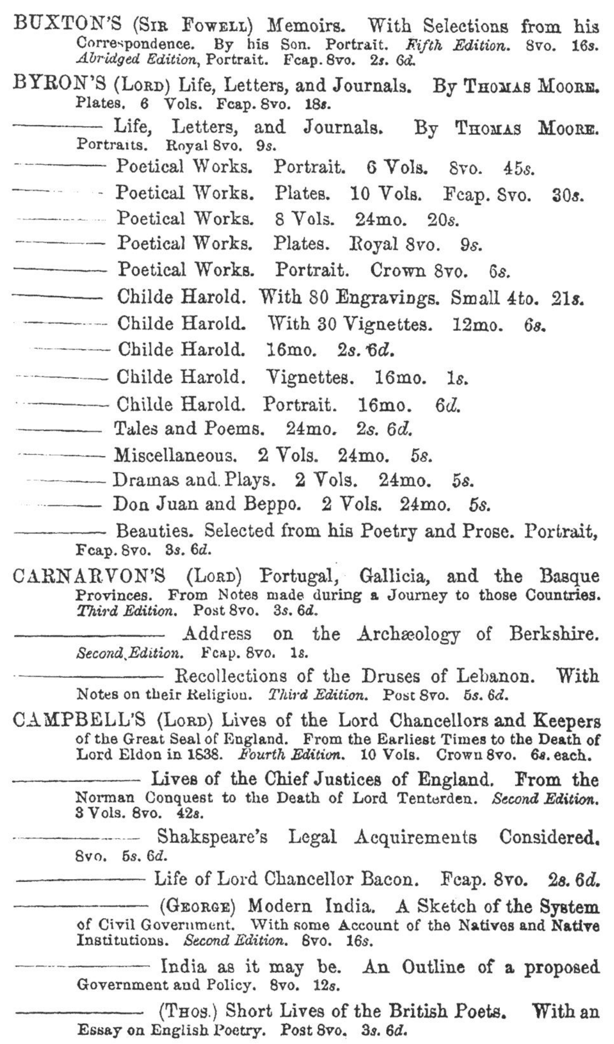

BUXTON'S (Sir Fowell) Memoirs. With Selections from his Correspondence. By his Son. Portrait. *Fifth Edition.* 8vo. 16s. *Abridged Edition*, Portrait. Fcap. 8vo. 2s. 6d.

BYRON'S (Lord) Life, Letters, and Journals. By Thomas Moore. Plates. 6 Vols. Fcap. 8vo. 18s.

——— Life, Letters, and Journals. By Thomas Moore. Portraits. Royal 8vo. 9s.

——— Poetical Works. Portrait. 6 Vols. 8vo. 45s.

——— Poetical Works. Plates. 10 Vols. Fcap. 8vo. 30s.

——— Poetical Works. 8 Vols. 24mo. 20s.

——— Poetical Works. Plates. Royal 8vo. 9s.

——— Poetical Works. Portrait. Crown 8vo. 6s.

——— Childe Harold. With 80 Engravings. Small 4to. 21s.

——— Childe Harold. With 30 Vignettes. 12mo. 6s.

——— Childe Harold. 16mo. 2s. 6d.

——— Childe Harold. Vignettes. 16mo. 1s.

——— Childe Harold. Portrait. 16mo. 6d.

——— Tales and Poems. 24mo. 2s. 6d.

——— Miscellaneous. 2 Vols. 24mo. 5s.

——— Dramas and Plays. 2 Vols. 24mo. 5s.

——— Don Juan and Beppo. 2 Vols. 24mo. 5s.

——— Beauties. Selected from his Poetry and Prose. Portrait, Fcap. 8vo. 3s. 6d.

CARNARVON'S (Lord) Portugal, Gallicia, and the Basque Provinces. From Notes made during a Journey to those Countries. *Third Edition.* Post 8vo. 3s. 6d.

——— Address on the Archæology of Berkshire. *Second Edition.* Fcap. 8vo. 1s.

——— Recollections of the Druses of Lebanon. With Notes on their Religion. *Third Edition.* Post 8vo. 5s. 6d.

CAMPBELL'S (Lord) Lives of the Lord Chancellors and Keepers of the Great Seal of England. From the Earliest Times to the Death of Lord Eldon in 1838. *Fourth Edition.* 10 Vols. Crown 8vo. 6s. each.

——— Lives of the Chief Justices of England. From the Norman Conquest to the Death of Lord Tenterden. *Second Edition.* 3 Vols. 8vo. 42s.

——— Shakspeare's Legal Acquirements Considered. 8vo. 5s. 6d.

——— Life of Lord Chancellor Bacon. Fcap. 8vo. 2s. 6d.

——— (George) Modern India. A Sketch of the System of Civil Government. With some Account of the Natives and Native Institutions. *Second Edition.* 8vo. 16s.

——— India as it may be. An Outline of a proposed Government and Policy. 8vo. 12s.

——— (Thos.) Short Lives of the British Poets. With an Essay on English Poetry. Post 8vo. 3s. 6d.

CALVIN'S (JOHN) Life. With Extracts from his Correspondence. By THOMAS H. DYER. Portrait. 8vo. 15*s.*

CALLCOTT'S (LADY) Little Arthur's History of England. 130*th Thousand.* With 20 Woodcuts. Fcap. 8vo. 2*s.* 6*d.*

CARMICHAEL'S (A. N.) Greek Verbs. Their Formations, Irregularities, and Defects. *Second Edition.* Post 8vo. 8*s.* 6*d.*

CASTLEREAGH (THE) DESPATCHES, from the commencement of the official career of the late Viscount Castlereagh to the close of his life. Edited by the MARQUIS OF LONDONDERRY. 12 Vols. 8vo. 14*s.* each.

CATHCART'S (SIR GEORGE) Commentaries on the War in Russia and Germany, 1812-13. Plans. 8vo. 14*s.*

——— Military Operations in Kaffraria, which led to the Termination of the Kaffir War. *Second Edition.* 8vo. 12*s.*

CAVALCASELLE (G. B.). Notices of the Early Flemish Painters; Their Lives and Works. Woodcuts. Post 8vo. 12*s.*

CHAMBERS' (G. F.) Handbook of Descriptive and Practical Astronomy. Illustrations. Post 8vo. 12*s.*

CHANTREY (SIR FRANCIS). Winged Words on Chantrey's Woodcocks. Edited by JAS. P. MUIRHEAD. Etchings. Square 8vo. 10*s.* 6*d.*

CHARMED ROE (THE); or, The Story of the Little Brother and Sister. By OTTO SPECKTER. Plates. 16mo. 5*s.*

CHURTON'S (ARCHDEACON) Gongora. An Historical Essay on the Age of Philip III. and IV. of Spain. With Translations. Portrait. 2 Vols. Small 8vo. 15*s.*

CLAUSEWITZ'S (CARL VON) Campaign of 1812, in Russia. Translated from the German by LORD ELLESMERE. Map. 8vo. 10*s.* 6*d.*

CLIVE'S (LORD) Life. By REV. G. R. GLEIG, M.A. Post 8vo. 3*s.* 6*d.*

COBBOLD'S (REV. R. H.) Pictures of the Chinese drawn by themselves. With 24 Plates. Crown 8vo. 9*s.*

COLCHESTER (THE) PAPERS. The Diary and Correspondence of Charles Abbott, Lord Colchester, Speaker of the House of Commons, 1802-1817. Edited by HIS SON. Portrait. 3 Vols. 8vo. 42*s.*

COLERIDGE'S (SAMUEL TAYLOR) Table-Talk. *Fourth Edition.* Portrait. Fcap. 8vo. 6*s.*

——— (HENRY NELSON) Introductions to the Greek Classic Poets. *Third Edition.* Fcap. 8vo. 5*s.* 6*d.*

——— (SIR JOHN) on Public School Education, with especial reference to Eton. *Third Edition.* Fcap. 8vo. 2*s.*

COLONIAL LIBRARY. [See Home and Colonial Library.]

COOKERY (MODERN DOMESTIC). Founded on Principles of Economy and Practical Knowledge, and adapted for Private Families. By a Lady *New Edition.* Woodcuts. Fcap. 8vo. 5*s.*

CORNWALLIS (THE). Papers and Correspondence during the American War,—Administrations in India,—Union with Ireland, and Peace of Amiens. Edited by CHARLES ROSS. *Second Edition.* 3 Vols. 8vo. 63*s.*

CRABBE'S (REV. GEORGE) Life, Letters, and Journals. By his SON. Portrait. Fcap. 8vo. 3*s.*

——— Poetical Works. With his Life. Plates. 8 Vols. Fcap. 8vo. 24*s.*

——— Life and Poetical Works. Plates. Royal 8vo. 7*s.*

CROKER'S (J. W.) Progressive Geography for Children. *Fifth Edition.* 18mo. 1*s.* 6*d.*

——— Stories for Children, Selected from the History of England. *Fifteenth Edition.* Woodcuts. 16mo. 2*s.* 6*d.*

——— Boswell's Life of Johnson. Including the Tour to the Hebrides. Portraits. Royal 8vo. 10*s.*

——— LORD HERVEY'S Memoirs of the Reign of George the Second, from his Accession to the death of Queen Caroline. Edited with Notes. *Second Edition.* Portrait. 2 Vols. 8vo. 21*s.*

——— Essays on the Early Period of the French Revolution. 8vo. 15*s.*

——— Historical Essay on the Guillotine. Fcap. 8vo. 1*s.*

CROMWELL (OLIVER) and John Bunyan. By ROBERT SOUTHEY. Post 8vo. 2*s.*

CROWE'S (J. A.) Notices of the Early Flemish Painters; their Lives and Works. Woodcuts. Post 8vo. 12*s.*

CUNNINGHAM'S (ALLAN) Life of Sir David Wilkie. With his Journals and Critical Remarks on Works of Art. Portrait. 3 Vols. 8vo. 42*s.*

——— Poems and Songs. Now first collected and arranged, with Biographical Notice. 24mo. 2*s.* 6*d.*

——— (CAPT. J. D.) History of the Sikhs. From the Origin of the Nation to the Battle of the Sutlej. *Second Edition.* Maps. 8vo. 15*s.*

CURETON (REV. W.) Remains of a very Ancient Recension of the Four Gospels in Syriac, hitherto unknown in Europe. Discovered, Edited, and Translated. 4to. 24*s.*

CURTIUS' (PROFESSOR) Student's Greek Grammar, for the use of Colleges and the Upper Forms. Translated from the German. Edited by DR. WM. SMITH. Post 8vo.

——— Smaller Greek Grammar, abridged from the above, 12mo.

CURZON'S (HON. ROBERT) Visits to the Monasteries of the Levant. *Fourth Edition.* Woodcuts. Post 8vo. 15*s.*

——— ARMENIA AND ERZEROUM. A Year on the Frontiers of Russia, Turkey, and Persia. *Third Edition.* Woodcuts. Post 8vo. 7*s.* 6*d.*

CUST'S (GENERAL) Annals of the Wars of the Nineteenth Century —1800–15. 4 Vols. Fcap. 8vo. 5*s.* each.

——— Annals of the Wars of the Eighteenth Century. 5 Vols. Fcap. 8vo. 5*s.* each.

DARWIN'S (CHARLES) Journal of Researches into the Natura History and Geology of the Countries visited during a Voyage round the World. *Tenth Thousand.* Post 8vo. 9*s.*

——— Origin of Species by Means of Natural Selection; or, the Preservation of Favoured Races in the Struggle for Life. *Seventh Thousand.* Post 8vo. 14*s.*

——— Various Contrivances by which Orchids are Fertilised through Insect Agency, and as to the good of Intercrossing. Woodcuts. Post 8vo. 9*s.*

DAVIS' (NATHAN) Ruined Cities within Numidian and Carthaginian Territories. Map and Illustrations. 8vo. 16*s.*

DAVY'S (SIR HUMPHRY) Consolations in Travel; or, Last Days of a Philosopher. *Fifth Edition.* Woodcuts. Fcap. 8vo. 6*s.*

——— Salmonia; or, Days of Fly Fishing. With some Account of the Habits of Fishes belonging to the genus Salmo. *Fourth Edition.* Woodcuts. Fcap. 8vo. 6*s.*

DELEPIERRE'S (OCTAVE) History of Flemish Literature and its celebrated Authors. From the Twelfth Century to the present Day. 8vo. 9s.

DENNIS' (GEORGE) Cities and Cemeteries of Etruria. Plates. 2 Vols. 8vo. 42s.

DIXON'S (HEPWORTH) Story of the Life of Lord Bacon. Portrait. Fcap. 8vo. 7s. 6d.

DOG-BREAKING; the Most Expeditious, Certain, and Easy Method, whether great excellence or only mediocrity be required. By LIEUT.-COL. HUTCHINSON. *Third Edition.* Woodcuts. Post 8vo. 9s.

DOMESTIC MODERN COOKERY. Founded on Principles of Economy and Practical Knowledge, and adapted for Private Families. *New Edition.* Woodcuts. Fcap. 8vo. 5s.

DOUGLAS'S (GENERAL SIR HOWARD) Treatise on the Theory and Practice of Gunnery. *Fifth Edition.* Plates. 8vo. 21s.

——— Treatise on Military Bridges, and the Passages of Rivers in Military Operations. *Third Edition.* Plates. 8vo. 21s.

——— Naval Warfare with Steam. *Second Edition.* 8vo. 8s. 6d.

——— Modern Systems of Fortification, with special reference to the Naval, Littoral, and Internal Defence of England. Plans. 8vo. 12s.

——— Life and Adventures; from Notes, Conversations, and Correspondence. By S. W. FULLOM. Portrait. 8vo. 15s.

DRAKE'S (SIR FRANCIS) Life, Voyages, and Exploits, by Sea and Land. By JOHN BARROW. *Third Edition.* Post 8vo. 2s.

DRINKWATER'S (JOHN) History of the Siege of Gibraltar, 1779-1783. With a Description and Account of that Garrison from the Earliest Periods. Post 8vo. 2s.

DU CHAILLU'S (PAUL B.) EQUATORIAL AFRICA, with Accounts of the Manners and Customs of the People, and of the Chase of the Gorilla, the Nest-building Ape, Chimpanzee, Crocodile, &c. *Tenth Thousand.* Illustrations. 8vo. 21s.

DUDLEY'S (EARL OF) Letters to the late Bishop of Llandaff. *Second Edition.* Portrait. 8vo. 10s. 6d.

DUFFERIN'S (LORD) Letters from High Latitudes, being some Account of a Yacht Voyage to Iceland, &c., in 1856. *Fourth Edition.* Woodcuts. Post 8vo. 9s.

DURHAM'S (ADMIRAL SIR PHILIP) Naval Life and Services. By CAPT. ALEXANDER MURRAY. 8vo. 5s. 6d.

DYER'S (THOMAS H.) Life and Letters of John Calvin. Compiled from authentic Sources. Portrait. 8vo. 15s.

——— History of Modern Europe, from the taking of Constantinople by the Turks to the close of the War in the Crimea. Vols. 1 & 2. 8vo. 30s.

EASTLAKE'S (SIR CHARLES) Italian Schools of Painting. From the German of KUGLER. Edited, with Notes. *Third Edition.* Illustrated from the Old Masters. 2 Vols. Post 8vo. 30s.

EASTWICK'S (E. B.) Handbook for Bombay and Madras, with Directions for Travellers, Officers, &c. Map. 2 Vols. Post 8vo. 24s.

EDWARDS' (W. H.) Voyage up the River Amazon, including a Visit to Para. Post 8vo. 2s.

EGERTON'S (HON. CAPT. FRANCIS) Journal of a Winter's Tour in India; with a Visit to Nepaul. Woodcuts. 2 Vols. Post 8vo. 18s.

ELDON'S (Lord) Public and Private Life, with Selections from his Correspondence and Diaries. By Horace Twiss. *Third Edition.* Portrait. 2 Vols. Post 8vo. 21*s.*

ELIOT'S (Hon. W. G. C.) Khans of the Crimea. Being a Narrative of an Embassy from Frederick the Great to the Court of Krim Gerai. Translated from the German. Post 8vo. 6*s.*

ELLIS (Rev. W.) Visits to Madagascar, including a Journey to the Capital, with notices of Natural History, and Present Civilisation of the People. *Fifth Thousand.* Map and Woodcuts. 8vo. 16*s.*

——— (Mrs.) Education of Character, with Hints on Moral Training. Post 8vo. 7*s.* 6*d.*

ELLESMERE'S (Lord) Two Sieges of Vienna by the Turks. Translated from the German. Post 8vo. 2*s.*

——— Second Campaign of Radetzky in Piedmont. The Defence of Temeswar and the Camp of the Ban. From the German. Post 8vo. 6*s.* 6*d.*

——— Campaign of 1812 in Russia, from the German of General Carl Von Clausewitz. Map. 8vo. 10*s.* 6*d.*

——— Pilgrimage, and other Poems. Crown 4to. 24*s.*

——— Essays on History, Biography, Geography, and Engineering. 8vo. 12*s.*

ELPHINSTONE'S (Hon. Mountstuart) History of India—the Hindoo and Mahomedan Periods. *Fourth Edition.* Map. 8vo. 18*s.*

ENGLAND (History of) from the Peace of Utrecht to the Peace of Versailles, 1713–83. By Lord Mahon. *Library Edition,* 7 Vols. 8vo. 93*s.*; or *Popular Edition,* 7 Vols. Post 8vo. 35*s.*

——— From the First Invasion by the Romans, down to the 14th year of Queen Victoria's Reign. By Mrs. Markham. 118*th Edition.* Woodcuts. 12mo. 6*s.*

——— Social, Political, and Industrial, in the 19th Century. By W. Johnston. 2 Vols. Post 8vo. 18*s.*

ENGLISHWOMAN IN AMERICA. Post 8vo. 10*s.* 6*d.*

——— RUSSIA. Woodcuts. Post 8vo. 10*s.* 6*d.*

EOTHEN; or, Traces of Travel brought Home from the East. *A New Edition.* Post 8vo. 7*s.* 6*d.*

ERSKINE'S (Admiral) Journal of a Cruise among the Islands of the Western Pacific, including the Fejees, and others inhabited by the Polynesian Negro Races. Plates. 8vo. 16*s.*

ESKIMAUX and English Vocabulary, for Travellers in the Arctic Regions. 16mo. 3*s.* 6*d.*

ESSAYS FROM "THE TIMES." Being a Selection from the Literary Papers which have appeared in that Journal. *Seventh Thousand.* 2 vols. Fcap. 8vo. 8*s.*

EXETER'S (Bishop of) Letters to the late Charles Butler, on the Theological parts of his Book of the Roman Catholic Church; with Remarks on certain Works of Dr. Milner and Dr. Lingard, and on some parts of the Evidence of Dr. Doyle. *Second Edition.* 8vo. 16*s.*

FAIRY RING; A Collection of Tales and Stories. From the German. By J. E. Taylor. Illustrated by Richard Doyle. *Second Edition.* Fcap. 8vo.

FALKNER'S (Fred.) Muck Manual for the Use of Farmers. A Treatise on the Nature and Value of Manures. *Second Edition.* Fcap. 8vo. 5*s.*

FAMILY RECEIPT-BOOK. A Collection of a Thousand Valuable and Useful Receipts. Fcap. 8vo. 5*s.* 6*d.*

FANCOURT'S (Col.) History of Yucatan, from its Discovery to the Close of the 17th Century. With Map. 8vo. 10*s.* 6*d.*

FARRAR'S (Rev. A. S.) Science in Theology. Sermons Preached before the University of Oxford. 8vo. 9*s.*

——— Critical History of Free Thought in reference to the Christian Religion. Being the Bampton Lectures, 1862. 8vo. 16*s.*

——— (F. W.) Origin of Language, based on Modern Researches. Fcap. 8vo. 5*s.*

FEATHERSTONHAUGH'S (G. W.) Tour through the Slave States of North America, from the River Potomac to Texas and the Frontiers of Mexico. Plates. 2 Vols. 8vo. 26*s.*

FELLOWS' (Sir Charles) Travels and Researches in Asia Minor, more particularly in the Province of Lycia. *New Edition.* Plates. Post 8vo. 9*s.*

FERGUSSON'S (James) Palaces of Nineveh and Persepolis Restored: an Essay on Ancient Assyrian and Persian Architecture. Woodcuts. 8vo. 16*s.*

——— Handbook of Architecture. Being a Concise and Popular Account of the Different Styles prevailing in all Ages and Countries in the World. With a Description of the most remarkable Buildings. With 850 Illustrations. 8vo. 26*s.*

——— History of the Modern Styles of Architecture, completing the above work. With 312 Illustrations. 8vo. 31*s.* 6*d.*

FERRIER'S (T. P.) Caravan Journeys in Persia, Afghanistan, Herat, Turkistan, and Beloochistan, with Descriptions of Meshed, Balk, and Candahar, &c. *Second Edition.* Map. 8vo. 21*s.*

——— History of the Afghans. Map. 8vo. 21*s.*

FISHER'S (Rev. George) Elements of Geometry, for the Use of Schools. *Fifth Edition.* 18mo. 1*s.* 6*d.*

——— First Principles of Algebra, for the Use of Schools. *Fifth Edition.* 18mo. 1*s.* 6*d.*

FLOWER GARDEN (The). An Essay. By Rev. Thos. James. Reprinted from the "Quarterly Review." Fcap. 8vo. 1*s.*

FORBES' (C. S.) Iceland; its Volcanoes, Geysers, and Glaciers. Illustrations. Post 8vo. 14*s.*

FORD'S (Richard) Handbook for Spain, Andalusia, Ronda, Valencia, Catalonia, Granada, Gallicia, Arragon, Navarre, &c. *Third Edition.* 2 Vols. Post 8vo. 30*s.*

——— Gatherings from Spain. Post 8vo. 3*s.* 6*d.*

FORSTER'S (John) Arrest of the Five Members by Charles the First. A Chapter of English History re-written. Post 8vo. 12*s.*

——— Debates on the Grand Remonstrance, 1641. With an Introductory Essay on English freedom under the Plantagenet and Tudor Sovereigns. *Second Edition.* Post 8vo. 12*s.*

——— Oliver Cromwell, Daniel De Foe, Sir Richard Steele, Charles Churchill, Samuel Foote. Biographical Essays. *Third Edition.* Post 8vo. 12*s.*

FORSYTH'S (William) Hortensius, or the Advocate: an Historical Essay on the Office and Duties of an Advocate. Post 8vo. 12*s.*

——— History of Napoleon at St. Helena. From the Letters and Journals of Sir Hudson Lowe. Portrait and Maps. 3 Vols. 8vo. 45*s.*

FORTUNE'S (ROBERT) Narrative of Two Visits to the Tea Countries of China, between the years 1843-52, with full Descriptions of the Tea Plant. *Third Edition.* Woodcuts. 2 Vols. Post 8vo. 18*s.*

——— Chinese, Inland, on the Coast, and at Sea. A Narrative of a Third Visit in 1853-56. Woodcuts. 8vo. 16*s.*

——— Yedo and Peking, with Notices of Natural Productions, Agriculture, Horticulture, and Trade of those Countries, and other Things met with by the Way. Illustrations. 8vo.

FRANCE (HISTORY OF). From the Conquest by the Gauls to the Death of Louis Philippe. By Mrs. MARKHAM. 56*th Thousand.* Woodcuts. 12mo. 6*s.*

FRENCH (THE) in Algiers; The Soldier of the Foreign Legion—and the Prisoners of Abd-el-Kadir. Translated by Lady DUFF GORDON. Post 8vo. 2*s.*

GALTON'S (FRANCIS) Art of Travel; or, Hints on the Shifts and Contrivances available in Wild Countries. *Third Edition.* Woodcuts. Post 8vo. 7*s.* 6*d.*

GEOGRAPHICAL (THE) Journal. Published by the Royal Geographical Society of London. 8vo.

GERMANY (HISTORY OF). From the Invasion by Marius, to the present time. By Mrs. MARKHAM. *Fifteenth Thousand.* Woodcuts. 12mo. 6*s.*

GIBBON'S (EDWARD) History of the Decline and Fall of the Roman Empire. *A New Edition.* Preceded by his Autobiography. Edited, with Notes, by Dr. WM. SMITH. Maps. 8 Vols. 8vo. 60*s.*

——— (The Student's Gibbon); Being an Epitome of the above work, incorporating the Researches of Recent Commentators. By Dr. WM. SMITH. *Ninth Thousand.* Woodcuts. Post 8vo. 7*s.* 6*d.*

GIFFARD'S (EDWARD) Deeds of Naval Daring; or, Anecdotes of the British Navy. New Edition. Fcap. 8vo.

GOLDSMITH'S (OLIVER) Works. A New Edition. Printed from the last editions revised by the Author. Edited by PETER CUNNINGHAM. Vignettes. 4 Vols. 8vo. 30*s.* (Murray's British Classics.)

GLEIG'S (REV. G. R.) Campaigns of the British Army at Washington and New Orleans. Post 8vo. 2*s.*

——— Story of the Battle of Waterloo. Compiled from Public and Authentic Sources. Post 8vo. 3*s.* 6*d.*

——— Narrative of Sir Robert Sale's Brigade in Affghanistan, with an Account of the Seizure and Defence of Jellalabad. Post 8vo. 2*s.*

——— Life of Robert Lord Clive. Post 8vo. 3*s.* 6*d.*

——— Life and Letters of General Sir Thomas Munro. Post 8vo. 3*s.* 6*d.*

GORDON'S (SIR ALEX. DUFF) Sketches of German Life, and Scenes from the War of Liberation. From the German. Post 8vo. 3*s.* 6*d.*

——— (LADY DUFF) Amber-Witch: the most interesting Trial for Witchcraft ever known. From the German. Post 8vo. 2*s.*

——— French in Algiers. 1. The Soldier of the Foreign Legion. 2. The Prisoners of Abd-el-Kadir. From the French. Post 8vo. 2*s.*

GOUGER'S (HENRY) Personal Narrative of Two Years' Imprisonment in Burmah. *Second Edition.* Woodcuts. Post 8vo. 12*s.*

GRANT'S (ASAHEL) Nestorians, or the Lost Tribes; containing Evidence of their Identity, their Manners, Customs, and Ceremonies; with Sketches of Travel in Ancient Assyria, Armenia, and Mesopotamia; and Illustrations of Scripture Prophecy. *Third Edition.* Fcap. 8vo. 6*s.*

GRENVILLE (THE) PAPERS. Being the Public and Private Correspondence of George Grenville, including his PRIVATE DIARY. Edited by W. J. SMITH. 4 Vols. 8vo. 16s. each.

GREEK GRAMMAR FOR SCHOOLS. Abridged from Matthiæ. By BISHOP BLOMFIELD. *Ninth Edition*, revised by Rev. J. EDWARDS. 2mo. 3s.

GREY'S (SIR GEORGE) Polynesian Mythology, and Ancient Traditional History of the New Zealand Race. Woodcuts. Pos 8vo. 10s. 6d.

GROTE'S (GEORGE) History of Greece. From the Earliest Times to the close of the generation contemporary with the death of Alexander the Great. *Fourth Edition.* Portrait and Maps. 8 vols. 8vo. 112s.

——— (MRS.) Memoir of the Life of the late Ary Scheffer. *Second Edition.* Portrait. Post 8vo. 8s. 6d.

——— Collected Papers in Prose and Verse (Original and Reprinted.) 8vo. 10s. 6d.

HALLAM'S (HENRY) Constitutional History of England, from the Accession of Henry the Seventh to the Death of George the Second. *Seventh Edition.* 3 Vols. 8vo. 30s.

——— History of Europe during the Middle Ages. *Tenth Edition.* 3 Vols. 8vo. 30s.

——— Literary History of Europe, during the 15th, 16th and 17th Centuries. *Fourth Edition.* 3 Vols. 8vo. 36s.

——— Literary Essays and Characters. Selected from the last work. Fcap. 8vo. 2s.

——— Historical Works. History of England,—Middle Ages of Europe,—Literary History of Europe. 10 Vols. Post 8vo. 6s. each.

——— (ARTHUR) Remains; in Verse and Prose. With Preface, Memoir, and Portrait. Fcap. 8vo. 7s. 6d.

HAMILTON'S (JAMES) Wanderings in Northern Africa, Benghazi, Cyrene, the Oasis of Siwah, &c. Woodcuts. Post 8vo. 12s.

HAMPDEN'S (BISHOP) Philosophical Evidence of Christianity, or the Credibility obtained to a Scripture Revelation from its Coincidence with the Facts of Nature. 8vo. 9s. 6d.

HARCOURT'S (EDWARD VERNON) Sketch of Madeira; with Map and Plates. Post 8vo. 8s. 6d.

HART'S ARMY LIST. (*Quarterly and Annually.*) 8vo. 10s. 6d. and 21s.

HAY'S (J. H. DRUMMOND) Western Barbary, its wild Tribes and savage Animals. Post 8vo. 2s.

HEBER'S (BISHOP) Journey through the Upper Provinces of India, From Calcutta to Bombay, with a Journey to Madras and the Southern Provinces. *Twelfth Edition.* 2 Vols. Post 8vo. 7s.

——— Poetical Works. *Sixth Edition.* Portrait. Fcap. 8vo. 6s.

——— Parish Sermons. *Sixth Edition.* 2 Vols. Post 8vo. 16s.

——— Sermons Preached in England. *Second Edition.* 8vo.

——— Hymns for the Weekly Church Service of the Year. *Twelfth Edition.* 16mo. 2s.

HAND-BOOK—TRAVEL-TALK. English, German, French, and Italian. 18mo. 3*s.* 6*d.*

—— NORTH GERMANY, HOLLAND, BELGIUM, and the Rhine to Switzerland. Map. Post 8vo. 10*s.*

—— SOUTH GERMANY, Bavaria, Austria, Styria, Salzberg, the Austrian and Bavarian Alps, the Tyrol, Hungary, and the Danube, from Ulm to the Black Sea. Map. Post 8vo. 10*s.*

—— PAINTING. The German, Flemish, and Dutch Schools. Edited by DR. WAAGEN. Woodcuts. 2 Vols. Post 8vo. 24*s.*

—— LIVES OF THE EARLY FLEMISH PAINTERS, with Notices of their Works. By CROWE and CAVALCASELLE. Illustrations. Post 8vo. 12*s.*

—— SWITZERLAND, Alps of Savoy, and Piedmont. Maps. Post 8vo. 9*s.*

—— FRANCE, Normandy, Brittany, the French Alps, the Rivers Loire, Seine, Rhone, and Garonne, Dauphiné, Provence, and the Pyrenees. Maps. Post 8vo. 10*s.*

—— PARIS AND ITS ENVIRONS. Map. Post 8vo. (*Nearly Ready.*)

—— SPAIN, Andalusia, Ronda, Granada, Valencia, Catalonia, Gallicia, Arragon, and Navarre. Maps. 2 Vols. Post 8vo. 30*s.*

—— PORTUGAL, LISBON, &c. Map. Post 8vo.

—— NORTH ITALY, Piedmont, Liguria, Venetia, Lombardy, Parma, Modena, and Romagna. Map. Post 8vo. 12*s.*

—— CENTRAL ITALY, Lucca, Tuscany, Florence, The Marches, Umbria, and the Patrimony of St. Peter's. Map. Post 8vo. 10*s.*

—— ROME AND ITS ENVIRONS. Map. Post 8vo. 9*s.*

—— SOUTH ITALY, Two Sicilies, Naples, Pompeii, Herculaneum, and Vesuvius. Map. Post 8vo. 10*s.*

—— SICILY, Palermo, Messina, Catania, Syracuse, Etna, and the Ruins of the Greek Temples. Map. Post 8vo. (*In the Press.*)

—— PAINTING. The Italian Schools. From the German of KUGLER. Edited by Sir CHARLES EASTLAKE, R.A. Woodcuts. 2 Vols. Post 8vo. 30*s.*

—— LIVES OF THE EARLY ITALIAN PAINTERS, AND PROGRESS OF PAINTING IN ITALY, from CIMABUE to BASSANO. By Mrs. JAMESON Woodcuts. Post 8vo. 12*s.*

—— DICTIONARY OF ITALIAN PAINTERS. By A LADY. Edited by RALPH WORNUM. With a Chart. Post 8vo. 6*s.* 6*d.*

—— GREECE, the Ionian Islands, Albania, Thessaly, and Macedonia. Maps. Post 8vo. 15*s.*

—— TURKEY, Malta, Asia Minor, Constantinople, Armenia, Mesopotamia, &c. Maps. Post 8vo. (*In the Press.*)

—— EGYPT, Thebes, the Nile, Alexandria, Cairo, the Pyramids, Mount Sinai, &c. Map. Post 8vo. 15*s.*

—— SYRIA & PALESTINE, Peninsula of Sinai, Edom, and Syrian Desert. Maps. 2 Vols. Post 8vo. 24*s.*

—— BOMBAY AND MADRAS. Map. 2 Vols. Post 8vo. 24*s.*

—— DENMARK, NORWAY and SWEDEN. Maps. Post 8vo. 15*s.*

—— RUSSIA, THE BALTIC AND FINLAND. Maps. Post 8vo. 12*s.*

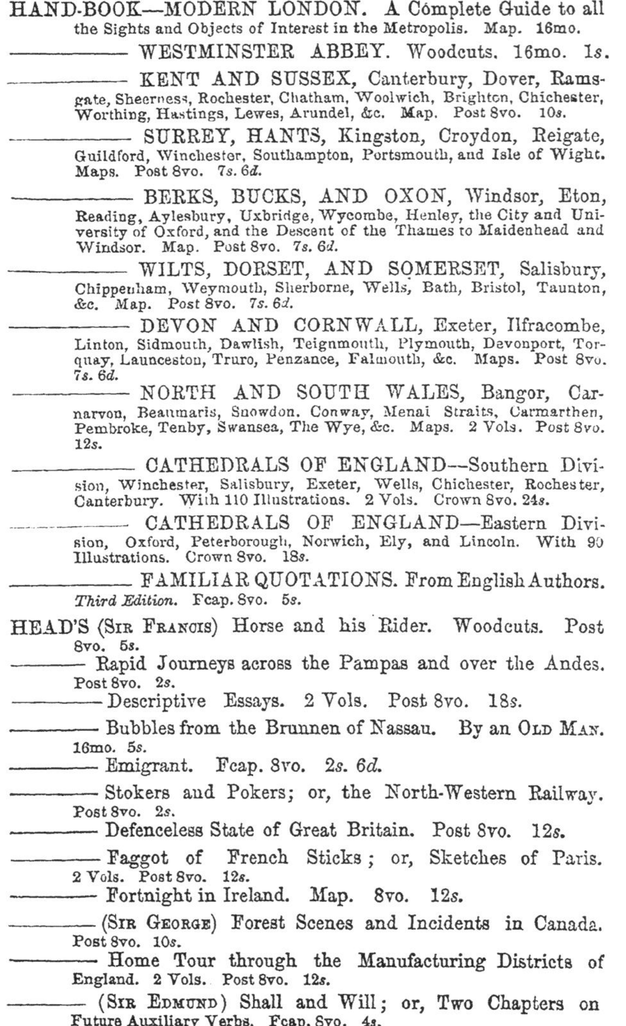

HAND-BOOK—MODERN LONDON. A Cômplete Guide to all the Sights and Objects of Interest in the Metropolis. Map. 16mo.

——— WESTMINSTER ABBEY. Woodcuts. 16mo. 1*s.*

——— KENT AND SUSSEX, Canterbury, Dover, Ramsgate, Sheerness, Rochester, Chatham, Woolwich, Brighton, Chichester, Worthing, Hastings, Lewes, Arundel, &c. Map. Post 8vo. 10*s.*

——— SURREY, HANTS, Kingston, Croydon, Reigate, Guildford, Winchester, Southampton, Portsmouth, and Isle of Wight. Maps. Post 8vo. 7*s.* 6*d.*

——— BERKS, BUCKS, AND OXON, Windsor, Eton, Reading, Aylesbury, Uxbridge, Wycombe, Henley, the City and University of Oxford, and the Descent of the Thames to Maidenhead and Windsor. Map. Post 8vo. 7*s.* 6*d.*

——— WILTS, DORSET, AND SOMERSET, Salisbury, Chippenham, Weymouth, Sherborne, Wells, Bath, Bristol, Taunton, &c. Map. Post 8vo. 7*s.* 6*d.*

——— DEVON AND CORNWALL, Exeter, Ilfracombe, Linton, Sidmouth, Dawlish, Teignmouth, Plymouth, Devonport, Torquay, Launceston, Truro, Penzance, Falmouth, &c. Maps. Post 8vo. 7*s.* 6*d.*

——— NORTH AND SOUTH WALES, Bangor, Carnarvon, Beaumaris, Snowdon, Conway, Menai Straits, Carmarthen, Pembroke, Tenby, Swansea, The Wye, &c. Maps. 2 Vols. Post 8vo. 12*s.*

——— CATHEDRALS OF ENGLAND—Southern Division, Winchester, Salisbury, Exeter, Wells, Chichester, Rochester, Canterbury. With 110 Illustrations. 2 Vols. Crown 8vo. 24*s.*

——— CATHEDRALS OF ENGLAND—Eastern Division, Oxford, Peterborough, Norwich, Ely, and Lincoln. With 90 Illustrations. Crown 8vo. 18*s.*

——— FAMILIAR QUOTATIONS. From English Authors. *Third Edition.* Fcap. 8vo. 5*s.*

HEAD'S (Sir Francis) Horse and his Rider. Woodcuts. Post 8vo. 5*s.*

——— Rapid Journeys across the Pampas and over the Andes. Post 8vo. 2*s.*

——— Descriptive Essays. 2 Vols. Post 8vo. 18*s.*

——— Bubbles from the Brunnen of Nassau. By an Old Man. 16mo. 5*s.*

——— Emigrant. Fcap. 8vo. 2*s.* 6*d.*

——— Stokers and Pokers; or, the North-Western Railway. Post 8vo. 2*s.*

——— Defenceless State of Great Britain. Post 8vo. 12*s.*

——— Faggot of French Sticks; or, Sketches of Paris. 2 Vols. Post 8vo. 12*s.*

——— Fortnight in Ireland. Map. 8vo. 12*s.*

——— (Sir George) Forest Scenes and Incidents in Canada. Post 8vo. 10*s.*

——— Home Tour through the Manufacturing Districts of England. 2 Vols. Post 8vo. 12*s.*

——— (Sir Edmund) Shall and Will; or, Two Chapters on Future Auxiliary Verbs. Fcap. 8vo. 4*s.*

HEIRESS (THE) in Her Minority; or, The Progress of Character. By the Author of "BERTHA'S JOURNAL." 2 Vols. 12mo. 18*s.*

HERODOTUS. A New English Version. Edited with Notes and Essays, historical, ethnographical, and geographical. By Rev. G. RAWLINSON, assisted by SIR HENRY RAWLINSON and SIR J. G. WILKINSON. *Second Edition.* Maps and Woodcuts. 4 Vols. 8vo. 48*s.*

HERVEY'S (LORD) Memoirs of the Reign of George the Second, from his Accession to the Death of Queen Caroline. Edited, with Notes, by MR. CROKER. *Second Edition.* Portrait. 2 Vols. 8vo. 21*s.*

HESSEY (REV. DR.). Sunday—Its Origin, History, and Present Obligations. Being the Bampton Lectures for 1860. *Second Edition.* 8vo. 16*s.*

HICKMAN'S (WM.) Treatise on the Law and Practice of Naval Courts-Martial. 8vo. 10*s.* 6*d.*

HILLARD'S (G. S.) Six Months in Italy. 2 Vols. Post 8vo. 16*s.*

HOLLWAY'S (J. G.) Month in Norway. Fcap. 8vo. 2*s.*

HONEY BEE (THE). An Essay. By REV. THOMAS JAMES. Reprinted from the "Quarterly Review." Fcap. 8vo. 1*s.*

HOOK'S (DEAN) Church Dictionary. *Eighth Edition.* 8vo. 16*s.*

——— Discourses on the Religious Controversies of the Day. 8vo. 9*s.*

——— (THEODORE) Life. By J. G. LOCKHART. Reprinted from the "Quarterly Review." Fcap. 8vo. 1*s.*

HOOKER'S (Dr. J. D.) Himalayan Journals; or, Notes of an Oriental Naturalist in Bengal, the Sikkim and Nepal Himalayas, the Khasia Mountains, &c. *Second Edition.* Woodcuts. 2 Vols. Post 8vo. 18*s.*

HOOPER'S (LIEUT.) Ten Months among the Tents of the Tuski; with Incidents of an Arctic Boat Expedition in Search of Sir John Franklin. Plates. 8vo. 14*s.*

HOPE'S (A. J. BERESFORD) English Cathedral of the Nineteenth Century. With Illustrations. 8vo. 12*s.*

HORACE (Works of). Edited by DEAN MILMAN. With 300 Woodcuts. Crown 8vo. 21*s.*

——— (Life of). By DEAN MILMAN. Woodcuts, and coloured Borders. 8vo. 9*s.*

HOSPITALS AND SISTERHOODS. By a LADY. Fcap. 8vo. 3*s.* 6*d.*

HUME'S (DAVID) History of England, from the Invasion of Julius Cæsar to the Revolution of 1688. Abridged for Students. Correcting his errors, and continued to 1858. *Twenty-fifth Thousand.* Woodcuts. Post 8vo. 7*s.* 6*d.*

HUTCHINSON (COL.) on the most expeditious, certain, and easy Method of Dog-Breaking. *Third Edition.* Woodcuts. Post 8vo. 9*s.*

HUTTON'S (H. E.) Principia Græca; an Introduction to the Study of Greek. Comprehending Grammar, Delectus, and Exercise-book, with Vocabularies. *Second Edition.* 12mo. 3*s.*

HOME AND COLONIAL LIBRARY. A Series of Works adapted for all circles and classes of Readers, having been selected for their acknowledged interest and ability of the Authors. Post 8vo. Published at 2*s.* and 3*s.* 6*d.* each, and arranged under two distinctive heads as follows:—

CLASS A.

HISTORY, BIOGRAPHY, AND HISTORIC TALES.

1. SIEGE OF GIBRALTAR. By JOHN DRINKWATER. 2*s.*
2. THE AMBER-WITCH. By LADY DUFF GORDON. 2*s.*
3. CROMWELL AND BUNYAN. By ROBERT SOUTHEY. 2*s.*
4. LIFE OF SIR FRANCIS DRAKE. By JOHN BARROW.
5. CAMPAIGNS AT WASHINGTON. By REV. G. R. GLEIG. 2*s.*
6. THE FRENCH IN ALGIERS. By LADY DUFF GORDON. 2*s.*
7. THE FALL OF THE JESUITS. 2*s.*
8. LIVONIAN TALES. 2*s.*
9. LIFE OF CONDE. By LORD MAHON. 3*s.* 6*d.*
10. SALE'S BRIGADE. By REV. G. R. GLEIG. 2*s.*
11. THE SIEGES OF VIENNA. By LORD ELLESMERE. 2*s.*
12. THE WAYSIDE CROSS. By CAPT. MILMAN. 2*s.*
13. SKETCHES OF GERMAN LIFE. By SIR A. GORDON. 3*s.* 6*d.*
14. THE BATTLE OF WATERLOO. By REV. G. R. GLEIG. 3*s.* 6*d.*
15. AUTOBIOGRAPHY OF STEFFENS. 2*s.*
16. THE BRITISH POETS. By THOMAS CAMPBELL. 3*s.* 6*d.*
17. HISTORICAL ESSAYS. By LORD MAHON. 3*s.* 6*d.*
18. LIFE OF LORD CLIVE. By REV. G. R. GLEIG. 3*s.* 6*d.*
19. NORTH - WESTERN RAILWAY. By SIR F. B. HEAD. 2*s.*
20. LIFE OF MUNRO. By REV. G. R. GLEIG. 3*s.* 6*d.*

CLASS B.

VOYAGES, TRAVELS, AND ADVENTURES.

1. BIBLE IN SPAIN. By GEORGE BORROW. 3*s.* 6*d.*
2. GIPSIES OF SPAIN. By GEORGE BORROW. 3*s.* 6*d.*

3 & 4. JOURNALS IN INDIA. By BISHOP HEBER. 2 Vols. 7*s.*

5. TRAVELS IN THE HOLY LAND. By IRBY and MANGLES. 2*s.*
6. MOROCCO AND THE MOORS. By J. DRUMMOND HAY. 2*s.*
7. LETTERS FROM THE BALTIC. By a LADY. 2*s.*
8. NEW SOUTH WALES. By MRS. MEREDITH. 2*s.*
9. THE WEST INDIES. By M. G. LEWIS. 2*s.*
10. SKETCHES OF PERSIA. By SIR JOHN MALCOLM. 3*s.* 6*d.*
11. MEMOIRS OF FATHER RIPA. 2*s.*

12 & 13. TYPEE AND OMOO. By HERMANN MELVILLE. 2 Vols. 7*s.*

14. MISSIONARY LIFE IN CANADA. By REV. J. ABBOTT. 2*s.*
15. LETTERS FROM MADRAS. By a LADY. 2*s.*
16. HIGHLAND SPORTS. By CHARLES ST. JOHN. 3*s.* 6*d.*
17. PAMPAS JOURNEYS. By SIR F. B. HEAD. 2*s.*
18. GATHERINGS FROM SPAIN. By RICHARD FORD. 3*s.* 6*d.*
19. THE RIVER AMAZON. By W. H. EDWARDS. 2*s.*
20. MANNERS & CUSTOMS OF INDIA. By REV. C. ACLAND. 2*s.*
21. ADVENTURES IN MEXICO. By G. F. RUXTON. 3*s.* 6*d.*
22. PORTUGAL AND GALLICIA. By LORD CARNARVON. 3*s.* 6*d.*
23. BUSH LIFE IN AUSTRALIA. By Rev. H. W. HAYGARTH. 2*s.*
24. THE LIBYAN DESERT. By BAYLE ST. JOHN. 2*s.*
25. SIERRA LEONE. By a LADY. 3*s.* 6*d.*

*** Each work may be had separately.

IRBY AND MANGLES' Travels in Egypt, Nubia, Syria, and the Holy Land. Post 8vo. 2*s.*

JAMES' (Rev. Thomas) Fables of Æsop. A New Translation, with Historical Preface. With 100 Woodcuts by Tenniel and Wolf. *Thirty-eighth Thousand.* Post 8vo. 2*s.* 6*d.*

JAMESON'S (Mrs.) Lives of the Early Italian Painters, from Cimabue to Bassano, and the Progress of Painting in Italy. *New Edition.* With Woodcuts. Post 8vo. 12*s.*

JERVIS'S (Capt.) Manual of Operations in the Field. Post 8vo. 9*s.* 6*d.*

JESSE'S (Edward) Scenes and Occupations of Country Life. *Third Edition.* Woodcuts. Fcap. 8vo. 6*s.*

——— Gleanings in Natural History. *Eighth Edition.* Fcap. 8vo. 6*s.*

JOHNSON'S (Dr. Samuel) Life. By James Boswell. Including the Tour to the Hebrides. Edited by the late Mr. Croker. Portraits. Royal 8vo. 10*s.*

——— Lives of the most eminent English Poets. Edited by Peter Cunningham. 3 vols. 8vo. 22*s.* 6*d.* (Murray's British Classics.)

JOHNSTON'S (Wm.) England: Social, Political, and Industrial, in 19th Century. 2 Vols. Post 8vo. 18*s.*

JONES' (Rev. R.) Literary Remains. With a Prefatory Notice. By Rev. W. Whewell, D.D. Portrait. 8vo. 14*s.*

JOURNAL OF A NATURALIST. *Fourth Edition.* Woodcuts. Post 8vo. 9*s.* 6*d.*

JOWETT (Rev. B.) on St. Paul's Epistles to the Thessalonians, Galatians, and Romans. *Second Edition.* 2 Vols. 8vo. 30*s.*

KEN'S (Bishop) Life. By A Layman. *Second Edition.* Portrait. 2 Vols. 8vo. 18*s.*

——— Exposition of the Apostles' Creed. Extracted from his "Practice of Divine Love." *New Edition.* Fcap. 1*s.* 6*d.*

——— Approach to the Holy Altar. Extracted from his "Manual of Prayer" and "Practice of Divine Love." *New Edition.* Fcap. 8vo. 1*s.* 6*d.*

KING'S (Rev. S. W.) Italian Valleys of the Alps; a Tour through all the Romantic and less-frequented "Vals" of Northern Piedmont. Illustrations. Crown 8vo. 18*s.*

——— (Rev. C. W.) Antique Gems; their Origin, Use, and Value, as Interpreters of Ancient History, and as illustrative of Ancient Art. Illustrations. 8vo. 42*s.*

KING EDWARD VIth's Latin Grammar; or, an Introduction to the Latin Tongue, for the Use of Schools. *Sixteenth Edition.* 12mo. 3*s.* 6*d.*

——— First Latin Book; or, the Accidence, Syntax, and Prosody, with an English Translation for the Use of Junior Classes. *Fourth Edition.* 12mo. 2*s.* 6*d.*

KNAPP'S (J. A.) English Roots and Ramifications; or, the Derivation and Meaning of Divers Words. Fcap. 8vo. 4*s.*

KUGLER'S Italian Schools of Painting. Edited, with Notes, by SIR CHARLES EASTLAKE. *Third Edition.* Woodcuts. 2 Vols. Post 8vo. 30*s.*

——— German, Dutch, and Flemish Schools of Painting. Edited, with Notes, by DR. WAAGEN. *Second Edition.* Woodcuts. 2 Vols. Post 8vo. 24*s.*

LABARTE'S (M. JULES) Handbook of the Arts of the Middle Ages and Renaissance. With 200 Woodcuts. 8vo. 18*s.*

LABORDE'S (LEON DE) Journey through Arabia Petræa, to Mount Sinai, and the Excavated City of Petræa,—the Edom of the Prophecies. *Second Edition.* With Plates. 8vo. 18*s.*

LANE'S (E. W.) Manners and Customs of the Modern Egyptians. *Fifth Edition.* Edited by E. STANLEY POOLE. Woodcuts. 8vo. 18*s.*

LATIN GRAMMAR (KING EDWARD VITH'S). For the Use of Schools. *Fifteenth Edition.* 12mo. 3*s.* 6*d.*

——— First Book (KING EDWARD VITH'S); or, the Accidence, Syntax, and Prosody, with English Translation for Junior Classes. *Fourth Edition.* 12mo. 2*s.* 6*d.*

LAYARD'S (A. H.) Nineveh and its Remains. Being a Narrative of Researches and Discoveries amidst the Ruins of Assyria. With an Account of the Chaldean Christians of Kurdistan; the Yezedis, or Devil-worshippers; and an Enquiry into the Manners and Arts of the Ancient Assyrians. *Sixth Edition.* Plates and Woodcuts. 2 Vols. 8vo. 36*s.*

——— Nineveh and Babylon; being the Result of a Second Expedition to Assyria. *Fourteenth Thousand.* Plates. 8vo. 21*s.* Or *Fine Paper*, 2 Vols. 8vo. 30*s.*

——— Popular Account of Nineveh. 15*th Edition.* With Woodcuts. Post 8vo. 5*s.*

LESLIE'S (C. R.) Handbook for Young Painters. With Illustrations. Post 8vo. 10*s.* 6*d.*

——— Autobiographical Recollections, with Selections from his Correspondence. Edited by TOM TAYLOR. Portrait. 2 Vols. Post 8vo. 18*s.*

——— Life of Sir Joshua Reynolds. With an Account of his Works, and a Sketch of his Cotemporaries. By TOM TAYLOR. 2 Vols. 8vo. (*In the Press.*)

LEAKE'S (COL.) Topography of Athens, with Remarks on its Antiquities. *Second Edition.* Plates. 2 Vols. 8vo. 30*s.*

——— Travels in Northern Greece. Maps. 4 Vols. 8vo. 60*s.*

——— Disputed Questions of Ancient Geography. Map. 8vo. 6*s.* 6*d.*

——— Numismata Hellenica, and Supplement. Completing a descriptive Catalogue of Twelve Thousand Greek Coins, with Notes Geographical and Historical. With Map and Appendix. 4to. 63*s.*

——— Peloponnesiaca. 8vo. 15*s.*

——— On the Degradation of Science in England. 8vo. 3*s.* 6*d.*

LEXINGTON (THE) PAPERS; or, Some Account of the Courts of London and Vienna at the end of the 17th Century. Edited by HON. H. MANNERS SUTTON. 8vo. 14*s.*

LETTERS FROM THE BALTIC. By a LADY. Post 8vo. 2*s.*

——— MADRAS. By a LADY. Post 8vo. 2s.

——— SIERRA LEONE. By a LADY. Post 8vo. 3*s.* 6*d.*

——— Head Quarters; or, The Realities of the War in the Crimea. By a STAFF OFFICER. Plans. Post 8vo. 6*s.*

LEWIS' (SIR G. C.) Essay on the Government of Dependencies. 8vo. 12*s.*

——— Glossary of Provincial Words used in Herefordshire and some of the adjoining Counties. 12mo. 4*s.* 6*d.*

——— (LADY THERESA) Friends and Contemporaries of the Lord Chancellor Clarendon, illustrative of Portraits in his Gallery. With a Descriptive Account of the Pictures, and Origin of the Collection. Portraits. 3 Vols. 8vo. 42*s.*

——— (M. G.) Journal of a Residence among the Negroes in the West Indies. Post 8vo. 2*s.*

LIDDELL'S (DEAN) History of Rome. From the Earliest Times to the Establishment of the Empire. With the History of Literature and Art. 2 Vols. 8vo. 28*s.*

——— Student's History of Rome. Abridged from the above Work. *Twentieth Thousand.* With Woodcuts. Post 8vo. 7*s.* 6*d.*

LINDSAY'S (LORD) Lives of the Lindsays; or, a Memoir of the Houses of Crawfurd and Balcarres. With Extracts from Official Papers and Personal Narratives. *Second Edition.* 3 Vols. 8vo. 24*s.*

——— Report of the Claim of James, Earl of Crawfurd and Balcarres, to the Original Dukedom of Montrose, created in 1488. Folio. 15*s.*

——— Scepticism; a Retrogressive Movement in Theology and Philosophy. 8vo. 9*s.*

LISPINGS from LOW LATITUDES; or, the Journal of the Hon. Impulsia Gushington. With 24 Plates, 4to.

LITTLE ARTHUR'S HISTORY OF ENGLAND. By LADY CALLCOTT. 120*th Thousand.* With 20 Woodcuts. Fcap. 8vo. 2*s.* 6*d.*

LIVINGSTONE'S (REV. DR.) Missionary Travels and Researches in South Africa; including a Sketch of Sixteen Years' Residence in the Interior of Africa, and a Journey from the Cape of Good Hope to Loanda on the West Coast; thence across the Continent, down the River Zambesi, to the Eastern Ocean. *Thirtieth Thousand.* Map, Plates, and Index. 8vo. 21*s.*

——— Popular Account of Travels in South Africa. Condensed from the above. Map and Illustrations. Post 8vo. 6*s.*

LIVONIAN TALES. By the Author of "Letters from the Baltic." Post 8vo. 2*s.*

LOCKHART'S (J. G.) Ancient Spanish Ballads. Historical and Romantic. Translated, with Notes. *Illustrated Edition.* 4to. 21*s.* Or, *Popular Edition,* Post 8vo. 2*s.* 6*d.*

——— Life of Robert Burns. *Fifth Edition.* Fcap. 8vo. 3*s.*

LONDON'S (BISHOP OF). Dangers and Safeguards of Modern Theology. Containing Suggestions to the Theological Student under present difficulties. *Second Edition.* 8vo. 9*s.*

LOUDON'S (Mrs.) Instructions in Gardening for Ladies. With Directions and Calendar of Operations for Every Month. *Eighth Edition.* Woodcuts. Fcap. 8vo. 5*s.*

——— Modern Botany; a Popular Introduction to the Natural System of Plants. *Second Edition.* Woodcuts. Fcap. 8vo. 6*s.*

LOWE'S (Sir Hudson) Letters and Journals, during the Captivity of Napoleon at St. Helena. By William Forsyth. Portrait. 3 Vols. 8vo. 45*s.*

LUCKNOW: A Lady's Diary of the Siege. *Fourth Thousand.* Fcap. 8vo. 4*s.* 6*d.*

LYELL'S (Sir Charles) Principles of Geology; or, the Modern Changes of the Earth and its Inhabitants considered as illustrative of Geology. *Ninth Edition.* Woodcuts. 8vo. 18*s.*

——— Visits to the United States, 1841-46. *Second Edition.* Plates. 4 Vols. Post 8vo. 24*s.*

——— Geological Evidences of the Antiquity of Man. With 50 Illustrations. 8vo. 14*s.*

MAHON'S (Lord) History of England, from the Peace of Utrecht to the Peace of Versailles, 1713—83. *Library Edition,* 7 Vols. 8vo. 93*s.* *Popular Edition,* 7 Vols. Post 8vo. 35*s.*

——— Life of William Pitt, with Extracts from his MS. Papers. *Second Edition.* Portraits. 4 Vols. Post 8vo. 42*s.*

——— Miscellanies. Post 8vo. 5*s.*

——— "Forty-Five;" a Narrative of the Rebellion in Scotland. Post 8vo. 3*s.*

——— History of British India from its Origin till the Peace of 1783. Post 8vo. 3*s.* 6*d.*

——— Spain under Charles the Second; or, Extracts from the Correspondence of the Hon. Alexander Stanhope, British Minister at Madrid from 1690 to 1700. *Second Edition.* Post 8vo. 6*s.* 6*d.*

——— Life of Louis, Prince of Condé, surnamed the Great. Post 8vo. 3*s.* 6*d.*

——— Life of Belisarius. *Second Edition.* Post 8vo. 10*s.* 6*d.*

——— Historical and Critical Essays. Post 8vo. 3*s.* 6*d.*

——— Story of Joan of Arc. Fcap. 8vo. 1*s.*

——— Addresses Fcap. 8vo. 1*s.*

McCLINTOCK'S (Capt. Sir F. L.) Narrative of the Discovery of the Fate of Sir John Franklin and his Companions in the Arctic Seas. *Twelfth Thousand.* Illustrations. 8vo. 16*s.*

McCOSH (Rev. Dr.) on the Intuitive Convictions of the Mind inductively investigated. 8vo. 12*s.*

McCULLOCH'S (J. R.) Collected Edition of Ricardo's Political Works. With Notes and Memoir. *Second Edition.* 8vo. 16*s.*

MAINE (H. Sumner) on Ancient Law: its Connection with the Early History of Society, and its Relation to Modern Ideas. *Second Edition.* 8vo. 12*s.*

MALCOLM'S (Sir John) Sketches of Persia. *Third Edition.* Post 8vo. 3*s.* 6*d.*

MANSEL (Rev. H. L.) Limits of Religious Thought Examined. Being the Bampton Lectures for 1858. *Fourth Edition.* Post 8vo. 7*s.* 6*d.*

MANTELL'S (Gideon A.) Thoughts on Animalcules; or, the Invisible World, as revealed by the Microscope. *Second Edition.* Plates. 16mo. 6*s.*

MANUAL OF SCIENTIFIC ENQUIRY, Prepared for the Use of Officers and Travellers. By various Writers. Edited by Sir J. F. HERSCHEL and Rev. R. MAIN. *Third Edition.* Maps. Post 8vo. 9s. (*Published by order of the Lords of the Admiralty.*)

MARKHAM'S (MRS.) History of England. From the First Invasion by the Romans, down to the fourteenth year of Queen Victoria's Reign. 156*th Edition.* Woodcuts. 12mo. 6s.

——— History of France. From the Conquest by the Gauls, to the Death of Louis Philippe. *Sixtieth Edition.* Woodcuts. 12mo. 6s.

——— History of Germany. From the Invasion by Marius, to the present time. *Fifteenth Edition.* Woodcuts. 12mo. 6s.

——— History of Greece. From the Earliest Times to the Roman Conquest. By DR. WM. SMITH. Woodcuts. 16 mo. 3s. 6d.

——— History of Rome, from the Earliest Times to the Establishment of the Empire. By DR. WM. SMITH. Woodcuts. 16mo. 3s. 6d.

——— (CLEMENTS, R.) Travels in Peru and India, for the purpose of collecting Cinchona Plants, and introducing Bark into India. Maps and Illustrations. 8vo. 16s.

MARKLAND'S (J. H.) Reverence due to Holy Places. *Third Edition.* Fcap. 8vo. 2s.

MARRYAT'S (JOSEPH) History of Modern and Mediæval Pottery and Porcelain. With a Description of the Manufacture. *Second Edition.* Plates and Woodcuts. 8vo. 31s. 6d.

——— (HORACE) Two Years Residence in Jutland, the Danish Isles, and Copenhagen. Illustrations. 2 Vols. Post 8vo. 24s.

——— One Year in Sweden, including a Visit to the Isle of Gothland. Illustrations. 2 Vols. Post 8vo. 28s.

MATTHIÆ'S (AUGUSTUS) Greek Grammar for Schools. Abridged from the Larger Grammar. By Blomfield. *Ninth Edition.* Revised by EDWARDS. 12mo. 3s.

MAUREL'S (JULES) Essay on the Character, Actions, and Writings of the Duke of Wellington. *Second Edition.* Fcap. 8vo. 1s. 6d.

MAWE'S (H. L.) Journal of a Passage from the Pacific to the Atlantic. 8vo. 12s.

MAXIMS AND HINTS on Angling and Chess. To which is added the Miseries of Fishing. By RICHARD PENN. *New Edition.* Woodcuts. 12mo. 1s.

MAYNE'S (R. C.) Four Years in British Columbia and Vancouver Island. Its Forests, Rivers, Coasts, and Gold Fields, and its Resources for Colonisation. Map and Illustrations. 8vo. 16s.

MAYO'S (DR.) Pathology of the Human Mind. Fcap. 8vo. 5s. 6d.

MELVILLE'S (HERMANN) Typee and Omoo; or, Adventures amongst the Marquesas and South Sea Islands. 2 Vols. Post 8vo. 7s.

MENDELSSOHN'S Life. By JULES BENEDICT. 8vo. 2s. 6d.

MEREDITH'S (MRS. CHARLES) Notes and Sketches of New South Wales, during a Residence from 1839 to 1844. Post 8vo. 2s.

——— Tasmania, during a Residence of Nine Years. With Illustrations. 2 Vols. Post 8vo. 18s.

MERRIFIELD (MRS.) on the Arts of Painting in Oil, Miniature, Mosaic, and Glass; Gilding, Dyeing, and the Preparation of Colours and Artificial Gems, described in several old Manuscripts. 2 Vols. 8vo. 30s.

MESSIAH (THE). By Author of the "Life of Bishop Ken." Map. 8vo. 18*s.*

MILLS' (ARTHUR) India in 1858; A Summary of the Existing Administration—Political, Fiscal, and Judicial; with Laws and Public Documents, from the earliest to the present time. *Second Edition.* With Coloured Revenue Map. 8vo. 10*s.* 6*d.*

MILMAN'S (DEAN) History of Latin Christianity; including that of the Popes to the Pontificate of Nicholas V. *Second Edition.* 6 Vols. 8vo. 72*s.*

——— History of the Jews, brought down to Modern Times. 3 Vols. 8vo.

——— Character and Conduct of the Apostles considered as an Evidence of Christianity. 8vo. 10*s.* 6*d.*

——— Life and Works of Horace. With 300 Woodcuts. *New Edition.* 2 Vols. Crown 8vo. 30*s.*

——— Poetical Works. Plates. 3 Vols. Fcap. 8vo. 18*s.*

——— Fall of Jerusalem. Fcap. 8vo. 1*s.*

——— (CAPT. E. A.) Wayside Cross; or, the Raid of Gomez. A Tale of the Carlist War. Post 8vo. 2*s.*

MITCHELL'S (THOMAS) Plays of Aristophanes. With English Notes. FROGS. 8vo. 15*s.*

MODERN DOMESTIC COOKERY. Founded on Principles of Economy and Practical Knowledge, and adapted for Private Families. *New Edition.* Woodcuts. Fcap. 8vo. 5*s.*

MOLTKE'S (BARON) Russian Campaigns on the Danube and the Passage of the Balkan, 1828-9. Plans. 8vo. 14*s.*

MONASTERY AND THE MOUNTAIN CHURCH. By Author of "Sunlight through the Mist." Woodcuts. 16mo. 4*s.*

MOORE'S (THOMAS) Life and Letters of Lord Byron. *Cabinet Edition.* Plates. 6 Vols. Fcap. 8vo. 18*s.*

——— Life and Letters of Lord Byron. Portraits. Royal 8vo. 9*s.*

MOTLEY'S (J. L.) History of the United Netherlands: from the Death of William the Silent to the Synod of Dort. Embracing the English-Dutch struggle against Spain; and a detailed Account of the Spanish Armada. *Fourth Thousand.* Portraits. 2 Vols. 8vo. 30*s.*

MOZLEY'S (REV. J. B.) Treatise on the Augustinian Doctrine of Predestination. 8vo. 14*s.*

——— Primitive Doctrine of Baptismal Regeneration. 8vo. 7*s.* 6*d.*

MUCK MANUAL (The) for the Use of Farmers. A Practical Treatise on the Chemical Properties, Management, and Application of Manures. By FREDERICK FALKNER. *Second Edition.* Fcap. 8vo. 5*s.*

MUNDY'S (GEN.) Pen and Pencil Sketches during a Tour in India. *Third Edition.* Plates. Post 8vo. 7*s.* 6*d.*

——— (ADMIRAL). H.M.S. Hannibal at Palermo and Naples, during the Italian Revolution, with Notices of Garibaldi, Francis II., and Victor Emmanuel. Post 8vo. 12*s.*

MUNRO'S (GENERAL SIR THOMAS) Life and Letters. By the REV. G. R. GLEIG. Post 8vo. 3*s.* 6*d.*

MURCHISON'S (SIR RODERICK) Russia in Europe and the Ural Mountains; Geologically Illustrated. With Coloured Maps, Plates, Sections, &c. 2 Vols. Royal 4to.

——— Siluria; or, a History of the Oldest Rocks containing Organic Remains. *Third Edition.* Map and Plates. 8vo. 42*s.*

MURRAY'S RAILWAY READING. For all classes of Readers.

[*The following are published:*]

WELLINGTON. By LORD ELLESMERE. 6*d.*
NIMROD ON THE CHASE, 1*s.*
ESSAYS FROM "THE TIMES." 2 Vols. 8*s.*
MUSIC AND DRESS. 1*s.*
LAYARD'S ACCOUNT OF NINEVEH. 5*s.*
MILMAN'S FALL OF JERUSALEM. 1*s.*
MAHON'S "FORTY-FIVE." 3*s.*
LIFE OF THEODORE HOOK. 1*s.*
DEEDS OF NAVAL DARING. 2 Vols. 5*s.*
THE HONEY BEE. 1*s.*
JAMES' ÆSOP'S FABLES. 2*s.* 6*d.*
NIMROD ON THE TURF. 1*s.* 6*d.*
OLIPHANT'S NEPAUL. 2*s.* 6*d.*
ART OF DINING. 1*s.* 6*d.*
HALLAM'S LITERARY ESSAYS. 2*s.*
MAHON'S JOAN OF ARC. 1*s.*
HEAD'S EMIGRANT. 2*s.* 6*d.*
NIMROD ON THE ROAD. 1*s.*
WILKINSON'S ANCIENT EGYPTIANS. 12*s.*
CROKER ON THE GUILLOTINE. 1*s.*
HOLLWAY'S NORWAY. 2*s.*
MAUREL'S WELLINGTON. 1*s.* 6*d.*
CAMPBELL'S LIFE OF BACON. 2*s.* 6*d.*
THE FLOWER GARDEN. 1*s.*
LOCKHART'S SPANISH BALLADS. 2*s.* 6*d.*
LUCAS ON HISTORY. 6*d.*
BEAUTIES OF BYRON. 3*s.*
TAYLOR'S NOTES FROM LIFE. 2*s.*
REJECTED ADDRESSES. 1*s.*
PENN'S HINTS ON ANGLING. 1*s.*

MURRAY'S (CAPT. A.) Naval Life and Services of Admiral Sir Philip Durham. 8vo. 5*s.* 6*d.*

MUSIC AND DRESS. Two Essays, by a Lady. Reprinted from the "Quarterly Review." Fcap. 8vo. 1*s.*

NAPIER'S (SIR WM.) English Battles and Sieges of the Peninsular War. *Third Edition.* Portrait. Post 8vo. 10*s.* 6*d.*

——— Life and Letters. Edited by H. A. BRUCE, M.P. Portraits. 2 Vols. Crown 8vo.

——— Life of General Sir Charles Napier; chiefly derived from his Journals, Letters, and Familiar Correspondence. *Second Edition.* Portraits. 4 Vols. Post 8vo. 48*s.*

NAUTICAL ALMANACK (The). Royal 8vo. 2*s.* 6*d.* (*Published by Authority.*)

NAVY LIST (The Quarterly). (*Published by Authority.*) Post 8vo. 2*s.* 6*d.*

NELSON (ROBERT), Memoir of his Life and Times. By Rev. C. T. SECRETAN, M.A. Portrait. 8vo. 10*s.* 6*d.*

NEWBOLD'S (LIEUT.) Straits of Malacca, Penang, and Singapore. 2 Vols. 8vo. 26*s.*

NEWDEGATE'S (C. N.) Customs' Tariffs of all Nations; collected and arranged up to the year 1855. 4to. 30*s.*

NICHOLLS' (SIR GEORGE) History of the English Poor-Laws. 2 Vols. 8vo. 28*s.*

——— History of the Irish Poor-Law. 8vo. 14*s.*

——— History of the Scotch Poor-Law. 8vo. 12*s.*

——— (Rev. H. G.) Historical and Descriptive Account of the Forest of Dean: from Sources Public, Private, Legendary, and Local. Woodcuts, &c. Post 8vo. 10*s.* 6*d.*

NICOLAS' (SIR HARRIS) Historic Peerage of England. Exhibiting the Origin, Descent, and Present State of every Title of Peerage which has existed in this Country since the Conquest. Being a New Edition of the "Synopsis of the Peerage." Revised and Continued to the Present Time. By WILLIAM COURTHOPE, Somerset Herald. 8vo. 30*s.*

NIMROD On the Chace—The Turf—and The Road. Reprinted from the "Quarterly Review." Woodcuts. Fcap. 8vo. 3*s.* 6*d.*

O'CONNOR'S (R.) Field Sports of France; or, Hunting, Shooting, and Fishing on the Continent. Woodcuts. 12mo. 7*s.* 6*d.*

OXENHAM'S (REV. W.) English Notes for Latin Elegiacs; designed for early Proficients in the Art of Latin Versification, with Prefatory Rules of Composition in Elegiac Metre. *Fourth Edition.* 12mo. 3*s.* 6*d*

PAGET'S (JOHN) Hungary and Transylvania. With Remarks on their Condition, Social, Political, and Economical. *Third Edition.* Woodcuts. 2 Vols. 8vo. 18*s.*

PARIS' (Dr.) Philosophy in Sport made Science in Earnest; or, the First Principles of Natural Philosophy inculcated by aid of the Toys and Sports of Youth. *Eighth Edition.* Woodcuts. Post 8vo. 7*s.* 6*d.*

PEEL'S (SIR ROBERT) Memoirs. Left in MSS. Edited by EARL STANHOPE and the Right Hon. EDWARD CARDWELL. 2 Vols. Post 8vo. 7*s.* 6*d.* each.

PEILE'S (REV. DR.) Agamemnon and Choephorœ of Æschylus. A New Edition of the Text, with Notes. *Second Edition.* 2 Vols. 8vo. 9*s.* each.

PENN'S (RICHARD) Maxims and Hints for an Angler and Chess-player. *New Edition.* Woodcuts. Fcap. 8vo. 1*s.*

PENROSE'S (F. C.) Principles of Athenian Architecture, and the Optical Refinements exhibited in the Construction of the Ancient Buildings at Athens, from a Survey. With 40 Plates. Folio. 5*l.* 5*s.*

PERCY'S (JOHN, M.D.) Metallurgy; or, the Art of Extracting Metals from their Ores and adapting them to various purposes of Manufacture. *First Division* — Slags, Fire-Clays, Fuel-Copper, Zinc, and Brass. Illustrations. 8vo. 21*s.*

PERRY'S (SIR ERSKINE) Bird's-Eye View of India. With Extracts from a Journal kept in the Provinces, Nepaul, &c. Fcap. 8vo. 5*s.*

PHILLIPS' (JOHN) Memoirs of William Smith, LL.D. (the Geologist). Portrait. 8vo. 7*s.* 6*d.*

——— Geology of Yorkshire, The Yorkshire Coast, and the Mountain-Limestone District. Plates. 4to. Part I., 20*s.*—Part II., 30*s.*

——— Rivers, Mountains, and Sea Coast of Yorkshire. With Essays on the Climate, Scenery, and Ancient Inhabitants of the Country. *Second Edition,* with 36 Plates. 8vo. 15*s.*

——— (March.) Jurisprudence. 8vo.

PHILPOTT'S (BISHOP) Letters to the late Charles Butler, on the Theological parts of his "Book of the Roman Catholic Church;" with Remarks on certain Works of Dr. Milner and Dr. Lingard, and on some parts of the Evidence of Dr. Doyle. *Second Edition.* 8vo. 16*s.*

PHIPPS' (HON. EDMUND) Memoir, Correspondence, Literary and Unpublished Diaries of Robert Plumer Ward. Portrait. 2 Vols. 8vo. 28*s.*

POPE'S (ALEXANDER) Life and Works. *A New Edition.* Containing nearly 500 unpublished Letters. Edited with a NEW LIFE, Introductions and Notes. By REV. WHITWELL ELWIN. Portraits. Vol. I. 8vo. (*In the Press.*)

PORTER'S (REV. J. L.) Five Years in Damascus. With Travels to Palmyra, Lebanon, and other Scripture Sites. Map and Woodcuts. 2 Vols. Post 8vo. 21*s.*

——— Handbook for Syria and Palestine: including an Account of the Geography, History, Antiquities, and Inhabitants of these Countries, the Peninsula of Sinai, Edom, and the Syrian Desert. Maps. 2 Vols. Post 8vo. 24*s.*

——— (MRS.) Rational Arithmetic for Schools and for Private Instruction. 12mo. 3*s.* 6*d.*

PRAYER-BOOK (The Illustrated), with 1000 Illustrations of Borders, Initials, Vignettes, &c. Medium 8vo. 21*s.*

PRECEPTS FOR THE CONDUCT OF LIFE. Extracted from the Scriptures. *Second Edition.* Fcap. 8vo. 1*s.*

PRINSEP'S (Jas.) Essays on Indian Antiquities, Historic, Numismatic, and Palæographic, with Tables. Edited by Edward Thomas. Illustrations. 2 Vols. 8vo. 52*s.* 6*d.*

PROGRESS OF RUSSIA IN THE EAST. An Historical Summary, continued to the Present Time. *Third Edition.* Map. 8vo. 6*s.* 6*d.*

PUSS IN BOOTS. With 12 Illustrations; for Old and Young. By Otto Speckter. 16mo. 1*s.* 6*d.*; or Coloured, 2*s.* 6*d.*

QUARTERLY REVIEW (The). 8vo. 6*s.*

RAWLINSON'S (Rev. George) Herodotus. A New English Version. Edited with Notes and Essays. Assisted by Sir Henry Rawlinson and Sir J. G. Wilkinson. *Second Edition.* Maps and Woodcut. 4 Vols. 8vo. 48*s.*

——— Historical Evidences of the truth of the Scripture Records stated anew, with special reference to the Doubts and Discoveries of Modern Times; the Bampton Lectures for 1859. *Second Edition.* 8vo. 14*s.*

——— Five Great Monarchies of the Ancient World. Or the History, Geography, and Antiquities of Chaldæa, Assyria, Babylonia, Media, and Persia. Illustrations. Vol. I. 8vo. 16*s.*

REJECTED ADDRESSES (The). By James and Horace Smith. *New Edition.* Fcap. 8vo. 1*s.*, or *Fine Paper*, with Portrait, fcap. 8vo, 5*s.*

RICARDO'S (David) Political Works. With a Notice of his Life and Writings. By J. R. M'Culloch. *New Edition.* 8vo. 16*s.*

RIPA'S (Father) Memoirs during Thirteen Years' Residence at the Court of Peking. From the Italian. Post 8vo. 2*s.*

ROBERTSON'S (Canon) History of the Christian Church, From the Apostolic Age to the Concordat of Worms, A.D. 1123. *Second Edition.* 3 Vols. 8vo. 38*s.*

——— Life of Becket. Illustrations. Post 8vo. 9*s.*

ROBINSON'S (Rev. Dr.) Biblical Researches in the Holy Land. Being a Journal of Travels in 1838, and of Later Researches in 1852. Maps. 3 Vols. 8vo. 36*s.*

ROMILLY'S (Sir Samuel) Memoirs and Political Diary. By his Sons. *Third Edition.* Portrait. 2 Vols. Fcap. 8vo. 12*s.*

ROSS'S (Sir James) Voyage of Discovery and Research in the Southern and Antarctic Regions, 1839-43. Plates. 2 Vols. 8vo. 36*s.*

ROWLAND'S (David) Manual of the English Constitution; a Review of its Rise, Growth, and Present State. Post 8vo. 10*s.* 6*d.*

RUNDELL'S (Mrs.) Domestic Cookery, founded on Principles of Economy and Practice, and adapted for Private Families. *New and Revised Edition.* Woodcuts. Fcap. 8vo. 5*s.*

RUSSELL'S (J. Rutherfurd, M.D.) Art of Medicine—Its History and its Heroes. Portraits. 8vo. 14*s.*

RUSSIA; A Memoir of the Remarkable Events which attended the Accession of the Emperor Nicholas. By Baron M. Korff, Secretary of State. 8vo. 10*s.* 6*d.* (*Published by Imperial Command.*)

RUXTON'S (George F.) Travels in Mexico; with Adventures among the Wild Tribes and Animals of the Prairies and Rocky Mountains. Post 8vo. 3*s.* 6*d.*

SALE'S (Lady) Journal of the Disasters in Affghanistan. Post 8vo. 12*s.*

——— (Sir Robert) Brigade in Affghanistan. With an Account of the Defence of Jellalabad. By Rev. G. R. Gleig. Post 8vo. 2*s.*

SANDWITH'S (HUMPHRY) Siege of Kars and Resistance by the Turkish Garrison under General Williams. Post 8vo. 3s. 6d.

SCOTT'S (G. GILBERT) Secular and Domestic Architecture, Present and Future. *Second Edition.* 8vo. 9s.

——— (Master of Baliol) Sermons Preached before the University of Oxford. Post 8vo. 8s. 6d.

SCROPE'S (WILLIAM) Days of Deer-Stalking; with some Account of the Red Deer. *Third Edition.* Woodcuts. Crown 8vo. 20s.

——— Days and Nights of Salmon Fishing in the Tweed; with a short Account of the Salmon. *Second Edition.* Woodcuts. Royal 8vo. 31s. 6d.

——— (G. P.) Memoir of Lord Sydenham, and his Administration in Canada. *Second Edition.* Portrait. 8vo. 9s. 6d.

——— Geology and Extinct Volcanoes of Central France. *Second Edition.* Illustrations. Medium 8vo. 30s.

SELF-HELP. With Illustrations of Character and Conduct. By SAMUEL SMILES. *Fifty-fifth Thousand.* Post 8vo. 6s.

SENIOR'S (N. W.) Suggestions on Popular Education. 8vo. 9s.

SHAFTESBURY (LORD CHANCELLOR); Memoirs of his Early Life. With his Letters, &c. By W. D. CHRISTIE. Portrait. 8vo. 10s. 6d.

SHAW'S (J. F.) Outlines of English Literature for Students. *Second Edition.* Revised. Post 8vo. (*In the Press.*)

SIERRA LEONE; Described in Letters to Friends at Home. By A LADY. Post 8vo. 3s. 6d.

SIMMONS on Courts-Martial. *5th Edition.* Adapted to the New Mutiny Act and Articles of War, the Naval Discipline Act, and the Criminal Law Consolidation Acts. 8vo.

SMILES' (SAMUEL) Lives of British Engineers; from the Earliest Period to the Death of Telford; with an account of their Principal Works, and a History of Inland Communication in Britain. *Sixth Thousand.* Portraits and Illustrations. 2 Vols. 8vo. 42s.

——— George and Robert Stephenson. Forming the Third Volume of "Lives of British Engineers." *Fourth Thousand.* Portraits and Illustrations. Medium 8vo. 21s.

——— Story of the Life of George Stephenson. Woodcuts. *Eighteenth Thousand.* Post 8vo. 6s.

——— Self-Help. With Illustrations of Character and Conduct. *Fifty-fifth Thousand.* Post 8vo. 6s.

——— Workmen's Earnings, Savings, and Strikes. *Fifth Thousand.* Fcap. 8vo. 1s. 6d.

SOMERVILLE'S (MARY) Physical Geography. *Fifth Edition.* Portrait. Post 8vo. 9s.

——— Connexion of the Physical Sciences. *Ninth Edition.* Woodcuts. Post 8vo. 9s.

SOUTH'S (JOHN F.) Household Surgery; or, Hints on Emergencies. *Seventeenth Thousand.* Woodcuts. Fcp. 8vo. 4s. 6d.

SOUTHEY'S (ROBERT) Book of the Church. *Seventh Edition.* Post 8vo. 7s. 6d.

——— Lives of Bunyan and Cromwell. Post 8vo. 2s.

SPECKTER'S (OTTO) Puss in Boots. With 12 Woodcuts. Square 12mo. 1s. 6d. plain, or 2s. 6d. coloured.

——— Charmed Roe; or, the Story of the Little Brother and Sister. Illustrated. 16mo.

SMITH'S (DR. WM.) Dictionary of the Bible; its Antiquities, Biography, Geography, and Natural History. *Second Edition.* Woodcuts. Vol. I. 8vo. 42s.

——— Greek and Roman Antiquities. *2nd Edition.* Woodcuts. 8vo. 42s.

——— Greek and Roman Biography and Mythology. Woodcuts. 3 Vols. 8vo 5l. 15s. 6d.

——— Greek and Roman Geography. Woodcuts. 2 Vols. 8vo. 30s.

——— New Latin-English Dictionary. Based upon the Works of Forcellini and Freund. *Ninth Thousand.* 8vo. 21s.

——— Smaller Latin-English Dictionary. *Twenty-fifth Thousand.* Square 12mo. 7s. 6d.

——— New Classical Dictionary. *6th Edition.* 750 Woodcuts. 8vo. 18s.

——— Smaller Classical Dictionary. *Twentieth Thousand.* 200 Woodcuts. Crown 8vo. 7s. 6d.

——— Smaller Dictionary of Antiquities. *Twentieth Thousand.* 200 Woodcuts. Crown 8vo. 7s. 6d.

——— Principia Latina—Part I. A Grammar, Delectus, and Exercise Book, with Vocabularies. *3rd Edition.* 12mo. 3s. 6d.

——— Principia Latina—Part II. A Reading-book, Mythology, Geography, Roman Antiquities, and History. With Notes and Dictionary. *Second Edition.* 12mo. 3s. 6d.

——— Principia Latina.—Part III. A Latin Poetry Book. Containing:—Easy Hexameters and Pentameters; Eclogæ Ovidianæ; Latin Prosody. 12mo. 3s. 6d.

——— Latin-English Vocabulary; applicable for those reading Phædrus, Cornelius Nepos, and Cæsar. *Second Edition.* 12mo. 3s. 6d.

——— Principia Græca; a First Greek Course. A Grammar, Delectus, and Exercise-book with Vocabularies. By H. E. HUTTON, M.A. *3rd Edition.* 12mo. 3s. 6d.

——— Student's Greek Grammar. Translated from the German of Professor CURTIUS. Post 8vo.

——— Smaller Greek Grammar, for the use of the Middle and Lower Forms. Abridged from the above work. 12mo.

——— Student's Latin Grammar, for the use of Colleges and the Upper Forms in Schools. Post 8vo.

——— Smaller Latin Grammar, for the use of the Middle and Lower Forms. Abridged from the above work. 12mo.

STANLEY'S (CANON) Lectures on the History of the Eastern Church. *Second Edition.* Plans. 8vo. 16s.

——— Lectures on the History of the Jewish Church. From ABRAHAM TO SAMUEL. Plans. 8vo. 16s.

——— Sermons on the Unity of Evangelical and Apostolical Teaching. *Second Edition.* Post 8vo. 7s. 6d.

——— St. Paul's Epistles to the Corinthians, with Notes and Dissertations. *Second Edition.* 8vo. 18s.

——— Historical Memorials of Canterbury. *Third Edition.* Woodcuts. Post 8vo. 7s. 6d.

——— Sinai and Palestine, in Connexion with their History. *Sixth Edition.* Map. 8vo. 16s.

——— Bible in the Holy Land. Being Extracts from the above work. *Second Edition.* Woodcuts. Fcp. 8vo. 2s. 6d.

——— ADDRESSES AND CHARGES OF BISHOP STANLEY. With Memoir. *Second Edition.* 8vo 10s. 6d.

——— Sermons Preached during the Tour of H.R.H. the Prince of Wales in the East, with Notices of some of the Localities Visited. 8vo.

ST. JOHN'S (CHARLES) Wild Sports and Natural History of the Highlands. Post 8vo. 3*s*. 6*d*.

———— (BAYLE) Adventures in the Libyan Desert and the Oasis of Jupiter Ammon. Woodcuts. Post 8vo. 2*s*.

STANHOPE'S (EARL) Life of William Pitt. With Extracts from his MS. Papers. *Second Edition*. Portraits. 2 Vols. Post 8vo. 42*s*.

———— Miscellanies. Post 8vo. 5*s*.

STEPHENSONS' (GEORGE and ROBERT) Lives. Forming the Third Volume of Smiles' "Lives of British Engineers." Portrait and Illustrations. 8vo. 21*s*.

STOTHARD'S (THOS.) Life. With Personal Reminiscences. By Mrs. BRAY. With Portrait and 60 Woodcuts. 4to.

STREET'S (G. E.) Brick and Marble Architecture of Italy in the Middle Ages. Plates. 8vo. 21*s*.

STRIFE FOR THE MASTERY. Two Allegories. With Illustrations. Crown 8vo. 6*s*.

STUDENT'S HUME. A History of England from the Invasion of Julius Cæsar to the Revolution of 1688. Based on the Work by DAVID HUME. Continued to 1858. *Twenty-fifth Thousand*. Woodcuts. Post 8vo. 7*s*. 6*d*.

*** A Smaller History of England. 12mo. 3*s*. 6*d*.

———— HISTORY OF FRANCE; From the Earliest Times to the Establishment of the Second Empire, 1852. Woodcuts. Post 8vo. 7*s*. 6*d*.

———— HISTORY OF GREECE; from the Earliest Times to the Roman Conquest. With the History of Literature and Art. By WM. SMITH, LL.D. *20th Thousand*. Woodcuts. Crown 8vo. 7*s*. 6*d*. (Questions. 2*s*.)

*** A SMALLER HISTORY OF GREECE. 12mo. 3*s*. 6*d*.

———— HISTORY OF ROME; from the Earliest Times to the Establishment of the Empire. With the History of Literature and Art. By H. G. LIDDELL, D.D. *20th Thousand*. Woodcuts. Crown 8vo. 7*s*. 6*d*.

*** A SMALLER HISTORY OF ROME. 12mo. 3*s*. 6*d*.

———— GIBBON; an Epitome of the History of the Decline and Fall of the Roman Empire. Incorporating the Researches of Recent Commentators. *9th Thousand*. Woodcuts. Post 8vo. 7*s*. 6*d*.

———— MANUAL OF ANCIENT GEOGRAPHY. Based on the larger Dictionary of Greek and Roman Geography. Woodcuts. Post 8vo. 9*s*.

———— ENGLISH LANGUAGE. By GEORGE P. MARSH. Edited by Dr. WM. SMITH. Post 8vo. 7*s*. 6*d*.

SWIFT'S (JONATHAN) Life, Letters, Journals, and Works. By JOHN FORSTER. 8vo. (*In Preparation*.)

SYME'S (JAS.) Principles of Surgery. *Fourth Edition*. 8vo. 14*s*.

TAIT'S (BISHOP) Dangers and Safeguards of Modern Theology. 8vo. 9*s*.

TAYLOR'S (HENRY) Notes from Life. Fcap. 8vo. 2*s*.

THOMSON'S (ARCHBISHOP) Sermons Preached in Lincoln's Inn Chapel. 8vo. 10*s*. 6*d*.

———— (DR.) Story of New Zealand; Past and Present—Savage and Civilised. *Second Edition*. Illustrations. 2 Vols. Post 8vo. 24*s*.

THREE-LEAVED MANUAL OF FAMILY PRAYER; arranged so as to save the trouble of turning the Pages backwards and forwards. Royal 8vo. 2*s.*

TICKNOR'S (GEORGE) History of Spanish Literature. With Criticisms on particular Works, and Biographical Notices of Prominent Writers. *Second Edition.* 3 Vols. 8vo. 24*s.*

TOCQUEVILLE'S (M. DE) State of France before the Revolution, 1789, and on the Causes of that Event. Translated by HENRY REEVE, ESQ. 8vo. 14*s.*

TREMENHEERE'S (H. S.) Political Experience of the Ancients, in its bearing on Modern Times. Fcap. 8vo. 2*s.* 6*d.*

——— Notes on Public Subjects, made during a Tour in the United States and Canada. Post 8vo. 10*s.* 6*d.*

——— Constitution of the United States compared with our own. Post 8vo. 9*s.* 6*d.*

TRISTRAM'S (H. B.) Great Sahara; or, Wanderings South of the Atlas Mountains. Illustrations. Post 8vo. 15*s.*

TWISS' (HORACE) Public and Private Life of Lord Chancellor Eldon, with Selections from his Correspondence. Portrait. *Third Edition.* 2 Vols. Post 8vo. 21*s.*

TYNDALL'S (JOHN) Glaciers of the Alps. Being a Narrative of various Excursions among them, and an Account of Three Years' Observations and Experiments on their Motion, Structure, and General Phenomena. Woodcuts. Post 8vo. 14*s.*

TYTLER'S (PATRICK FRASER) Memoirs. By REV. J. W. BURGON, M.A. *Second Edition.* 8vo. 9*s.*

UBICINI'S (M. A.) Letters on Turkey and its Inhabitants—the Moslems, Greeks, Armenians, &c. Translated by LADY EASTHOPE. 2 Vols. Post 8vo. 21*s.*

VAUGHAN'S (REV. DR.) Sermons preached in Harrow School. 8vo. 10*s.* 6*d.*

VENABLES' (REV. R. L.) Domestic Scenes in Russia during a Year's Residence, chiefly in the Interior. *Second Edition.* Post 8vo. 5*s.*

VOYAGE to the Mauritius and back, touching at the Cape of Good Hope and St. Helena. By Author of "PADDIANA." Post 8vo. 9*s.* 6*d.*

WAAGEN'S (DR.) Treasures of Art in Great Britain. Being an Account of the Chief Collections of Paintings, Sculpture, Manuscripts, Miniatures, &c. &c., in this Country. Obtained from Personal Inspection during Visits to England. 3 Vols. 8vo. 36*s.*

——— Galleries and Cabinets of Art in England. Being an Account of more than Forty Collections, visited in 1854-56. With Index. 8vo. 18*s.*

WADDINGTON'S (DEAN) Condition and Prospects of the Greek Church. *New Edition.* Fcap. 8vo. 3*s.* 6*d.*

WAKEFIELD'S (E. J.) Adventures in New Zealand. With some Account of the Beginning of the British Colonisation of the Island. Map. 2 Vols. 8vo. 28*s.*

WALKS AND TALKS. A Story-book for Young Children. By AUNT IDA. With Woodcuts. 16mo. 5*s.*

WALSH'S (SIR JOHN) Practical Results of the Reform Bill of 1832. 8vo. 5*s.* 6*d.*

WARD'S (ROBERT PLUMER) Memoir, Correspondence, Literary and Unpublished Diaries and Remains. By the HON. EDMUND PHIPPS. Portrait. 2 Vols. 8vo. 28*s.*

WATT'S (James) Life. Incorporating the most interesting passages from his Private and Public Correspondence. By James P. Muirhead, M.A. *Second Edition.* Portrait. 8vo. 16s.

——— Origin and Progress of his Mechanical Inventions. Illustrated by his Correspondence. By J. P. Muirhead. Plates. 3 Vols. 8vo. 45s.

WELLINGTON'S (The Duke of) Despatches during his various Campaigns. Compiled from Official and other Authentic Documents. By Col. Gurwood, C.B. *New Enlarged Edition.* 8 Vols. 8vo. 21s. each.

——— Supplementary Despatches, and other Papers. Edited by his Son. Vols. I. to IX. 8vo. 20s. each.

——— Selections from his Despatches and General Orders. By Colonel Gurwood. 8vo. 18s.

——— Speeches in Parliament. 2 Vols. 8vo. 42s.

WILKIE'S (Sir David) Life, Journals, Tours, and Critical Remarks on Works of Art, with a Selection from his Correspondence. By Allan Cunningham. Portrait. 3 Vols. 8vo. 42s.

WILKINSON'S (Sir J. G.) Popular Account of the Private Life, Manners, and Customs of the Ancient Egyptians. *New Edition.* Revised and Condensed. With 500 Woodcuts. 2 Vols. Post 8vo. 12s.

——— Dalmatia and Montenegro; with a Journey to Mostar in Hertzegovina, and Remarks on the Slavonic Nations. Plates and Woodcuts. 2 Vols. 8vo. 42s.

——— Handbook for Egypt.—Thebes, the Nile, Alexandria, Cairo, the Pyramids, Mount Sinai, &c. Map. Post 8vo. 15s.

——— On Colour, and on the Necessity for a General Diffusion of Taste among all Classes; with Remarks on laying out Dressed or Geometrical Gardens. With Coloured Illustrations and Woodcuts. 8vo. 18s.

——— (G. B.) Working Man's Handbook to South Australia; with Advice to the Farmer, and Detailed Information for the several Classes of Labourers and Artisans. Map. 18mo. 1s. 6d.

WILSON'S (Daniel, D.D., Bishop of Calcutta) Life, with Extracts from his Letters and Journals. By Rev. Josiah Bateman. *New and Condensed Edition.* Illustrations. Post 8vo. 9s.

——— (Genl. Sir Robert) Secret History of the French Invasion of Russia, and Retreat of the French Army, 1812. *Second Edition.* 8vo. 15s.

——— Private Diary of Travels, Personal Services, and Public Events, during Missions and Employments in Spain, Sicily, Turkey, Russia, Poland, Germany, &c. 1812-14. 2 Vols. 8vo. 26s.

——— Life. Edited from Autobiographical Memoirs. Containing an Account of his Birth, Parentage, Early Life, Entrance into Army, Various Campaigns, and Diplomatic Services, down to the Peace of Tilsit. Portrait. 2 Vols. 8vo. 26s.

WOOD'S (Lieut.) Voyage up the Indus to the Source of the River Oxus, by Kabul and Badakhshan. Map. 8vo. 14s.

WORDSWORTH'S (Canon) Journal of a Tour in Athens and Attica. *Third Edition.* Plates. Post 8vo. 8s. 6d.

——— Pictorial, Descriptive, and Historical Account of Greece, with a History of Greek Art, by G. Scharf, F.S.A. *New Edition.* With 600 Woodcuts. Royal 8vo. 28s.

WORNUM (Ralph). A Biographical Dictionary of Italian Painters: with a Table of the Contemporary Schools of Italy. By a Lady. Post 8vo. 6s. 6d.

WROTTESLEY'S (Lord) Thoughts on Government and Legislation. Post 8vo. 7s. 6d.

YOUNG'S (Dr. Thos.) Life and Miscellaneous Works, edited by Dean Peacock and John Leitch. Portrait and Plates. 4 Vols. 8vo. 15s. each.

BRADBURY AND EVANS, PRINTERS, WHITEFRIARS.

Printed in Great Britain by
Amazon.co.uk, Ltd.,
Marston Gate.